LOCAL PARTNERSHIPS FOR SOCIAL INCLUSION?

Jim Walsh
Sarah Craig
Des McCafferty

Oak Tree Press

Dublin

in association with

Combat Poverty Agency

Oak Tree Press
Merrion Building
Lower Merrion Street
Dublin 2, Ireland
www.oaktreepress.com

First published as Working Paper, *The Role of Local Partnerships in Promoting Social Inclusion: Ireland*, by the European Foundation for the Improvement of Living and Working Conditions (1998).

A catalogue record of this book is available from the British Library.

ISBN 1 86076 119 4

For rights of translation or reproduction, application should be made to the Director, European Foundation for the Improvement of Living and Working Conditions, Wyattville Road, Loughlinstown, Co Dublin, Ireland

This study forms part of the Combat Poverty Agency's Research Series, in which it is No. 26. The views expressed in this report are the authors' own and not necessarily those of the Combat Poverty Agency.

Printed in the Republic of Ireland
by Colour Books Ltd.

Contents

List of Tables and Figures

Glossary of Abbreviations

ABR	Area Based Response to Long-term Unemployment
ADM	Area Development Management
APIRD	Area Programme for Integrated Rural Development
CDO	community development organisation
CDP	Community Development Programme
CEB	city/county enterprise boards
CEP	Community Employment Programme
COMTEC	Community Training and Employment Consortia
CPA	Combat Poverty Agency
CSF	Community Support Framework
CSSC	Catholic Social Services Council
CWC	Community Workers' Co-operative
EAPN	European Anti-Poverty Network
EFILWC	European Foundation for the Improvement of Living and Working Conditions
ESRI	Economic and Social Research Institute
EU	European Union
FÁS	Foras Áiseanna Saothair — National Training and Employment Authority
GGLD	Global Grant for Local Development
IBEC	Irish Business and Employers' Confederation
ICTU	Irish Congress of Trade Unions
IFA	Irish Farmers' Association
IFI	International Fund for Ireland

INOU	Irish National Organisation of the Unemployed
IPCLD	Interdepartmental Policy Committee on Local Development
IRDT	Irish Resource Development Trust
IRL	Irish Rural Link
LDP	local development partnership
LEP	local enterprise partnership
LSP	local service partnership
LDSG	local development strategy groups
LEDA	Local employment development action
LEP	Local Enterprise Programme
LES	Local Employment Service
Leader	Liaisons entre actions de developpement de l'economie rurale
MABS	Money Advice and Budgeting Service
NGO	non-governmental organisation
NESC	National Economic and Social Council
NESF	National Economic and Social Forum
NSSB	National Social Service Board
OECD	Organisation for Economic Cooperation and Development
PCW	Programme for Competitiveness and Work
PESP	Programme for Economic and Social Progress
PIDDA	Programme for Integrated Development in Disadvantaged Areas
PPR	Programme for Peace and Reconciliation
URP	urban renewal partnership
VEC	Vocational Educational Committee
YEA	Youth Employment Agency

Preface

The Combat Poverty Agency[1] is delighted to participate in this important European study on the role of local partnerships in promoting social inclusion, under the auspices of the European Foundation for the Improvement in Living and Working Conditions. The Agency has been to the forefront in developing and assessing the potential of local partnerships as a tool for tackling social exclusion under various EU and national initiatives. This study enhances the Agency's knowledge and understanding of local partnerships by situating the Irish experience in the comparative context of similar social inclusion strategies in other European countries.

The opportunity to work with the European Foundation and its network of research associates in other European countries was a key attraction of this study for the Agency. In particular, the research has enhanced the Agency's capacity to facilitate the exchange of knowledge and good practice with other EU member states and with the European Commission strategies and policies to promote social inclusion.

The study was managed for the Agency by one of our research officers, Jim Walsh, who is also the principal author of the report. Another Agency research officer, Sarah Craig, and Des McCafferty, head of geography in Mary Immaculate College, University of Limerick, undertook two of the case studies (Tallaght Partnership and South Kerry Development Partnership respectively). Other Agency staff involved in the study were Helen Johnston, head of research, and Margaret Barry, head of projects.

---

[1] The Agency provides a statutory centre of expertise on policy advice, research, information and project support in relation to poverty in Ireland. It seeks the prevention and decrease of poverty and social exclusion and the reduction of inequality by striving for change which will promote a fairer and more just, equitable and inclusive society.

The Agency wishes to thank all those who contributed to the study: the eight projects chosen as illustrative examples and case studies of local partnerships and the various key informants representing government, the social partners, the community and voluntary sector and policy analysts/researchers. The Agency also acknowledges the support of the European Foundation in undertaking the research and in disseminating the final report, in particular the role played by Wendy Ó Conghaile and Robert Anderson who expertly managed the overall study and the research team involved. The maps in the report were provided by GAMMA (Maura McGinn), Des McCafferty and Trutz Haase.

December 1998

Executive Summary

This research report examines the role of local partnerships in promoting social inclusion in Ireland. It was undertaken by the Combat Poverty Agency as part of a wider European study, initiated and funded by the European Foundation for the Improvement of Living and Working Conditions. The European research contained ten national reports, five smaller national reviews and a synthesis European report. The research utilised a working definition of local partnership to guide its research as follows:

> a formal organisational framework for policy making and implementation, which mobilises a coalition of interests and the commitment of a range of partners, around a common agenda and multi-dimensional action programme, to combat social exclusion and promote social inclusion.

Ireland is amongst those countries where this model of local partnership is strongest, with various government programmes providing financial and technical support. The report assesses the application of this local partnership model in tackling social exclusion, canvasses the views of the various stakeholders as to its policy impact, and makes recommendations for the continued operation of local partnerships as an instrument of social inclusion. The research for the report draws on four main data sources: background research and policy reports, official documentation, detailed case studies and interviews with key policy actors.

The report details how the local partnership model has emerged as a national policy construct for tackling social exclusion, within a broader EU context. The socio-economic context for local partnerships was widespread and persistent unemployment, poverty and social exclusion in the 1980s and early 1990s. These problems were especially manifest in urban public housing estates and peripheral rural areas, and seemed immune to conventional policy measures. The policy response to these localised areas of disadvantage was shaped by a confluence of trends:

- Social partnership as a mechanism for policy-making and implementation;

- New sources of jobs through local enterprise and employment initiatives;

- Enhancement of welfare services through local co-ordination and delivery;

- Community empowerment and self-help as an important aid to government policy.

The result is a radical new localism in public policy, centred on three main themes: local multi-agency institutions, targeting and involvement of socially excluded groups in designated areas of disadvantage and local integrated plans combining enterprise initiatives and welfare measures. The main conduit for this new policy approach is the Local Development Programme, part of the joint government/EU Community Support Framework for the allocation of EU structural funds. Other smaller-scale programmes also foster a local partnership approach, focusing on specific issues such as rural decline, disadvantaged urban neighbourhoods, drugs, indebtedness and unemployment

These central programmes have given rise to a veritable explosion in local intervention, with upwards of 150 local partnerships in existence across four broad types: local development partnerships, urban regeneration partnerships, local employment and enterprise partnerships and local service partnerships. In addition, there are an estimated 200+ community development organisations which interact with and complement the local partnerships at the local level. Most of these new structures have a specific concern with issues of social exclusion, though their particular remit can vary enormously, covering issues such as enterprise and employment initiatives, local animation and capacity-building, physical regeneration, child and family services, and special initiatives with marginalised groups such as the homeless and drug users. Local partnerships also pursue an explicit equal opportunities policy in relation to discriminated groups such as women, travellers and people with a disability. This diversity of structures and activities is illustrated through eight examples of local partnerships and community development organisations, which operate in different spatial milieux and social contexts.

Local partnerships are not without their difficulties, however. The main problems identified are:

- Local partnerships are primarily a creature of central government and are heavily dependent on external funding and direction for their activities;

- Local partnerships function largely independent both of one another and of local government, leading to a lack of local co-ordination and public accountability;

- The linkages between local partnerships and local and national policy networks are informal and haphazard, with little systematic transfer of learning and good practice;

- The management practices and operating methods of local partnerships are highly variable, with inadequate investment in organisational training and development.

The research looks in a more detailed way at the operation and impact of local partnerships through three in-depth case studies: the PAUL Partnership Limerick, the Tallaght Partnership and the South Kerry Development Partnership. These case studies reveal the influence of local and programme factors on the origins, activities and resources of local partnerships. They also examine their representational structures, decision-making procedures and working methods, along with their linkages with other agencies and programmes. An assessment of the practical outcomes and the policy impact of these local partnerships is also presented, based on the findings of evaluation reports and interviews with the actors involved.

The report concludes with an overview of the experience of local partnership to date. It notes a major contradiction in this new localism: the encouragement of local initiative and policy-making on one hand and the retention by central government of overall control and direction over policy on the other. The report also argues for a better conceptualisation of what local partnerships are about, identifying four sources of synergy: enhancing the pool of local resources; making services more effective and efficient; promoting what is referred to as "social capitalism"; and finally, building local consensus and shared decision-making. The balance between these synergies varies depending on the priorities of individual local partnerships.

The report also makes recommendations as to how the effectiveness of local partnerships can be enhanced in terms of structure, process and strategy. In this regard, it is important to remember that the local partnership model is still only being built in Ireland, and therefore requires ongoing reflection, innovation and adjustment. The report therefore suggests that the organic diversity of local partnerships should be respected, while at the same time strengthening procedures for representation and communication. The management structures and culture of local partnerships must be continually reviewed to reflect the diverse philosophies and capacities of their partners. Also, local partnerships should avoid catch-all short-term strategies and develop long-term priorities which link local concerns and national policies. In this regard, there needs to be greater horizontal partnership with other tiers of government.

The report also outlines ways in which the various stakeholders involved with local partnerships could enhance their support for this policy measure. The key responsibility here lies with central government which has primarily promoted and funded this new model. It now needs to put in place procedures which will sustain the innovative work of local partnerships in tackling social exclusion, including ongoing funding, institutional recognition and transfer of learning and good practice. The government should also devise a strategic framework for local development, with clear linkages with regional, rural and urban development policies. At the European level, there is a need to enhance the policy framework for local partnerships, in particular through including local partnership as a delivery mechanism in the reformed structural funds. Also, the social inclusion remit should be mainstreamed in other policy areas relating to employment, agriculture, rural development, urban society and consumer protection.

In addition, there are policy implications for the other agencies involved in local partnerships. For the trade unions and business, these involve the development of pro-active local structures for engaging with the work of local partnerships. The key challenges for the community and voluntary sector relate to the structures and resources required to participate effectively in local partnerships. Meanwhile, state agencies and local government must underpin the valuable work of its representatives on local partnerships with greater delegation of powers and resources to local partnerships and a commitment to institutionalising new ways of working.

The local partnership experiment is entering a crucial stage in its evolution. In the first instance, there is an urgent need to consolidate the rapid expansion that has taken place in local partnerships, both the internal procedures of partnerships and their external linkages with other local bodies. At the same time, the policy environment continues to evolve, with discussions underway on the new national plan, an on-going programme for reform of local government, the implementation of the National Anti-Poverty Strategy and its application at the local level, and finally, the emerging debate about the future direction of national social partnership, in particular the relationship between the voluntary and community sector and the state. Since it is the nature of local partnerships that they are at the cutting edge of policy, it is likely that the next few years will inevitably bring about major changes in their role and structure.

The European synthesis report on this research is entitled *Local partnership: a successful strategy for social cohesion?*. It is available in full and summary form from the European Foundation for the Improvement of Living and Working Conditions. National reports are also available from the Foundation for Austria, Belgium, Finland, France, Germany, Greece, Portugal, Spain and the United Kingdom, along with summary reviews for Denmark, Italy, Netherlands, Luxembourg and Sweden.

Part 1

National Overview

Chapter 1

Introduction

Objectives and Content of the Research Report

Overall Framework

This research report forms part of a transnational study initiated and funded by the European Foundation for the Improvement in Living and Working Conditions on the role of local partnerships in promoting social inclusion in the EU. The study is designed to draw together the experiences and lessons of local partnership approaches to promoting social inclusion in the member states. The specific aims of the research are:

- to document and assess the extent to which the partnership model is being applied within EU member states in programmes concerned with promoting social inclusion;

- to document and analyse the perceptions of public, private, voluntary and community partners concerning the success of such partnerships and the problems they have encountered;

- to develop recommendations to assist policy makers and other interested parties in the future development of partnerships aimed at tackling social exclusion.

The emphasis in the research programme is on partnership structures which promote social inclusion at the local level, while having cognisance of the wider policy framework of partnership relationships and social inclusion programmes at national and European levels. The research programme contains four phases:

- national reviews of local partnership approaches to social inclusion;

- detailed case studies of a select number of local partnerships;

- synthesis review of the development and implementation of the partnership approach across member states, the implications for different partners and the policy implications at European, national and local levels;

- dissemination of the results and recommendations of the research.

The research programme includes in-depth studies of 10 countries, including Ireland, and summary reports for an additional 4 countries.[1] The programme adopted a common working definition of a local partnership and applied a standard research methodology to examining this phenomenon throughout Europe. As expected, there were considerable differences in the extent to which local partnership as a mechanism for promoting social inclusion is used in the different member states. Ireland is amongst those countries where local partnership is strongest, due to central government support. The Irish report thus presents a very rich and varied account of local partnership as a policy mechanism for promoting social inclusion.

National Report for Ireland

This report details the evolution, experience and some examples of local partnership approaches to promoting social inclusion in Ireland. It looks at the following issues:

- the background and policy context for local partnerships, including the roles played by the various government and social actors in promoting this new approach;

- the programmes for and forms of local partnership;

---

[1] Detailed studies are available for Austria, Belgium, Finland, France, Germany, Greece, Ireland, Portugal, Spain and the United Kingdom. Summary studies are available for Denmark, Italy, Netherlands, Luxembourg and Sweden.

- the range of local partnership approaches through the presentation of eight illustrative examples, detailing their mobilisation, membership, funding, remit and achievements;

- the views of the key actors about the successes and problems of local partnerships;

- the practice of local partnership through the in-depth examination of three case studies, involving interviews with key participants covering the perspectives of the different partners, the formal and informal aspects of partnership working and the benefits and drawbacks to this model of organisation in promoting social inclusion;

- the policy and practice issues for the future development of local partnerships.

The report was compiled using a diversity of data sources: evaluative reports on local partnerships; documentation produced by the promoters of local partnership and by local partnerships themselves; interviews with the key actors at a policy level; and visits to and interviews with personnel involved in local partnerships. The bulk of the fieldwork for the research was carried out from September to December 1995, with some supplementary material gathered in 1996 and 1997. A first draft of the report was completed in November 1996 and was subsequently revised and updated before a final draft was submitted to the European Foundation in May 1997. The report was approved for dissemination in late 1997.

Key Concepts in the Report

Local Partnerships

The focus on the study is on the innovative organisational structure referred to as a local partnership. This structure is a new public policy construct and reflects both EU and national government influences. For the purposes of this research, a local partnership is defined as:

a formal organisational framework for policy-making and implementation, which mobilises a coalition of interests and the commitment of a range of partners, around a common agenda and multi-dimensional action programme, to combat social exclusion and promote social inclusion.

This description does not represent a definitive model of local partnership; rather it is devised as an operational guide to identify comparable structures across the various EU countries in the research. Application of this definition in the Irish context was relatively straightforward given the strong government commitment for local partnerships as a policy instrument. By contrast, other countries have more diverse forms of partnership, reflecting the primacy of local or regional factors in the emergence of this organisational form. The study concentrates then on formal partnerships rather than informal alliances, involving a diversity of interests that support a joint programme of action. Other aspects of the definition are less well defined: for example, the extent to which social exclusion is the sole objective or one of a number of objectives, and the geographical scale at which a local partnership operates.

Social Exclusion / Social Inclusion

A second key theme is that of social exclusion/inclusion.[2] The scale and nature of poverty in the 1980s and 1990s has prompted researchers and policy-makers to develop a new and more complex concept to comprehend this phenomenon. Social exclusion refers to a process whereby certain groups experience an accumulation of poverty and disadvantage, which thereby excludes them from participation in common aspects of everyday life. The emphasis is thus on the structural causes of poverty (e.g. education system) and on the interrelationships between individual, familial and communal disadvantage. Social inclusion, as the opposite of social

---

[2] The official title for the study refers to "social cohesion", which is part of the parlance for addressing regional inequalities under the EU structural funds. In Ireland, a more appropriate term is considered to be "social inclusion", which focuses on the specific situation of groups excluded from the labour market and other aspects of society.

exclusion, refers to a process whereby all members of a society are enabled to participate in its social, economic and cultural activities, to their maximum ability and choice. Not surprisingly, there is more information and analysis about social exclusion than social inclusion. However, as this study is looking at strategies for countering social exclusion, the emphasis is on social inclusion.

Equal Opportunities

A cross-cutting theme of the research is that of equality of opportunity. Equal opportunities policy involves an active commitment to addressing inequalities based on gender, sexual orientation, disability, age, nationality, ethnic origin, religion or marital status. In Ireland, the two main dimensions of equal opportunities relate to gender (i.e. discrimination against women) and ethnicity (ie discrimination against travellers). Other issues, such as disability, age, sexual orientation, nationality, religion or marital status, have in general received far less consideration in the realm of social inclusion, though in principle have similar merit.

Contents of Report

The report has two main parts. Part 1 presents the national context for local partnerships and contains chapters 2 to 5. Chapter 2 sets the historical and policy scene for local partnership and social inclusion. Chapter 3 details the various programmes that have promoted partnership strategies for social inclusion and the array of local structures that now exist. Some illustrative examples of these are presented in chapter 4. Chapter 5 presents the views of the key stakeholders regarding partnership and social inclusion. Part 2 looks at the practice of local partnerships promoting social inclusion. Its three chapters (6, 7 and 8) contain selected case studies reflecting a diversity of programmes and geographical settings: suburban Dublin (Tallaght Partnership), large provincial city (PAUL Partnership in Limerick city) and rural (South Kerry Development Partnership). Finally, chapter 9 draws out the main conclusions of the study and sets out recommendations for improving the effectiveness of local partnerships and for enhancing the policy context in which local partnerships operate.

Chapter 2

Background and Policy Context

Introduction

This section outlines the social and policy context for the evolution of local partnership approaches to promoting social inclusion in Ireland. It begins by tracing Ireland's recent economic performance and highlights the emergence of widespread and persistent poverty and associated problems as reflected in the term social exclusion. A second theme is the institutional factors that have shaped the policy response to emerging patterns of social exclusion. These are:

- concept of social partnership (social corporatism);

- local development and employment initiatives as a job creation strategy;

- local co-ordination and delivery of welfare and employment services;

- an enhanced role for the traditional community sector.

There is an important EU input to this new policy approach, though often this has been refashioned to meet national exigencies.[1] In most instances, however, the motivation for policy reform has been indigenous and reflects a growing localism in Irish public policy as a means of responding to the concentrated incidence of unemployment and poverty in the 1980s.

---

[1] A separate report which sets out the EU policy context for the emergence of local partnerships as instruments for promoting social inclusion was also prepared as part of this research programme.

Social Context

Recent Economic Performance

Ireland has experienced a major transformation of its economy and society since the early 1960s. In this period, Ireland ended its experimentation with economic autarchy and embraced a strategy of economic development based on free trade, foreign industrial investment and membership of the EU. The state was the driving force in this policy shift, guided by a modernising elite within the civil service and supported by political and business interests. In order to attract foreign manufacturing industry, the state provided generous fiscal incentives, along with an unrestricted repatriation of profits. Accompanying this economic strategy was a rapid expansion in the welfare state, with an increase in employment in the public sector and the state-sponsored private sector, an expansion in education as the mechanism for allocating opportunities, and a growth in general welfare services (income support, health, housing, etc). Reflecting this high level of public involvement in the economy, government expenditure accounted for over 60 per cent of GNP by the late 1980s (Breen *et al*, 1990; O'Connell and Rottman, 1992).

This modernisation process has not been without its problems, especially in regard to the management of the public finances, the creation of employment and the competitiveness of the economy. In order to address these issues, central government initiated a succession of tripartite agreements with employers and trade unions in the late 1980s and early 1990s. These partnership policy agreements, together with significant investment from the EU and favourable external conditions, have generated a period of unprecedented economic growth and job creation and left Ireland well-placed for membership of the EU economic and monetary union in 1998.[2] This recent success has led to the coining of the

---

[2] GNP increased by an average of over 6 per cent in the years 1994-6, while employment grew by 140,000 in the same period (12 per cent). This has resulted in a fall in unemployment from 17 per cent to 13 per cent.

phrase "Celtic Tiger" by international commentators to describe the exceptional Irish economic performance. A further factor is the rapid and radical demographic change occurring in the population. This will see a significant fall in the economic dependency ratio, due to falling numbers of children, higher levels of labour market participation and increased worker productivity (J. Fitz-Gerald and T. Fahey, 1997). As a result of these improvements, Irish living standards have increased considerably, leading to a rapid convergence in per capita income as compared to the EU: from 72 per cent in 1990 to over 90 per cent by 1996, with the expectation Irish living standards will soon exceed the norm.

Poverty and Social Exclusion

Against the background of the current economic boom, it is ironic that poverty remains a persistent feature of Irish society. Worsening levels of poverty in the 1980s and early 1990s are documented by periodic income surveys conducted by the Central Statistics Office and the Economic and Social Research Institute. The latest of these (1994) reveals that 18.5 per cent of households, representing 20.7 per cent of the population, fall below an income poverty line set at 50 per cent of average household income (Callan *et al*, 1996). The trend over time is for an increase in poverty, especially in the percentage of people affected, which rose by a third between 1973 and 1994. However, a qualification to this pattern is that the extent to which households fell below the income poverty line decreased in the most recent period (1987-94). Also, if poverty lines are only adjusted in line with inflation, the growth in real incomes in this period has also helped to reduce the numbers on low incomes. Non-monetary indicators of deprivation can also be used to discern deep-rooted poverty trends. Applying a combined set of basic deprivation measures — lack of heating, debt, absence of main meal, etc — and a relative income threshold of 60 per cent, reveals that up to 15 per cent of the population experience generalised deprivation due to lack of resources. This proportion of "consistently poor" shows a slight improvement on the 1987 figure of 15 per cent (*ibid*).

TABLE 2.1: TRENDS IN INCOME POVERTY (50 PER CENT OF AVERAGE INCOME), 1973-94

	Households (%)	Persons (%)
1973	18.3	15.5
1980	16.8	16.2
1987	16.3	18.9
1994	18.5	20.7

Source: Callan *et al*, 1996

The structural nature of poverty is evidenced by looking at the composition of poor households. The main group here is the unemployed, which accounts for a third of the total. This reflects both the high poverty risk for this group (60 per cent) and the significant number of unemployed households in the general population (10 per cent). Other large groups among the low-income population are those engaged in home duties (25 per cent) and the retired (10.5 per cent). In social class terms, half of poor households come from semi and unskilled manual background, considerably greater than their representation in the population at large at 36 per cent. In terms of household type, families are over-represented among those in poverty, accounting for 55 per cent of poor households as compared to only 40 per cent in the general population. Larger families and lone parent families have a particularly high risk of poverty (38 and 57 per cent respectively).

A feature of Irish unemployment is the high percentage of long-term unemployed (over 50 per cent of the total). Reflecting this situation is the uneven distribution of the burden of unemployment: a small group (4 per cent of adults) with a minimum of 5 years without work account for over half of all career unemployment (Nolan *et al*, 1994). Also, there is a concentrated incidence of unemployment in certain locations, with rates in excess of 50 per cent not uncommon. The burden of economic change has thus been carried by the traditional urban working class, whose opportunities for manual work have reduced, while at the same time being unable to compete, either socially or geographically, for the new skilled positions (Breen *et al*, 1990). A similar pattern is apparent in agriculture, where the status of small producers has been eroded as farm output is increasingly monopolised by a minority of larger and more efficient farmers, a process aided directly by state agriculture policy (Hannan and Commins, 1992). The problem here is less acute due to the opportunities for off-farm employment and the terminal demographic status of many affected farm households.

The unemployed are primarily distinguished by their low educational attainment and poor occupational skills, which in turn are linked with manual social class origins (Nolan *et al*, 1994). Social class inequalities are strongly perpetuated through the education system. Despite increased participation rates across all social groups with the advent of free second-level education (and more recently free third-level), inequality in educational outcomes has persisted (O'Connell and Rottman, 1992). In particular, there remains a persistent problem of early school leaving, with approximately 5 per cent of young people, almost exclusively from lower working class backgrounds, leaving school each year without basic qualifications. With the growth in credentialism, the consequences of educational disadvantage have increased over time, culminating in a risk of permanent exclusion from the labour market. There have been various government initiatives targeted at the unemployed, in particular temporary employment programmes. However, these have enjoyed minimal success, with their main achievement being to re-cycle the unemployed through intermittent periods of work and/or training (Breen, 1994).

The implications of increased levels of poverty are substantially different for women and other minority groups. In part, this arises from the changing profile of low-income households, with an increasing proportion of lone parents and households engaged in home duties. In part, it is due to women's economic dependency, a pattern that is institutionalised under the social welfare system. While women may be responsible for managing household expenses, the allocation of resources to the household is channelled through the male partner. There are also specific social factors that impact on poor women. For example, not alone do women carry the brunt of the psychological stress associated with poverty, they may also do without themselves to ensure other household members are adequately clothed and nourished. Lack of access to childcare, especially where women are parenting on their own, together with difficulties in participating in labour market programmes, further isolate poor women in the home (Daly, 1989). Another group that experiences a particularly extreme form of poverty is Travellers. This nomadic ethnic minority, numbering approximately 20,000, have very basic housing conditions, frequently residing in temporary roadside encampments with inadequate water, sanitation and heating facilities. In addition, Travellers suffer discrimination in terms of access to many public and private services (Task Force on Travellers, 1995).

A particular feature of poverty is its socio-spatial manifestation, notably the clustering of poor households in urban localities. The key mediating factor here is housing tenure, with a major cleavage apparent between the public rented and privately owned sectors in terms of class structure, employment status and income. Hence, local authority tenants are up to ten times more likely to be persistently poor than owner-occupiers, and 40 per cent of persistently poor households are to be found in the public rented sector, though accounting for only 12 per cent of all households (Nolan *et al*, 1997). This social polarisation is exacerbated by the spatial segregation of housing, in particular due to the construction of large public housing estates in suburban peripheries during the 1970s and 1980s. The concentrated incidence of income poverty is further compounded by inferior housing and other social problems attendant to ghettoisation (e.g. crime and vandalism, inadequate services and weak community structures), giving rise to a pattern of cumulative disadvantage. A further factor is the public stigma associated with such areas, which can result in discrimination in employment and financial services (Walsh, 1993). In rural areas, by contrast, the spatial expression of poverty is one of peripherality and social isolation, problems compounded by ageing population structures and underdeveloped transportation networks in rural Ireland (Curtin *et al*, 1996).

Poverty can also give rise to a process of social exclusion, whereby households are denied access to key societal resources. Some aspects of this have been elaborated upon through in-depth studies, such as restricted access to credit and financial services, fuel poverty and powerlessness. Low-income households are particularly associated with moneylending, a form of collected credit with very high interest and collection charges and which can also lead to an increased risk of indebtedness (Daly and Walsh, 1988). Fuel poverty is another emerging problem, as poor households are unable to generate adequate heat due to structural deficiencies with their accommodation (Quinn, 1994). Another aspect of poverty is its impact on people's self-esteem and self-confidence. The forced dependency on centralised welfare services to meet basic housing and other needs frequently has created feelings of stigma, disempowerment, hopelessness and alienation among recipients. The clientelist nature of the political system adds to people's feelings of marginalisation from the decision-making processes which affect their lives (O'Neill, 1992).

Policy Context

Social Partnership

Social partnership (or corporatism) is at the core of public policy in Ireland and underpins recent economic performance. Social partnership can be defined as the search for consensus on economic and social objectives between sectoral interests — trade unions, business, farming organisations — and government. In recent times, NGOs have been included in this social partnership for the first time. Social partnership has strong cross-party political support, as exemplified in the policy programmes of the current and previous governments. These outline a commitment to partnership relationships in all aspects of society — political, economic and social, with "full support to the development of economic and social partnership at all levels of Irish economic and social life." Social partnership has in effect been elevated to a shared political ideology, which infuses all aspects of public policy-making and with minimal dissent.

Social partnership is apparent at a number of levels:

1. **As a mechanism for agreeing wages and other policy matters** The strongest application of the social partnership principle is in the successive agreements between the social partners since 1987 on a wide range of economic and social policy priorities. The ability of this country to compete in an increasingly global economy is seen as being predicated, in part, on its capacity to respond to changing international conditions. Social partnership is presented as a means of strengthening this capacity, thereby enhancing prospects for economic and social progress. The first social partnership programme took place in extremely unfavourable economic conditions during the late 1980s — spiralling public expenditure, rising unemployment and declining real incomes. Despite this, agreement was reached on a policy of fiscal rectitude (including wage moderation), balanced by protection of the most vulnerable sectors in society and a phased reduction in employees' tax liability. Three other programmes have followed, with agreement on similar broad-based policies. Monitoring of these programmes is undertaken by a committee comprising the social partners and attached to the Department of the Taoiseach (prime minister).

2. **As a forum for discussion and debate on public policy** A second expression of social partnership is the involvement of the social partners in government advisory bodies. Two dedicated structures have been established in this regard: the National Economic and Social Council (NESC) and the National Economic and Social Forum (NESF). NESC is a long-standing body with a broad policy research brief, connected with the Taoiseach's Department. Its periodic overview reports on economic and social strategy have provided the springboard for the various national agreements described previously. NESF is a newer entity, distinguished by (i) the inclusion of politicians and NGOs in its membership and (ii)

the specific focus on unemployment and poverty issues. NESF has had some impact on policy issues (e.g. measures for the long-term unemployed). Once-off government fora on particular policy issues have also included representatives of the social partners, e.g. Expert Group on the Integration of the Tax and Welfare Systems, Commission on the Family.

3. **As a framework for policy implementation** In an important recent development, social partnership has been used as a framework for local action to tackle long-term unemployment, arising from the social partnership-brokered Programme for Economic and Social Progress (1991-93). Under this, projects were established in specific localities involving government agencies and social partner representatives, with the addition of local NGOs. These new structures were designed to replicate, at a local level, the national model of social partnership. However, they go beyond being simply fora for policy formation to acting as mechanisms for mobilising the resources of public agencies, employers and trade unions, together with local community and voluntary groups, to meet agreed objectives. This initiative significantly deepens the involvement of employers and trade unions in policy design, as well as broadening the range of interests involved.

4. **As a dialogue for reforms at industry level** A final expression of social partnership, which is still only at embryonic stage, is that of trade union-employer involvement at industry and company levels. The latter is mainly focused on enhancing employee participation in companies through consultation programmes, financial involvement and working life initiatives. Another aspect is the development of more effective social and eco-auditing for enterprises.

Social partnership is a pervasive force in public policy, despite the absence of any legal basis for negotiations between government and the social partners. Other potential constraints, such as the lack of a strong social democratic political tradition and the fragmented organisational make-up of the social partners, have also been overcome. The primary motivation for social partnership remains enhanced national competitiveness, with government (supported by all the main political parties at one stage or another) in the vanguard. Trade unions, more than employers, have been strong advocates of social partnership, concerned to have access to public policy formation at a time of general retrenchment (and in anticipation of negative outcomes for workers, as occurred in the UK at the time). Employers are less enthusiastic about extending the scope of social partnership, because of concerns over the additional public expenditures arising in social policy.

In recent times, the influence of social partnership has broadened, from an initial incarnation as a mechanism to agree wages and related policy issues at the national level to becoming a tool for policy implementation at the local level involving NGOs. There is widespread support for the applied dimension to social partnership at the local level. For government, it offers a structure to improve public provision for the unemployed at the local level, but in a developmental rather than bureaucratic fashion due to the active involvement of employers and trade unions. Localising social partnership is also of strategic importance to the trade unions, in that it provides a tangible expression of their public policy influence at a level which is otherwise sidelined by the process of centralised negotiation of agreements on pay and other issues. Employers are again more sceptical of the local dimension, which reflects the voluntaristic (as distinct from commercial) framework in which their role is defined.

Local Development and Employment Initiatives

There is an enhanced local dimension in economic policy in recent years, centred on local economic development and employment initiatives. The current support for local intervention is ironic in a state where central control of economic matters has been a defining feature of public administration. Furthermore, it has occurred in a context in which local government has atrophied, with restricted powers, a secondary role for elected representatives and an overwhelming dependence on central funding. This new localism is best exemplified by the Programme for Local Urban and

Rural Development under the Community Support Framework (CSF). However, localism is not simply an EU implant: the driving force for local development is central government, in particular the Department of the Taoiseach. The rationale for the enhanced local emphasis in economic policy is twofold. First, the need to address the spatial outcomes of economic restructuring. Macroeconomic restructuring has resulted in a growing spatial polarisation in living conditions between particular localities. In rural Ireland, the effects of the Common Agricultural Policy are to concentrate farm production among a minority of producers. In areas where farm structures are less efficient (due to demographic and economic factors), dependence on agriculture has become more and more unviable, despite the introduction of targeted farm income supports. At a local level, these problems are compounded by a decline in public and private services, the out-migration of young people and the threatened collapse of the local economy. A similar pattern is apparent in more urbanised areas, in this case arising from the increase in structural unemployment among unskilled workers. Here, the spatial dimension is mediated through an extremely polarised housing system, with a spatially isolated public rented sector catering almost exclusively for those dependent on welfare (primarily due to unemployment, but increasingly also arising from lone parenthood).

Second, a concern to identify new sources of jobs, especially in the informal services sector. There is a growing realisation of the indigenous dimension to economic development. Poor organisational capacity, together with limited access to capital and other resources, can hinder the development of particular localities and sectors. Various EU initiatives, such as LEDA and Leader, have been designed to overcome these local blockages to economic development. Ironically, there has been a long if officially neglected tradition of local initiative in Ireland. It was only in the late 1980s, however, as part of a re-assessment of economic policy, that there has been a renewed interest in "bottom-up" development as a means of economic diversification and environmental sustainability. This policy re-alignment is reflected in the estab-

lishment of new public programmes with a specific local enterprise remit. The case for a strengthened local input is added to by
the recent EU emphasis on subsidiarity.

The motivation for this policy shift in favour of local intervention is thus quite diverse. The new localism enjoys widespread
support across political viewpoints and sectoral interests, though
some doubts have been expressed about the economic efficiency of
devolution. Despite this, the centralist nature of public administration remains largely unaltered: government departments continue to be heavily involved in service delivery, although with a
more localised facade; the local input into the CSF is not reflected
in regional strategies; while the powers and revenue-generating
capacity of local government are still very restricted. In effect, reform of local administration is a project of central government
which seeks to mobilise local initiative while retaining a large degree of central control.

Local Co-ordination and Delivery of Welfare Services

The scale of poverty and social exclusion, despite an extensive
welfare effort, has caused a gradual re-appraisal of public policy
for tackling poverty. This has led to growing support for the introduction of innovative strategies which incorporate three main
themes: *multi-faceted* actions supported by relevant agencies; *targeting* of resources at specific areas or sectors of need; and *participation* of intended beneficiaries in the planning and delivery of
services. These themes are reflected in a succession of EU and national initiatives since the mid-1980s.

Multi-faceted interventions, supported by inter-agency working, were central to the rationale for the Poverty 3 programme, as
expressed in its core principles of multi-dimensionality and partnership. This was premised on the belief that those affected by
social exclusion had a multiplicity of needs. Furthermore, such a
multi-dimensional programme could only be delivered through the
cooperation of a variety of agencies, statutory and voluntary. This
distinctive approach of Poverty 3 was also widely championed by
the Combat Poverty Agency, to the extent that the theory of inte-

grated strategies ran ahead of the actual practice in the programme. There have also been a number of important Irish reports which have outlined the need for a multi-dimensional approach to social exclusion. The most important is the NESC 1991 strategy report, which stated:

> Currently, social policies and services operate on a "functional" or "departmental" basis (Health, Social Welfare and others) without any coherent attempt to integrate services at local levels. Clearly, many low income communities are affected by the services, and receive resources from a range of state agencies — local government, health boards, the Department of Social Welfare, FÁS, for example. The scope for area "renewal" and community based coordination must therefore be considerable. Evidence suggests that concerted, intensive programmes in small areas, containing elements of housing and environmental improvement, as well as retraining and employment schemes and "outreach" health and educational projects, can have an impact over and above the separate effects of individual programmes. Furthermore, the more closely involved are local communities in the planning and delivery of area based projects, the more they will reflect local needs and priorities (NESC, 1991, p. 74).

A similar conclusion was drawn in an interdepartmental report on urban crime and disorder, which highlighted the need for greater co-ordination of local services in disadvantaged areas. The theory of multi-dimensionality, as well as being reflected in mainstream government services, has also been applied in a number of special local programmes, largely focusing on labour market provision for disadvantaged youth and the long-term unemployed.

A second theme informing policy on social exclusion is a desire for greater targeting of resources, especially in an era of public expenditure constraint. Together with traditional means-testing strategies, area-based programmes have represented the most convenient way of achieving this goal, especially given the distinct spatial nature of poverty and unemployment, as conveyed by the common use of the term "unemployment blackspots". This rationale was especially used for the introduction of special employment measures for the long-term unemployed and the provision of additional educational resources for disadvantaged schools. Such policies were frequently linked with programmes of multi-faceted action.

The increased importance of measures which encourage the active participation of beneficiaries is a third element of policy reform. This is especially associated with the new-found emphasis in provision for the long-term unemployed on client-oriented counselling and guidance. It is also reflected in the general advocacy of client consultation and participation in the planning and delivery of services. Again, these concepts were very much associated with the EU poverty programmes, though also having an indigenous resonance based on a long-established tradition of community self-help. Examples of mainline departments which have promoted the participation of its users are the Department of Education (parental involvement) and the Department of the Environment (tenant participation). Locally, state bodies such as health boards, VECs, FÁS and local authorities, together with voluntary organisations (Society of St Vincent de Paul) have also placed greater emphasis on initiatives which encourage client activation, albeit in a more haphazard and less well resourced way. For instance, many VECs have supported community-based adult education initiatives which provide a range of courses in personal development, as well as in basic education and training.

This reassessment of policy for tackling social exclusion has recently been brought to a new level with the decision by government to formulate a national anti-poverty strategy (Ireland, 1997). The aim of the strategy is to achieve greater policy coordination across government departments and with other bodies on key poverty issues, e.g. unemployment, educational disadvantage, etc. A second goal is to audit all existing policies to assess their impact on poverty, e.g. housing, taxation, etc. In formulating the strategy, government has emphasised the participation of organisations representing the socially excluded. Furthermore, participation should become a routine feature of the design and implementation of government actions to tackle poverty. This initiative is still at its early phase and yet to have a concrete impact on public policy and, crucially, on the collection and allocation of public resources.

Community as an Official Actor in Public Policy

There is a long-standing tradition of community involvement in social and community services, enterprise development, and education and training provision, much of it associated with rural areas and the Catholic Church. This tradition has remained institutionally weak due to the underdeveloped nature of local government and the lack of national statutory recognition and support for community initiatives. During this century, there have been two major attempts at rural community-based economic and social renewal (Ó Cinnéide, 1985). The first of these was Horace Plunkett's co-operative movement, which sought to promote economic development by supporting producer co-operatives among farmers and fishermen. After initial success, the movement gradually succumbed to market forces, eventually leading to its takeover by agribusiness. The second initiative was Muintir na Tíre, a rural revitalisation movement pioneered by Canon John Hayes, which promoted community development as a means of meeting rural needs (e.g. local infrastructure, community facilities). Muintir na Tíre also entered a period of decline due to a combination of official indifference and changed economic and social circumstances, though in recent years it has sought to re-establish itself as a rural force, mainly in crime prevention and community enterprise.

In recent years, a more positive attitude towards community development has emerged on the part of government. The main promoters here have been the Combat Poverty Agency and the Department of Social Welfare in the welfare field and various government employment agencies in the economic arena. The Agency is designated as a national resource centre for community development. It has piloted a succession of community development initiatives, as well as providing small-scale funding and resource material for this sector. The Agency also advocates support for community development at a wider policy level. Arising from this and other factors, the Department of Social Welfare has incorporated support for community development as part of its more traditional income support activities. The centrepiece is a nationwide community development programme, along with funding for women's and other community projects. The Youth Employment Agency and, more recently FÁS, has supported local economic and employment activities through various community enterprise and community employment programmes. Some government departments have also begun to support community development activities in their own areas of competence.

As a result, community development initiatives have flourished in recent years, though less on the grand scale of earlier movements and more through sectoral initiatives. These can be categorised using the framework developed by Ó Cinnéide and Walsh (1990):

1. **Community social services.** These emerged in the 1960s as a hybrid of professional social services (funded by the state) and christian ideals of lay voluntary action (promoted by the Catholic Church). These were established on a county basis and, in some cases, grew to be very large organisations (eg Kilkenny Social Services Council). A national statutory body to support these councils was also established: the National Social Services Council (later renamed as the National Social Service Board). Over time, the importance of these councils has diminished somewhat as the state expanded its own social services capacity through a network of regional health boards. However, youth services and services for the elderly remained under local control. Another factor was a re-assessment by the Catholic Church of its involvement in social services. The result was a shift of emphasis from lay involvement to empowerment and self-help of disadvantaged groups. This is exemplified by the establishment of locally-managed family resource centres under the general auspices of the church.

2. **Community economic and employment initiatives.** These date from the late 1960s and early 1970s and were ini-

tially associated with rural, mainly Irish-speaking areas, where community co-operatives acted as vehicles for local economic development. While designed to be community-owned through a shareholder mechanism, the driving force was often the manager employed by the co-operatives. These organisations received some financial support from government agencies. Since the 1970s, the co-operatives have been in decline, due to internal management problems and inadequate public support. In addition to these co-operatives, there have also been a number of stand-alone community economic development projects, also in rural areas, such as Kiltimagh and Glencolumbkille. Though well-documented and somewhat idealised, these ventures were more the exception than the norm against a backdrop of almost universal support for foreign-based industrial development. A new wave of community employment projects was promoted as a response to the growth of unemployment in the 1980s. In both urban and rural areas, community groups initiated a range of actions — jobs clubs, enterprise centres, employment projects, etc — in order to enhance local employment. These initiatives were supported at national level by the Youth Employment Agency (YEA) and later by FÁS, the state training and employment authority. Community employment initiatives are also supported by private business, such as the Enterprise Trust (formerly the Irish Resource Development Trust) and the Ireland Funds. Community organisations also administer government employment and training schemes.

3. **Community anti-poverty projects.** These initiatives were first supported under the first and second EU poverty programmes. Central to the projects was the employment of professional community workers and their direct engagement with poor and disadvantaged groups. The main method of work was action-research, with workers guiding and prompting local actions. This often included confrontation with other interests, such as business, politicians and state officials. Less attention was given to developing a formal management structure, though this changed in the second poverty programme. An innovative feature of the projects was the establishment of

a national co-ordination mechanism, initially on an ad-hoc basis and later as a statutory agency (CPA). In the late 1980s, community anti-poverty work achieved a quantum step forward with the establishment by a government department of a national community development programme. This was later supplemented with support for other local initiatives.

4. **Community information and advice projects.** Since the 1980s, community information and advice projects have been developed in response to an increase in welfare dependency and an emerging emphasis on welfare rights. The primary remit of these projects is the provision of information on public services. Many also provide personal development and adult education courses. There are three main groupings: citizen information centres, centres for the unemployed and community/family resource centres. The first two categories are supported at national level: citizen information centres by the state National Social Service Board (NSSB) and centres for the unemployed by the Irish Congress of Trade Unions (ICTU). (There are also some specialist support networks, e.g. projects linked to Threshold, the voluntary housing advice agency.) The third category of information projects are more stand-alone, at best getting some localised and very limited support from social services councils, Vocational Education Committees or other statutory bodies. A major new development in the context of community information is the founding of locally-managed money advice and budgeting services by the Department of Social Welfare.

Some distinctive features of the current phase of community development can be identified. First, the increased state support for community organisations in order to achieve policy goals. This is reflected by the establishment of community sections in many state agencies (though with limited funds), the development of sectoral programmes targeted at community organisations and the creation of regional and national structures in support of community development. Other national bodies, such as the churches and trades unions, have also recognised the value of community initiatives. Second, the emergence of a corps of professionals with specific expertise in community development. These professionals embrace a diversity of skills and work methods: community work, social work, enterprise development, rural development, adult education and church ministry. This trend is supported by third-level colleges offering professional courses in community work, adult education, etc. Third, the growing diversity of practices and structures within the rubric of community development. These include community-based service provision with strong lay involvement, developmental activities with selective community input, and empowerment projects working with disadvantaged communities and groups as part of a wider social change strategy. Finally, the emergence of national networks of community practitioners and organisations, including the Community Workers' Co-operative (CWC), the Irish National Organisation of the Unemployed (INOU), the European Anti-Poverty Network (EAPN) and Irish Rural Link (IRL). These organisations provide a voice for community initiatives at national and EU levels.

Conclusion

This chapter outlined the rapid and radical transformation in the Irish economy since the 1960s. The modernised Irish economy is performing exceptionally well, with record levels of economic growth and job creation being reflected in rising living standards. Its down side, however, is a persistently high incidence of unemployment, with the burden being carried by those with low education and skill qualifications. Inequalities in the education system are rooted in a rigid system of class differentiation, which results in a limited mobility for a closeted working class at a time when this section of society is increasingly marginalised due to economic change. The resultant high incidence of poverty and generalised deprivation is compounded by gender and ethnic inequalities, socio-spatial segregation in urban and rural areas and differential access to key quality of life measures.

Four catalysts were identified in shaping the emergence of a new local approach to the problems of unemployment and social exclusion. The first of these was the application of a national model of social partnership to the local level as a mechanism of policy implementation. A second was the strengthening of the local dimension in economic policy, with a particular focus on micro-enterprise and other local employment initiatives. A third factor was the design of locally delivered multi-sectoral strategies in order to enhance the effectiveness of traditional welfare policies. And fourth, government recognition and support for local communities as legitimate actors in the provision of welfare services and the promotion of economic self-help.

Chapter 3

Programmes, Structures and Experiences of Local Partnerships

Introduction

This chapter begins by detailing the various government and EU programmes that have promoted local policy responses to issues of unemployment, poverty and social exclusion. Invariably, these programmes have required the establishment of new local institutional structures based on a broad concept of partnership. The programmes fall into two main categories: local service co-ordination and integrated local development. A second theme in the chapter is to describe the models of local partnership that currently exist and the links between these models. The chapter also outlines the institutional framework for local partnerships at the national and local levels. It concludes with a review of the local partnership experience to date, based on various research and evaluation studies.

Local Partnership Programmes to Tackle Unemployment and Social Exclusion

Numerous EU and Irish government programmes have promoted local intervention in recent years as a means of tackling social exclusion. There has also been some independent support for local initiatives from private and non-governmental bodies, but none from local or regional government. The local programmes can be categorised into two: those which promote greater local co-ordination in service provision and those which encourage local economic and social development. A common feature of both categories is the adoption of a broad partnership approach, though the specific nature of this varies considerably. The programmes also differ in the extent to which unemployment and social exclusion are the main focus.

Local Service Co-ordination

Various programmes have used the model of local partnerships as a means of reforming service provision for unemployed and other social excluded groups through inter-agency co-operation, integrated local planning and community involvement. Three are now terminated, all having being introduced on a pilot basis, five are currently in operation as mainstream government initiatives and a sixth is at a pilot stage. The three completed programmes had a limited number of projects and modest funding and included the EU Poverty 3 programme and two Irish government initiatives. Three of the current programmes seek to operate on a nationwide basis, though the lead-in time for this has been considerable. Partnership is incorporated in these programmes as a requirement for the integration of services, though the degree and composition of partnership varies considerably. The geographical scale of intervention varies in the programmes from the local community to city or county administrative boundaries. These local programmes are, in historical order:

- Community Training and Employment Consortia Programme (1985-87)

- Third EU Poverty Programme (1989-94)

- Community Development Programmes (1990-)

- Area Based Response to Long-term Unemployment (1991-93)

- Money Advice and Budgeting Service (1992-)

- Local Employment Service (1995-)

- Local drugs task forces (1996-)

- Integrated Services Initiative (1998-)

The main features of the various programmes are indicated in Table 3.1, along with short summaries of their operation and activities.

- **Community Training and Employment Consortia Programme (1985-87)** The pilot Community Training and Employment Consortia Programme (COMTEC) was established in 1985 by the Youth Employment Agency (YEA) to co-ordinate, at a local level, various youth employment services. Eight COMTECs were set up at the equivalent of a county level to formulate and implement a two-year plan. The COMTECs consisted of a consultative council, involving a range of local interests, and a planning unit, composed of representatives of the main statutory service providers. At national level, a multi-agency co-ordination group monitored the programme, and the YEA provided a management team and funding. The programme had three goals: co-ordination between agencies, local participation in the planning of services, and implementation of a local plan. Minimal additional resources were provided for the initiative (£350,000 or £20,000 per project per year), primarily for administrative costs, while staff were provided through secondment arrangements. Though the programme was discontinued beyond its pilot phase, it did mark a first attempt at exploring the potential of a local input into service planning and implementation and of a wider range of actors being involved in this process (Joyce and Daly, 1987).

- **Third EU Poverty Programme (1989–94)** The Third EU Poverty Programme (better known as Poverty 3) was an EU initiative to promote the social and economic integration of poverty groups. Its key themes were multi-dimensional or integrated action, partnership of key agencies and participation of intended beneficiaries. Two model action projects and an innovative project were set-up in Ireland, which were supported at a national level by an independent research and development unit and the Combat Poverty Agency (which also co-funded the projects). The two model actions involved the main local economic and social agencies in their management, including representatives of intended beneficiaries. The activities of each project were set out in a strategic plan, which was prepared following a consultative assessment of local needs and monitored through an on-going process of evaluation. A key aspect of Poverty 3 was its national and transnational mechanisms for the exchange of information and know-how. There was also a strong policy commitment in the programme, in that the projects were expected to be an instrument for policy innovation of local and national importance. Poverty 3, though ending in 1994, had a considerable legacy on policy-making in Ireland. Its key principles were incorporated into a government programme on integrated local development (see below), while some of its policy and practice innovations were mainstreamed at local and national levels. (Commins and Mernagh, 1994; Curtin, 1994; Harvey, 1994; O'Connell, 1994; Walsh, 1994, Nexus, 1995)

- **Community Development Programme (1990–)** The Community Development Programme (CDP) is administered by the Department of Social, Community and Family Affairs and dates from the late 1980s, when it was set up to provide mainstream funding for projects in the Second EU Poverty Programme. The programme is targeted at communities affected by high unemployment, poverty and disadvantage, with a small number of projects targeted at disadvantaged groups, such as Travellers, people with disabilities and women. The CDP has a specific focus on enhancing the capacity of local people to contribute to and to avail of existing services. The programme has expanded greatly since 1990, and now supports almost 90 local projects at a cost in excess of £6 million. The projects are locally-managed, with widespread community involvement, along with some representatives of local voluntary and statutory agencies. They act as resource centres for a range of community activities and provide personal development opportunities and support services for groups and individuals. Annual core funding is between £40,000 and £60,000, which is used to recruit professional community workers. The remit of the projects is to enable local individuals and groups to articulate their needs and to identify solutions to these needs, in conjunction with other interests.

- **Area Based Response to Long-term Unemployment (1991–93)** The Area Based Response to Long-term Unemployment (ABR) was a pilot initiative under the Programme for Economic and Social Progress, a policy agreement between government and the social partners. Its aim was to develop an integrated approach to long-term unemployment in specific localities. The ABR had three objectives: enhancing training and employment provision, assisting with small business start-ups and improving access to employment opportunities. Twelve areas were selected, a mix of urban and rural, and local "partnership companies" were established to design and implement an area action plan. A standard formula was applied in selecting the membership for the partnership companies comprising representatives of community groups, statutory agencies and the social partners. A feature of the partnerships was their support for community capacity-building so as to enhance local participation in the initiative. The ABR was supported by a national co-ordinating team, initially under the auspices of the Department of the Taoiseach and later as a separate entity known as Area Development Management. The main resource base for the local projects was to be derived from partner agencies, in particular the state sector, as the external budget averaged only £60,000 per year (though additional funds were subsequently made available under a global grant for local development — see below). At the end of the pilot phase, the programme was restructured and considerably extended as a sub-set of the local development programme (see below). (Craig and McKeown, 1994)

- **Money Advice and Budgeting Service (1992–)** An initiative of the Department of Social Welfare, the Money Advice and Budgeting Service (MABS) is a response to growing problems of moneylending and indebtedness. MABS provides intensive advice and support to people in order to overcome their debt problems. A feature of the service is the provision of a budgeting and savings facility in conjunction with credit unions. MABS also liaises with welfare agencies and creditors on behalf of clients. The service is managed locally by voluntary committees drawn from representatives of community, statutory and voluntary organisations. Over 40 projects are in operation on an almost nationwide basis, with a total budget of c.£2.5m. The local projects are linked together through an elaborate regional and national structure, which includes a national policy advisory committee linked to the Department of Social Welfare. (Nexus, 1993)

- **Local Employment Service (1995–)** The Department of Enterprise and Employment initiated the Local Employment Service (LES) following recommendations from the National Economic and Social Forum and a government task force on long-term unemployment. The service is intended to co-ordinate the work of statutory and community bodies offering employment services and also to provide personal counselling and advice to unemployed people. The delivery of the LES is closely linked to the Local Development Programme through the local development partnerships, which oversee the service through a sub-committee structure involving employers, unions, state agencies, unemployed and community groups. However, the day-to-day operation of the service is largely autonomous, with its own dedicated staff and budget. Eighteen LES have been established, and it is proposed to extend the service nationwide on a gradual basis. The Department of Enterprise and Employment initially co-ordinated the development of the service at national level, though this function is now being delegated to FÁS, the national training and employment agency. There is also a national advisory committee for the programme.

- **Local drugs task forces (1996-)** Local drugs task forces were set up in 1996 following the report of a government committee on the drug problem (Ministerial Task Force on Measures to Reduce the Demand for Drugs, 1996). Local drugs task forces have been established in designated areas where drugs-related problems are most acute (12 in Dublin and 1 in Cork). The remit of the task forces is to prepare a local strategy to tackle the drugs problem, which incorporates all existing and planned services and resources. Initial funding of £10 million has been allocated for the task forces to cover a start-up period of roughly two years, with average payments of between £550,000 and £900,000. Long-term funding for this initiative has yet to be decided. The membership of the task forces comprises statutory, community and voluntary agencies. A national drugs task force oversees the local task forces and addresses the policy issues arising from this local intervention. It comprises personnel from government departments and voluntary/community groups. The lead government department on this initiative is the Department of Tourism, Sport and Recreation, under the political leadership of a specified minister of state. This local drugs initiative is also monitored by a government sub-committee on social inclusion.

• **Integrated Services Initiative (1998–)** The aim of the pilot integrated delivery initiative is to develop new procedures for the better co-ordination of statutory service delivery, as the basis for developing models of best practice. Four neighbourhoods have been selected for this pilot phase, based on ranking of disadvantaged urban areas using Census-derived indicators of disadvantage. The first phase of the programme is to profile existing services, to assess the extent of integration and to identify duplication and gaps. This information will then be used to develop an action plan to enhance service co-ordination. This initiative is promoted by the Department of Tourism, Sport and Recreation, again under the political leadership of the minister of state for local development, and is managed on its behalf by ADM.

Similar local initiatives to tackle difficult social problems have also been promoted by other government departments, though on a smaller scale and without the new structures involved in the larger programmes. These include the Home-school-community Liaison Scheme by the Department of Education and Science, tenant participation in estate management by the Department of the Environment and Local Government and youth diversion projects by the Department of Justice, Equality and Law Reform.

TABLE 3.1: LOCAL SERVICE CO-ORDINATION PROGRAMMES WITH A PARTNERSHIP FOCUS*

	COMTEC (1985-87)	Third EU Poverty Programme (1989-94)	Community Development Programme (1990-)	Area Based Response to Long-term Unemployment (1991-3)	Money Advice and Budgeting Service (1992+)	Local Employment Service (1995+)	Local Drugs Task Forces (1996-)
Sponsor (Support Agency)	Youth Employment Agency	Combat Poverty Agency (Research and Development Unit)	Department of Social, Community and Family Affairs (Combat Poverty Agency and regional bodies)	Department of the Taoiseach (National Co-ordinating Team)	Department of Social Community and Family Affairs	Department of Enterprise, Trade and Employment	Department of Tourism, Sports and Recreation (National Drugs Strategy Team)
Focus	Disadvantaged young people	Social groups affected by poverty and social exclusion	Disadvantaged communities and groups	Long-term unemployed and those at risk of long-term unemployment	Households in debt	Unemployed	Disadvantaged areas with acute drug problems

* The Integrated Services Pilot Initiative is not featured in this table because of its small-scale nature.

	COMTEC (1985-87)	Third EU Poverty Programme (1989-94)	Community Development Programme (1990-)	Area Based Response to Long-term Unemployment (1991-3)	Money Advice and Budgeting Service (1992+)	Local Employment Service (1995+)	Local Drugs Task Forces (1996-)
Remit	Co-ordination of education and manpower services	Promotion of multi-dimensional initiatives	Community empowerment and social change	Co-ordination of employment services and enterprise promotion	Advice and assistance with debt management and access to credit	Co-ordination and provision of guidance, counselling and job placement services	Co-ordination of services
Structure	Local councils (8)	Model action projects (2) and innovatory initiatives (1)	Local projects (90+)	Local partnership companies (12)	Local management committees (40+)	Local management committees (14)	Local task forces (13)
Resources	£0.9m	£3.9m	£6m+	£3.8m	£2.5m	£5m	
Assessment	External (Joyce and Daly, 1987)	Internal (Curtin, 1994; O'Connell, 1994; Walsh, 1994) and external (Commins and Mernagh, 1994; Nexus, 1995)	External (Cullen, 1994)	External (Craig and McKeown, 1994)	External (Nexus, 1993, with a new review about to commence)	Due for publication	Underway

Local Socio-economic Development

Seven programmes have been established to promote local development. All but one of the programmes was or is EU promoted or funded, typically through the structural funds. As a result of the EU input, the scale of the programmes has been considerably greater that those focused on service co-ordination, both in terms of resources and projects. The commitment to evaluation in these programmes is less pronounced, as is local research. The broad remit of the programmes is on local socio-economic development, with a key emphasis on local job creation. However, the programmes differ to the extent to which this emphasis is part of a general strategy of local economic development or a targeted programme focusing on areas or groups experiencing social exclusion. The principal delivery mechanism is local partnerships, though using a variety of organisational forms. The various programmes are:

- Area Programme for Integrated Rural Development (1988-90)

- Leader I and II Community Initiative (1991-94;1995-99)

- Global Grant for Local Development (1992-95)

- Local Enterprise Programme (1993-)

- Urban Community Initiative (1996-99)

- Programme of Integrated Development in Disadvantaged Areas (1995-99)

- Programme for Peace and Reconciliation (1995-99)

Their main features and brief summaries of each programme are outlined below.

- **Area Programme for Integrated Rural Development (1988–90).** The Area Programme for Integrated Rural Development (APIRD) was established by the Department of Agriculture in 1988 on a pilot basis. Its objective was to improve employment opportunities, earning potential, quality of life and a sense of community in rural areas, principally by promoting local enterprise. Twelve locations were identified for the pilot phase and each area was allocated a rural development co-ordinator or animator. These professionals worked with a locally appointed "core group", consisting of individuals with relevant experience and a commitment to local development. The core group was responsible for deciding and implementing the development needs of the area. The programme was designed and managed at national level by two consultants, who together with government officials formed an overall "planning team". A feature of APIRD was the regular networking of participants in a model of sharing learning. Only very modest funding for technical assistance was made available under the initiative, together with staff costs. The intention was that the existing funding, services and expertise of public agencies would be locally negotiated. The key ingredients in APIRD were external guidance and animation, local voluntary know-how and networks, and self-motivated enterprise of individuals and groups. A proposal to extend this programme was subsequently deferred with the decision by the EU to introduce the Leader initiative (see below). (O'Malley, 1992)

Leader Community Initiative (1991-99). The EU Leader programme (including Leader I and II) is administered by the Department of Agriculture with EU co-funding. Leader is a follow-on to the pilot integrated rural development programme (see above). Its main features are "the development of a partnership dynamic, local animation and capacity building, and multi-dimensional planning (i.e. linking the social, environmental and economic dimensions of development)". The programme also provides financial assistance to enterprise and employment projects, mainly in rural tourism. The Leader initiative is co-ordinated at national level by government officials. A separate and independent network of Leader projects functions to exchange experience and to link with policymakers. Transnational contacts are also a feature of the programme. Leader II encompasses all of rural Ireland, with 34 groups approved for on-going funding and a number of

TABLE 3.2: LOCAL DEVELOPMENT PROGRAMMES WITH A PARTNERSHIP FOCUS*

	Area Programme for Integrated Rural Development (1988-90)	*Leader I and II Community Initiative (1991-94 and 1995-99)*	*Global Grant for Local Development (1992-95)*	*Local Enterprise Programme (1993-99)*	*Urban Community Initiative (1995-99)*	*Programme of Integrated Development in Disadvantaged Areas (1995-99)*	*Territorial Employment Pacts (1997-99)*
Sponsor (Support Agency)	Department of Agriculture (independent consultants)	Department of Agriculture and Food	Area Development Management	Department of Enterprise and Employment	Department of Tourism, Sports and Recreation	Area Development Management	Department of the Taoiseach
Focus	Rural communities	Rural communities	Selected and other local communities	Unemployed and entrepreneurs	Disadvantaged urban Communities	Disadvantaged and other local communities	Areas with high unemployment
Remit	Promotion of small businesses and other development activities	Promotion of small businesses and related development activities	Promotion of enterprise, employment, education and community initiatives	Promotion of small enterprises and an enterprise culture	Promotion of infrastructural, employment and community initiatives	Promotion of enterprise, employment, education and community initiatives	Co-ordination of local job creation opportunities

*The Peace and Reconciliation programme is not included here because it does not have a specific local partnership focus.

	Area Programme for Integrated Rural Development (1988-90)	Leader I and II Community Initiative (1991-94 and 1995-99)	Global Grant for Local Development (1992-95)	Local Enterprise Programme (1993-99)	Urban Community Initiative (1995-99)	Programme of Integrated Development in Disadvantaged Areas (1995-99)	Territorial Employment Pacts (1997-99)
Structure	Local support groups (12)	Local development groups (34)	Local partnership companies (12) and community groups (28)	Local enterprise boards (35)	Local steering committees (3)	Local partnership companies (38), community groups and sectoral bodies	Local and regional partnership structures
Resources	£1.5m	£77.3m	£8m	£61.3m under the LDP	£15.5m	£78.5m	£0.76m
Assessment	External (O'Malley, 1992)	External Leader 1(B Kearney et al, 1994); Leader 11 underway	External (Haase et al, 1996)	External underway	External underway	External underway	None to date

national sectoral organisations also being supported. (Leader I funded seventeen projects covering half the rural population, with a budget of £70 million over four years.) Innovative features of Leader II are a field inspectorate staff to monitor group activities, efforts to minimise duplication with existing agencies and a programme of on-going evaluation (Kearney *et al*, 1994).

- **Global Grant for Local Development (1992-95).** The Global Grant for Local Development (GGLD) was a joint initiative of the EU and the government to promote local socio-economic development. It was specifically targeted at the 12 local partnerships set up under the ABR, though it also supported local development projects in other areas, but at a lesser scale. The fund was managed by an intermediary company, Area Development Management (ADM), which included representatives of the different interests on its board. In all, £8 million was distributed to local development agencies, with partnership companies receiving on average £328,000 and other groups £115,000. The GGLD had three expenditure categories, enterprise creation and development (43 per cent), training, education and capacity building (48 per cent) and operational costs, mainly ADM (9 per cent). Co-funding of the global grant from statutory and private sources amounted to almost £9 million, giving a total expenditure of £17 million under the initiative. The successor of this initiative is the Integrated Development Programme, under the CSF (see below). (Haase *et al*, 1996)

- **Local Enterprise Programme (1993-99).** The Local Enterprise Programme (LEP) was initiated in 1993 by the Department of Enterprise and Employment to support micro-enterprises at the local level. The programme is delivered through city/county enterprise boards (CEBs), which comprise representatives of state agencies, local authorities (including elected officials), social partners and voluntary groups. Initially supported by central government, the scale of the programme was greatly enhanced when additional resources were secured under the Local Development Programme. Local enterprise boards also incorporate the modest resources and staff of a previous statutory initiative — county development teams — which had been operated by local authorities. The LEP has two main components: formulation of a strategic framework for local economic and enterprise development and provision of advice, support, management training and financial resources to micro-businesses. The planned investment in the programme is £111 million, with a target of 8,000 new jobs. The programme is directly managed by government, with external technical support for training and advice, organisational development and information exchange. (Department of Enterprise and Employment, 1996)

- **Programme of Integrated Development in Disadvantaged Areas (1995–99).** The Programme of Integrated Development in Disadvantaged Areas (PIDDA), a component of the Local Development Programme, is targeted at designated disadvantaged and other areas. It replaces two earlier programmes — the ABR and the GGLD — with a greatly enhanced resource base of £79 million (compared to £8 million). The programme promotes local socio-economic development through a variety of measures: enterprise creation, infrastructural works, education and training, services for the unemployed and community development. An added feature of the programme is its commitment to equality of opportunity, with a particular focus on gender issues. The programme is managed nationally by ADM, which assesses applications on the basis of local plans. ADM has issued detailed guidelines for the preparation of such plans, which highlights local involvement and commitment, organisational capacity and ability to mobilise local resources. The programme is delivered by 38 local partnerships set up in designated areas (Figures 3.1 and 3.2), along with another 33 local development organisations in non-designated areas (Figure 3.4). The programme also funds a number of national voluntary organisations working on sectoral issues, e.g. unemployment, enterprise development, childcare, Travellers, youth. There is a national committee to monitor the programme, and an external evaluation is underway.

FIGURE 3.1: LOCAL DEVELOPMENT PARTNERSHIPS IN DESIGNATED AREAS OF DISADVANTAGE — NON-DUBLIN

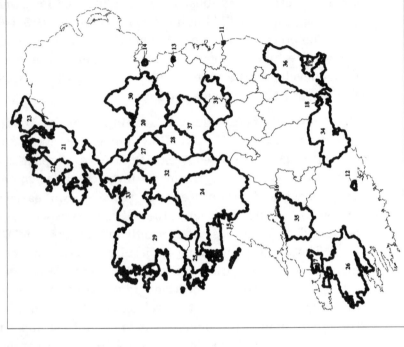

NO	NAME
11	Bray Partnership
12	Cork City Partnership
13	Drogheda Partnership
14	Dundalk Employment Partnership
15	Galway City Partnership
16	PAUL Partnership Limerick
17	Tra Li Partnership
18	Waterford Area Partnership
19	Wexford Area Partnership
20	Cavan Partnership
21	Donegal Local Development Company
22	Pairíocht Gaeltacht Thír Chonaill
23	Inishowen Partnership
24	Galway Rural Development Company
25	Pairíocht Chonamara
26	South Kerry Development Partnership
27	Leitrim Partnership
28	Longford Community Resources
29	Meitheal Mhaigheo
30	Monaghan Partnership
31	OAK Partnership
32	Roscommon County Partnership
33	Sligo Leader Partnership
34	Waterford Development Partnership
35	West Limerick Resources
36	Wexford County Partnership
37	Westmeath Community Development

FIGURE 3.2: LOCAL DEVELOPMENT PARTNERSHIPS IN DESIGNATED AREAS OF DISADVANTAGE — DUBLIN

NO	NAME
1	Ballyfermot Partnership
2	Ballymun Partnership
3	Blanchardstown Area Partnership
4	Clondalkin Partnership
5	KWCD Partnership
6	Southside Partnership
7	Finglas Partnership
8	Northside Partnership
9	Canal Communities Partnership
10	Tallaght Partnership
38	Dublin Inner City Partnership

FIGURE 3.3: LOCAL DEVELOPMENT GROUPS IN NON-DESIGNATED AREAS OF DISADVANTAGE

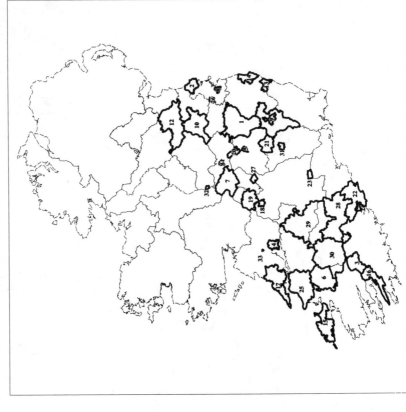

NO	NAME
1	Action South Kildare
2	Co-Operation Fingal (North)
3	Meitheal Muscraí
4	Obair
5	Portlaoise Community Action Network
6	Kerry Rural Development
7	West Offaly Integrated Development
8	Tercanore Community Enterprise Society
9	Ballon/Rathoe Development Assoc
10	Trim Initiative for Development & Enterprise
11	Tullamore Wider Options
12	North Meath Communities Development Assoc
13	Arklow Community Enterprise
14	Wicklow Working Together
15	Coiste Corca Dhuibhne
16	Bantry Integrated Development Group
17	Eiri Corca Baiscinn
18	Nenagh Community Network
19	Borrisokane Area Network Development
20	Mountmellic Community Development Assoc.
21	Castlecomer District Comm. Devt Network
22	East Cork Area Development
23	Clonmel Community Partnership
24	Carlow Area Network Devt Organisation
25	North Kerry Together
26	Lucan 2000
27	Roscrea 2000
28	Avondhu Development Group
29	Ballyhoura Community Partnership
30	I.R.D. Duhallow
31	Kilkenny Community Action Plan
32	Athlone Community Taskforce
33	Ennis West Partners

Urban Community Initiative (1996–99). UCI is an EU programme designed to address the needs of distressed urban areas. It combines employment and training initiatives with measures to improve the environment and community structures. A key theme in the programme is innovative management of urban areas, with a particular focus on an enhanced role for local authorities in tackling urban social exclusion. Three locations have been selected under the programme in Ireland: two in Dublin city and one in Cork city. In each area, a steering group comprising local authorities, local partnerships and other local agencies has been established to manage the programme. Nationally, the initiative is coordinated by the Department of the Taoiseach.

- **EU Territorial Employment Pact (1997–).** Territorial Employment Pacts (TEPs) are a recent EU initiative designed to maximise the job creation impact of the structural funds at local level through an approach based on local initiative, partnership, innovation and integration. A key objective of the pacts is to develop models of good practice for dissemination throughout the EU. In Ireland, four areas have been selected for implementation of TEPs: Dublin, Limerick city, Westmeath and Drogheda/Dundalk. Each pact area has to develop an action plan that identifies local job creation difficulties and opportunities and proposes training and other employment measures to address these. These plans have to be supported by the social partners, state agencies, local communities, local authorities, employers and other relevant interests. In Ireland, TEPs are closely linked to the Local Development Programme, with local development partnerships having responsibility for organising this initiative (except in Dublin where this is the task of the regional authority). Resources for the TEPs are fairly limited, amounting to 250,000 ECU or £190,000 per pact, which is for technical assistance in preparing the pact, employment of a local co-ordinator and transnational networking. The Department of the Taoiseach co-ordinates the TEPs at a national level, with other government departments and ADM having a support and information role.

- **Programme for Peace and Reconciliation (1995–99).** The Programme for Peace and Reconciliation (PPR) is a special EU initiative to promote social and economic development in Northern Ireland and the border counties in the Republic of Ireland, as a contribution to the process of peace and reconciliation. A number of measures in the programme relate to social inclusion, integrated local development and employment (11 out of 26). In the southern border region, two intermediary bodies (ADM and the Combat Poverty Agency) are responsible for administering these measures and an associated budget of £29 million (out of £66 million). The programme does not have an explicit local partnership focus, as the funding is available to a wide range of groups including community groups, local development organisations, statutory bodies and small businesses. In practice, however, local partnerships established under other programmes in the region have accessed the resources of the PPR for additional activities. (In Northern Ireland, by contrast, district partnerships were specifically established to administer the funds at a local level.) The programme has been extended from an initial three years to five, with more funding.

There are also other funding organisations that support local development initiatives, such as the International Fund for Ireland Communities in Action programme and various private funds such as the Enterprise Trust and the Ireland Funds. In addition, EU programmes such as Now, Integra, Youthstart and Adapt provide support for local employment initiatives.

Typology of Local Partnerships

There is a variety of local partnership structures arising from the various programmes outlined above. Within a broad generalisation of local partnership, a number of important distinctions can be identified using variables such as mobilisation, membership, remit and area (see Table 4.3) (Bailey, 1994). Mobilisation is the process whereby local development agencies are established. Two

TABLE 3.3: TYPOLOGY OF LOCAL PARTNERSHIP STRUCTURES

Name	*Local Development Partnerships (c65)*	*Local Enterprise and Employment Partnerships (c40)*	*Local Service Partnerships (c80)*	*Community Development Organisations (c200)*	*Urban Regeneration Partnerships (4)*
Funding	Local development programme	Local development programme	Central government, public agencies	Central government, local development programme	Urban programme
Mobilisation	Central government and local interests	Central government	Local interests and central government	Local interests	Central government and local interests
Membership	Local authorities, public agencies, social partners, community and voluntary groups	Local authorities, public agencies, social partners, politicians, community groups	Service providers (public and voluntary), community groups, service users, social partners	Residents, community and voluntary groups, business people, state professionals	Residents, voluntary organisations, politicians, local partnerships, local authorities, public agencies
Remit	Integrated socio-economic development	Micro-enterprise and local economic development	Local service co-ordination	Economic and community development	Physical, economic and social regeneration

Name	Local Development Partnerships (c65)	Local Enterprise and Employment Partnerships (c40)	Local Service Partnerships (c80)	Community Development Organisations (c200)	Urban Regeneration Partnerships (4)
Area	Designated local areas, mainly sub-county	Local government unit (county or city)	Local areas, mainly sub-county	Local community (neighbourhood, parish, town)	Local authority housing areas with 20,000-80,000 people
Examples	Tallaght Partnership, South Kerry Development Partnership, Ballyhoura Development, Blackwater Resource Development	Kildare County Enterprise Board, Limerick City Enterprise Board	Ballymun Task Force, Inner City Drugs Task Force, Ballyfermot Local Employment Service, Offaly Money Advice and Budgeting Service	Greater Blanchardstown Community Development Project, Pavee Point, Greater Mallow Area Development Partnership	Regeneration of Urban North Dublin, Cork Urban Steering Ctte, Ballymun Renewal

extremes can be distinguished: agencies established in response to an external initiative, whether government or other, and those which are inspired by local circumstances. Often times, a combination of the two can occur or, over time, an initial motivating factor is diluted by other exigencies. The make-up of local partnership agencies differs in terms of the range of interests involved and the balance of power between the actors/sectors. The remit refers to the types of issues taken on and the duration of these activities. A final variable is the geographical scale of operations — housing estate, locality or county. The critical factor is mobilisation, in that this will heavily influence the membership, remit and area of an agency. For example, a project initiated by central government is more likely to adopt a specified organisational structure, to deliver national policy objectives and to accept as given its boundaries of operation. The various local partnership categories are described below.

- **Local development partnerships (LDPs).** LDPs are a mechanism for delivering various local development programmes, such as the integrated local development strand of the Local Development Programme, the Leader programme and elements of the Peace and Reconciliation programme. Partnership is a defining feature of their organisational form, with membership drawn from a wide spectrum of interests, with the actual make-up depending on programme and local factors. The management of LDPs consists of a voluntary board of directors, usually with sectoral sub-committees, and a staff executive, some of whom are seconded from partner agencies. Their remit is integrated socio-economic development, including micro-enterprise, community capacity-building and measures to tackle social exclusion (unemployment, educational disadvantage, low-income farming). For this purpose, a local action plan is prepared, whose contents must be approved at central government level. LDPs operate in a defined area, though the size and population can vary considerably. In some cases, government criteria heavily influence their geographical remit (e.g. designated areas). Some of these bodies have evolved from community development organisation (CDOs) (see below). Frequently, these structures deliver more than one programme, with many rural LDPs having responsibility for both the Integrated Development and Leader programmes, and a smaller number in the border areas being in receipt of Peace and Reconciliation funding. There are an estimated 65 LDPs.

- **Local enterprise and employment partnerships (LEEPs).** LEEPs are strategic local employment and enterprise development bodies which mainly include the county/city enterprise boards, but also the territorial employment pacts and the Western Development Commission. They principally provide support for micro-enterprises and other employment initiatives under the aegis of the Local Development and other programmes. There is a precise formula for the membership of enterprise boards, which is overseen by central government. It consists of local authority representatives (including politicians), public enterprise agencies, social partners and community interests. Operationally, enterprise boards are heavily influenced by local authorities, with many of their staff drawn from this sector, while their chairperson is automatically the local authority manager. Enterprise boards are incorporated as companies limited by guarantee, though an added and rather unique feature is their statutory recognition as autonomous bodies under the aegis of the Department of Enterprise, Trade and Employment. The remit of LEEPs is to promote and assist small enterprise, though they also play a wider function through co-ordinating the work of local development agencies. LEEPs operate on the basis of a local action plan, usually drawn-up with the assistance of outside consultants, which is subject to central government approval. Their area of operation is coterminous with local government structures, either counties or county boroughs. LEEPS co-ordinate their activities with those of LDPs (and occasionally have overlapping membership), in order to minimise duplication. This category also includes the Western Development Commission, which promotes economic development in the west of Ireland through a £25 million investment fund, along with other strategic responsibilities.

- **Local service partnerships (LSPs).** LSPs are local co-ordinating structures that involve a diversity of service providers and community groups/service users. These networks are generally focused on specific issues: training and employment, indebtedness and access to credit, drugs, housing and childcare. They include local drugs task forces, money advice and budgeting services, local employment service networks, and the earlier Poverty 3, ABR and COMTEC projects would also have fallen into this grouping. LSPs are funded through special budget lines of individual government departments, though the amount of money involved is relatively limited and mainly funds staff. They are also expected to oversee the funding of public agencies that provide relevant services. The main remit of LSPs is to co-ordinate existing service provision and, where necessary, to provide additional services to meet specific local needs. This is achieved through the preparation and implementation of an integrated local strategy, following consultation with relevant interests. There is frequently a formal link between LSPs and LDPs. Thus, the local employment service network is structured as a sub-committee of LDPs, while LDPs nominate the chairperson and channel additional funding for local drug task forces. There are c.80 LSPs, including stand-alone initiatives such as the Ballymun Task Force.

- **Community development organisations (CDOs).** CDOs are a catch-all category of local community-based organisations engaged in economic, social and community development. They consist of rural integrated resource development projects, Gaeltacht-based community development co-operatives, local development groups, community development projects and miscellaneous other structures. In general, CDOs only receive project-specific funding, usually from a diversity of sources, including the local population, sectoral programmes (e.g. community enterprise, community employment, urban renewal, employment), private trusts (e.g. International Fund for Ireland) and global grants for local development. (The main exceptions to this are the Community Development Programme and the Local Development Programme.) They may be sponsored by an existing organisation, e.g. community council, or emerge as a loose alliance of local interests around a particular concern. Typically, a voluntary management committee oversees their work, with representation from diverse local interests, including statutory organisations, though without the formality of a partnership agreement. Their focus is twofold: generating local enterprise and employment and encouraging personal and community development. In rural areas, these two strands can be combined in the one organisational structure, while there are more likely to be separate functions in urban areas. Local factors almost exclusively determine their area of coverage, and there is a predominance of neighbourhood-based approaches, while some focus on a social group, e.g. homeless or Travellers. Over 100 CDOs are in existence in urban and rural areas.

- **Urban regeneration partnerships (URPs).** URPs are a relatively recent addition to the local partnership arena. Their distinctive focus is on the physical regeneration, along with social and economic improvements, in disadvantaged urban areas. URPs can be seen as multi-tiered partnerships which are made up of a number of local bodies, including local development partnerships and local authorities. Most are associated with the EU Urban programme, but also include two stand-alone initiatives, Ballymun Renewal and HARP (Historic Areas Renewal Project), which were established to promote urban regeneration in specific areas of Dublin city under the leadership of Dublin Corporation. URPs should be distinguished from central government-sponsored urban renewal initiatives that are primarily concerned with the commercial redevelopment of run-down inner city areas and have minimal input from local community or statutory interests (e.g. Temple Bar Properties, Custom House Docks Development Authority). A key feature of URPs is their focus on local authority housing estates, combining refurbishment and estate management initiatives with social and employment projects for the residents of these areas. Linked to this is the lead role played by local authorities, including public representatives, in the management and activities of URPs. At national level, the lead government department is the Department of Tourism, Sport and Recreation, with a secondary role for the Department of the Environment and Local Government.

Institutional Linkages for Local Partnerships

The institutional linkages governing local partnerships are outlined in Figure 3.4. The apex of this framework is represented by the Department of Tourism, Sport and Recreation, which has overall responsibility for local development initiatives. The main aspect of this is the management of the Local Development Programme, in liaison with the EU and a programme monitoring committee. The department is directly responsible for the subprogramme on integrated development in disadvantaged areas, for which it has devolved operational management to an independent intermediary body, Area Development Management (ADM), along with the drugs task forces and the integrated services pilot initiative (the operational management of which are also delegated to other bodies). The department retains the day-to-day management of the EU Urban programme. The Department also co-ordinates an interdepartmental policy committee on local development, which acts as a co-ordinating mechanism for government departments involved with local partnerships. This includes the Department of the Taoiseach, which up to 1997 was the lead government department, reflecting the social partnership origins of this model. At a political level, a minister of state in the Department of Tourism, Sport and Recreation, is charged with overseeing many of the local partnerships initiatives (e.g. local development, drugs, integrated services). This minister, in turn, reports to a cabinet sub-committee on social inclusion.

Other government departments involved in managing local partnership initiatives are the Department of Agriculture and Food (Leader programme), the Department of Enterprise, Trade and Employment (local enterprise programme and local employment service) and the Department of Social, Community and Family Affairs (community development programme and money advice and budgeting service). Various public service providers (national, regional and local) are also involved as partners in local partnerships, such as the national training and employment agency (FÁS), the regional health boards and the local committees responsible for vocational and adult education. Local government is also involved in local partnerships, though its status can vary from minor partner to being the lead body. Also, whether this involvement is channelled through executive staff or elected officials can differ in the various local structures. (There is no role for regional government, which in any case has extremely limited powers and resources.) Finally, there are county strategy groups, which provide a forum for local government, local development partnerships, enterprise boards and other local development bodies to co-ordinate their activities. These linkages are elaborated upon below.

FIGURE 3.4: INSTITUTIONAL LINKAGES FOR LOCAL PARTNERSHIPS

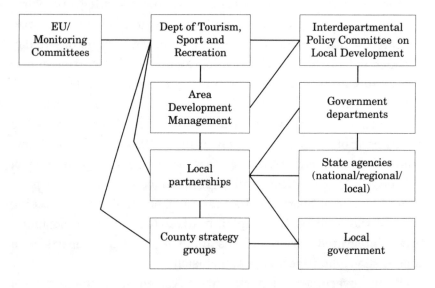

- **Department of Tourism, Sport and Recreation.** The Department of Tourism, Sport and Recreation is the lead government department for local partnership programmes. It only recently assumed this role when responsibility was removed from the Department of the Taoiseach and given to a

line government department. The Department of the Taoiseach initially assumed this role when negotiating a social
partnership agreement, the Programme for Economic and Social Progress (PESP), which gave rise to the ABR initiative. At
this time, the department established a co-ordinating team to
develop and support the initiative, which functioned as an
adjunct to its secretariat role in monitoring the PESP. As well
as an operational role under this initiative, the department
assumed co-ordination and animation functions in relation to
other government departments and agencies, whose roles
overlapped with local partnerships. It subsequently drew up
the Local Development Programme, established an interdepartmental policy group (see below), took on the management
of the Urban programme and had a minister of state for local
development. In 1997, following a change of government, the
majority of these responsibilities were handed over to a new
government department (Tourism, Sport and Recreation). The
Department is now responsible for overseeing the operation of
an integrated development programme, for drawing down
funds from the EU and for monitoring and evaluating the en-
tire programme.

- **Area Development Management.** Area Development
  Management (ADM) manages the implementation of the
  Programme of Integrated Development in Disadvantaged Areas, under an agreement between the Irish government and
  the EU. It is established as a private company, with its board
  of directors representing statutory, employer, trade union and
  community interests and is funded through a global grant.
  The functions of ADM are: (i) to approve, fund and monitor
  the activities of local development partnerships; (ii) to provide
  technical support in the establishment and operation of local
  partnerships; and (iii) to facilitate the dissemination of know-
  how and good practice within the programme. The staff of
  ADM comprises seconded personnel from statutory and other
  bodies and people directly recruited by the company. ADM
  also administers a pilot childcare initiative on behalf of the
  Department of Justice, Equality and Law Reform, which supports new local childcare services in disadvantaged areas.

ADM reports to the Department of the Taoiseach and is represented on the interdepartmental policy committee on local development. It also has links with the EU, government departments and state bodies in regard to local development issues.

- **Interdepartmental policy committee on local development.** An interdepartmental committee was initially established to formulate a local development programme under the EU-funded CSF. This was subsequently given a formal role to oversee the implementation of the local development programme, to co-ordinate the activities of various government departments involved in local initiatives and to provide a mechanism for linking local practice with national policy. The committee includes representatives of government departments, Area Development Management, Combat Poverty Agency and FÁS and is co-ordinated by the Department of Tourism, Sport and Recreation.

- **Other government departments.** Line government departments have become involved in local partnerships in two ways. First, some departments have undertaken local initiatives which incorporate, to varying degrees, features of the local partnership model. The most obvious examples of this are the Leader programme and the local enterprise boards. Many of these initiatives have an EU dimension, either in terms of providing resources or delivering a programme. A summary of the various departmental initiatives is:

  ◊ Department of Agriculture and Food — EU Leader Programme

  ◊ Department of Enterprise, Trade and Employment — Local Enterprise Programme

  ◊ Department of Social, Community and Family Affairs — Poverty 3/Community Development Programme

  ◊ Department of the Taoiseach – Territorial Employment Pacts

In many of these cases, government departments contract out the technical support aspects of their work to independent agencies. Departments are also responsible for commissioning an independent evaluation of the programmes they manage. A second engagement is where government departments have delegated the implementation of specific policy initiatives to local partnerships. Examples here include the new Local Employment Service (Department of Enterprise, Trade and Employment), welfare-to-work schemes (Department of Social, Community and Family Affairs) and an equal opportunities child-care initiative (Department of Equality and Law Reform). A third, and more informal linkage, is where government departments have worked with individual local partnerships on general policy initiatives, e.g. estate management and urban renewal (Department of the Environment and Local Government) or educational disadvantage (Department of Education and Science).

- **Public agencies and local government.** Another interface between local partnerships and the administrative system is the involvement of state agencies as partners in these local bodies. This category includes a central government department (Department of Social Welfare), national sectoral agencies (industrial development, training and employment), regional health boards, local educational bodies and local government. In almost all cases, the representatives of state agencies are staff, even where there are elected public representatives on the board of a state agency. Public agencies' main linkage with local partnerships is in regard to the provision of services. There is seldom a policy engagement, primarily because partner state agencies have little local discretion given their centralised nature (whether in structure or funding). Nor is there a funding relationship because of the financial constraints under which state agencies operate. An important recent development is the special status allocated to local government in the operation of the local co-ordination body for local partnerships, county strategy groups (see below).

- **County strategy groups.** County strategy groups (CSGs) co-
  ordinate the activities of the various local partnerships in operation at a local authority level. They are chaired by the
  manager of the relevant local authority and include representatives of LDPs, CEBs and LDOs, along with central government representatives (primarily the Department of the
  Taoiseach, which co-ordinates this initiative at national level).
  The functions of LDSGs are to exchange information, improve
  linkages and liaise with government on policy issues. The
  main output of CSGs is a "programme of co-ordination", which
  sets out the mechanisms for achieving its goals. They do not
  have an implementation capacity, operating on a voluntary
  basis and with affiliated groups to provide any administrative
  resources that are required. This aspect of the institutional
  framework for local partnerships is currently the subject of
  some amendment, with a stronger lead role envisaged for local
  government, including elected representatives.

There also exists a non-governmental institutional framework for
local partnerships through internal programme networks that are
independent of government. For example, the 38 local development partnerships in the integrated development sub-programme
have established a representative organisation known as Planet.
This grouping consists of chairpersons and managers and meets
on a quarterly basis. It also has a secretariat. The role of Planet is
to share experiences on the management of the programme and to
represent the views of the partnerships to ADM and national policy makers. Similar networks exist for the Leader, Urban, community development and local enterprise programmes.

European Union Role in Local Partnerships

The EU input into the evolution of local partnerships has and
continues to be considerable. The EU influence can be traced in
four ways. First, EU policy statements on social exclusion, equal
opportunities, rural development and unemployment have influenced the policy framework in Ireland. This reflects the positive
disposition to European ideas both in official circles and among

non-governmental agencies, including voluntary and community organisations (e.g. the European Anti-Poverty Network and the Community Workers' Co-operative). The fact that two Irish people have held the European Commission's social affairs portfolio is another important factor. This transfer of ideas is not one way, especially in recent times as the apparent success of Irish policies in regard to unemployment and local development is being widely trumpeted as a model for future action on these issues in Europe.

A second and more tangible factor is the EU structural funds that promote economic and social cohesion between the regions. These are highly important tools of economic and social policy given Ireland's status as an objective 1 region and the scale of funds which flows from this. The influence on local partnerships is most apparent in the current community support framework (CSF), where local development is one of the four guiding themes for allocation of EU funds. This programme provides £200 million for a combination of promotion of local enterprise, integrated development in disadvantaged areas and urban and village (physical) renewal. An addition to the CSF is the Programme for Peace and Reconciliation, which provides over £300 million for social and economic development in Northern Ireland and the southern border counties. This EU input is more than simply funds, however, as a portion of this money is allocated outside of the government administrative system through the mechanism of a global grant. This gives greater access to these resources by non-governmental bodies than would be the norm with mainline government expenditure. There is also a strong emphasis on subsidiarity (i.e. funding for regional and local authorities), though this principle has been largely negated by the continued control exercised by central government over the allocation and dispersal of EU funds. (Hence, a key reason for the importance of central government support in the enhanced funding for local partnerships.)

A third means of influence on local partnerships is through EU programmes such as Poverty 3, Leader, Urban and the Territorial Employment Pacts. These transnational initiatives support innovative actions at local level using an explicit partnership model.

The importance of these exemplar programmes was noted earlier, where they have provided the inspiration for both pilot and main-line government initiatives. For example, Poverty 3 pre-dated and helped to shape the ABR initiative and subsequently, the programme of integrated development. Leader, meanwhile, has been used to extend, on a nationwide basis, a government programme of rural development. Similarly, the new Urban programme is encouraging innovative approaches to the management of deprived urban areas, which is currently a key public policy issue.

A final source of influence are transnational networks and contacts between local partnerships. These occur in various forms: as an integral feature of EU programmes (e.g. Poverty 3, Leader, Urban); as stand-alone EU initiatives, such as "Quartiers en Crise", the network of urban areas; or as various one-off EU events, such as the annual employment week or thematic conferences. What they have in common is providing a mechanism for the transfer of experience and good practice with other EU countries. Examples of where local partnerships have picked up new ideas through these contacts include the Belgian Plato small business initiative which has been promoted by the Tallaght Partnership and the Dutch model of a tailored employment service which was picked up by the Northside Partnership.

The EU impact on local partnerships is multi-tiered: a general conscientisation of public policy; funding for local development initiatives; pilot programmes to identify new ways of tackling poverty and social exclusion; and mechanisms for the transfer of good practice. It is also important to recall the internal reasons why Ireland has proved a very fertile ground for receiving EU policies and practices, as were outlined in the last chapter. The administrative vacuum at the local level, into which EU programmes brought a new dynamic, and the role of EU transfers in a context of government financial stringency in the late 1980s/ early 1990s, are probably the most significant aspects of EU policy in terms of local partnerships. But there were also positive indigenous factors, such as the national commitment to social partnership and the political concern with the growth of "unemployment blackspots" and the acceleration of rural decline, which added a distinctive Irish flavour to EU policies.

Interestingly, the recent successes of the Irish economy (in terms of economic growth, job creation and fiscal management), together with its local initiatives on unemployment and local development, has reversed the traditional pupil-teacher relationship between Ireland and the EU. Increasingly, it is the EU, together with other bodies such as the OECD, which are now looking to Ireland for answers to the problems of poverty, unemployment and social exclusion in Europe and in the developed countries of the world.

The Experience and Lessons of Local Partnership

Local partnerships are playing an increasingly important role in Government and EU policy to tackle unemployment and social exclusion. Most of the programmes that have supported this new approach have been subject to in-depth evaluation, due to a combination of their pilot nature and the requirements of EU funding. What are the main lessons emerging from these studies on the use of local partnerships to promote social inclusion? Eleven issues are noted.

1. **Power and control over resources**. Local partnerships, in general, are non-statutory bodies and therefore without the power to enforce the implementation of an agreed local action plan. Their ability in this regard is dependent on their ability to exert an influence over the policies and budgets of partner agencies. However, statutory agencies have been most reluctant to surrender their already limited powers to local partnerships. The most local partnerships have aspired to is to have an informal say over the resource allocations of partner agencies, which is by necessity a grey area. To compensate for this, local partnerships have relied on access to external funds to undertake their work programmes, a pattern facilitated by the increased provision of such funding by government and the EU. Such funding has important short-term benefits: it gives partnerships their own discretionary funds and it also

provides a mechanism to lever additional local resources. In the longer-term, however, reliance on external funds may dilute the focus on effective use of existing partner resources and introduce a competitive relationship with other local bodies, including partner agencies, over access to such funds. There is also a question mark over the continued operation of these bodies in the post-1999 era of reduced structural funds (Joyce and Daly, 1987; Haase *et al*, 1996).

2. **Involvement of partner agencies.** It is important to differentiate between the role played by individual representatives in local partnerships and the contribution of partner agencies. Many representatives (though clearly not all) are personally committed to the work of local partnerships and bring a lot of goodwill and energy to their role. However, the degree to which such involvement is translated into meaningful support also depends on the willingness and capacity of the parent organisation to engage in joint local planning. National endorsement of local partnerships, while important, does not guarantee local involvement and may, in fact, dilute feelings of local ownership and participation. Thus, the failure to incorporate capacity-building measures into partnership programmes, with the exception of the community sector, has been a significant oversight. In addition, national-level factors, such as the relationships between government departments and the constraints attached to the provision of local resources, are perhaps even more important given the centralised nature of service planning and delivery. This observation also applies to the social partners, since these too are primarily centralist bodies. While all local partnership programmes have had an ad-hoc element of national-level support, this dimension has been inadequate to overcome institutional constraints. The recent establishment of an interdepartmental policy committee to co-ordinate the involvement of government departments and agencies in local partnerships is potentially an important innovation in this regard (Joyce and Daly, 1987; Commins and Mernagh, 1994; Craig and McKeown, 1994).

3. **Organisational effectiveness.** Much of the initial hype about local partnerships relates to their innovative organisational structures. Over time, however, this has given way to practical concerns about the effectiveness of these entities as decision-making and implementing bodies. Turning multi-agency structures involving many participants into dynamic and effective organisations is influenced by a number of factors: composition, management culture and skills, internal structures, development timescale and range of interests. One problem is that standardised models of local partnership have inadvertently created large and unwieldy local entities without a natural cohesion. Meanwhile, local partnerships bring together diverse and conflicting management cultures and contain quite differing levels of experience. Training and facilitation, along with the input of the chairpeople and managers, have a pivotal role in creating a cohesive management structure. Another organisational factor is the intricate internal structures in local partnerships which, while maximising opportunities for local participation in decision-making, pose serious challenges in regard to organisational effectiveness. Finally, the short timescale in which partnerships begin to function and the multiple geographical scales and diversity of interests of partner organisations are other considerations impacting on organisational effectiveness (Joyce and Daly 1987; Walsh, 1994).

4. **Community participation.** A key motif in local partnerships is providing a community input into public service policy and provision. Despite significant community involvement at various levels of local partnerships, concerns have been expressed as to costs of this involvement to participants and community groups and the actual impact of this input on decision-making. Three sets of factors have been identified in these regards: first, the level of back-up and resources provided to community participants involved in local partnerships; second, the linkages (selection, report back, etc) between community nominees, community organisations and the wider local community; and third, the decision-making procedures and management ethos adopted in local partnerships. Considerable

efforts have gone into enhancing the quality and representa-
tiveness of community participation through initiatives at national (e.g. provision of information and training, establishment of a forum of community directors) and local levels (e.g.
recoupment of expenses, employment of community liaison
staff, establishment of community forums). By contrast, much
less attention has focused on the governance procedures in local partnerships, in particular, how the seemingly consensual
nature of decision-making may conceal basic differences in the
ability of participants to influence decisions (Craig and McKeown, 1994; Haase *et al*, 1996, Walsh, 1996).

5. **Operating models for local partnerships.** Recent evaluations have helped to distinguish ways of working or operating
models for local partnerships, thus helping to clarify the intended benefits of these new structures for those involved.
These include: *service delivery*, where a partnership designs,
funds and delivers services itself, usually on a pilot basis. This
occurs where the local infrastructure is underdeveloped or
where there is an immediate need. Service delivery is especially important when a local partnership is seeking to establish an identity for itself. A second way of working for local
partnerships is an *agency approach*, where local partnerships
work with other local organisations (existing or new) to enhance the provision of services. In some cases, this can be
achieved through an existing body and in others, by establishing an new intermediary structure. A third approach is referred to as a *brokerage role*, where local partnerships act as
support agencies for service providers. Their function is needs
assessment, support, facilitation, planning and lobbying. The
objective here is to strengthen the existing infrastructure
through the medium of partnership. These operation models
are not mutually exclusive in that a local partnership may
combine all three. Equally, there is an evolutionary span, with
the brokerage approach representing the epoch of the partnership model (Craig and McKeown, 1994; Walsh, 1994).

6. **National support structures.** The provision of national
support and advice is a standard feature of centrally-devised
local partnership programmes. The means whereby this sup-

port and advice are provided and the range of services offered varies considerably between programmes. These services can include guidelines on programme activities; approval of plans and provision of funds; support and advice to individual partnerships; monitoring and evaluation of activities; and coordination of links between local partnerships on one hand and central government and the EU on the other. The functioning of these support structures has proven to be rather problematic in a number of ways. First, the required level of technical expertise may not be available in these structures. This applies where support structures consist exclusively of public servants, who may not have an adequate understanding of the requirements of local partnerships. Second, the often hybrid status of support structures can result in confusion as to their relationship with government departments and national agencies. A third issue relates to conflict between the various functions taken on by these bodies, in particular between funding and supervision tasks, training and development activities and policy-related functions (Commins and Mernagh, 1994; Walsh, 1994; Craig and McKeown, 1994).

7. **Linkages with local government.** A recurring theme in the literature relating to local partnerships is their emerging function as a form of local governance, an especially noteworthy feature in a such a traditionally centralist country as Ireland. Their status in this regard, however, is somewhat ambivalent due to their weak formal linkages with existing local government structures and their anomalous administrative status as quasi-public bodies (Harvey, 1994; NESC, 1995; OECD, 1996). A particular focus of concern here is the almost complete absence of elected local public representatives on local partnerships. Another issue relates to the multiplicity of local development agencies and scope for duplication of effort and resources. There is widespread agreement that, for the nascent form of local governance associated with partnerships to develop, these issues will have to be resolved. This has prompted various proposals for a "realignment" between local partnerships and local authorities from the *ex-ante* evaluation of the national development plan, NESC (1995), the Devolu-

tion Commission (1996), the OECD (1996), the Department of the Environment and Local Government (1996) and, most recently, the Task Force on the Integration of Local Government and Local Development (1998). However, such a realignment, in the absence of parallel reform of local government, may restrict the capacity and flexibility of local partnerships.

8. **National policy framework for local partnerships.** A strength of local partnerships is the support they have received at the highest level in the national policy framework. This has facilitated not alone the rapid development of these novel structures, but also the piloting of a number of important policy reforms, e.g. an enhanced temporary employment programme, innovative welfare-to-work measures and the new Local Employment Service. The other side of this coin is equally important: the capacity of the national framework to transfer local innovation into mainstream policy. Various reports have suggested that there are clear deficiencies, horizontally and vertically, which are limiting the impact of local partnerships on the national policy framework for tackling social exclusion (Commins and Mernagh, 1994; Haase *et al*, 1996; OECD, 1996). While addressing issues of policy and practice arising from local experience is a specific brief of the interdepartmental policy committee on local development, it lacks the means to implement this role. A recent OECD report has proposed an innovative proposal to address this weakness in national policy through a model of "democratic experimentalism" (OECD, 1996). This has two components: "simultaneous engineering" (horizontal and vertical transfer of innovation) and "benchmarking" (criteria for comparing the activities of various institutions). The feasibility of this approach has been questioned given the continued lack of clarity as to the status of local partnerships (Walsh, 1996). The recently launched national anti-poverty strategy may provide a more tangible key to improvements in the national policy arena.

9. **Good practice in local planning.** Local strategic planning is identified as a key dimension of the work of local partnerships in all programmes. This task poses considerable difficul-

ties, both technical and political. The first relates to the limited availability and poor quality of local data, with many problems being encountered where operational boundaries do not correspond to administrative ones. The development of appropriate mechanisms for ensuring community consultation is another challenging aspect of local planning. The second difficulty refers to the ability of local partnerships to adopt a strategic approach. In particular, how to move from having shopping lists of actions compiled by individual partners to preparing strategies which address, in an innovative and integrated way, key local issues. The haste with which local plans are often required to be drawn up and the limited technical competence in local partnerships to prepare such plans due to their voluntary management structure and small staff complements, add to this difficulty. While both the Combat Poverty Agency and ADM have produced guidelines in this regard, a common option is to rely on external consultants to undertake this task. This generates its own problems regarding the ownership of the plan and its suitability for local needs (Kearney *et al*, 1994; Haase *et al*, 1996). A key requirement is to add to the composite base of expertise in this critical area.

10. **Equal opportunities.** Considerable emphasis has been given to the participation of women and, to a lesser extent, of minority groups (e.g. Travellers, people with disabilities) in local partnerships, reflecting wider public policy concerns about equal opportunities. Various measures, including a government guideline regarding the gender composition of partnerships and the publication of a guide to gender equality in local partnerships, have been taken in pursuit of this policy goal. Despite this, recent research indicates that women remain under-represented on local partnerships (25 per cent of directors, 24 per cent of chairpeople and 29 per cent of managers), while there is almost no Traveller involvement at these levels. This anomaly is attributed to the exclusivist culture of partnerships, the specific barriers faced by women wishing to engage in partnership activity (e.g. access to childcare, their voluntary status) and the low status of women in many partner agencies (Faughnan *et al*, 1996). Less information is

available on the equal opportunity impact of the activities of local partnerships. The impression here is that while most local partnerships implement specific programmes targeted at women (e.g. childcare, community education), there is a lower priority given to addressing the employment and enterprise needs of women. Similarly, important initiatives have been taken with regard to Travellers and people with disabilities, but again there is considerable ground to be made up before these groups are integrated into the mainstream employment and enterprise activities of local partnerships.

11. **Spatial dimension.** Local partnership programmes have an implicit spatial dimension. This is reflected in two main ways: the identification of areas of disadvantage and the effectiveness of local action as a policy response to social exclusion. Recent research has shown that poverty is a spatially pervasive feature of Irish society. While much of policy is driven by a perception of poverty blackspots, such areas only contain a minority of poor people. Even when location is refined by tenure type (such as major urban local authority housing), only 30 per cent of low income households are still to be found in these areas (Williams *et al*, 1996). One policy response to this has been to extend the designation of disadvantaged areas to include half of the population of the state. This, of course, brings its own problems in terms of diluting the resource base and, hence, the impact of the initiative. Another problem is the nature of the data used to designate such areas, which relies largely on surrogate indicators of poverty and social exclusion. A second issue relates to the limitations of purely local intervention in tackling the structural problems producing poverty (e.g. educational disadvantage, etc). Indeed, areas with high unemployment and poverty are also the places where the obstacles to local development are greatest (Nolan and Callan, 1994, p. 328). A more viable course of action would therefore appear to be to separate those aspects of disadvantaged areas which are amenable to local intervention, for example through better provision and co-ordination of services, from those which require national-level action. Measures which improve the immediate quality of life (housing, crime)

in such areas should also be prioritised (Pringle, 1996; Walsh, 1996). Use of different scales of intervention (neighbourhood, local labour market, region) would be important aspects of a refined spatial approach.

Conclusion

This chapter has presented an overview of the policy and practice of local partnership. The key observations from this are fivefold. First, following a number of innovative and pilot local partnership programmes from the mid-1980s on, the government has made partnership-led local intervention an integral component of national economic and social policy. Second, numerous new structures have been set up at local level under this policy framework, which differ in terms of their mobilisation, structure, remit and area of operation. Third, there is a strong commitment to local partnership at central government level, with administrative and political leadership provided by the Department of the Taoiseach. Fourth, a minimal level of integration with local government is apparent in the institutional framework for local partnership, though this is the subject of review. Finally, various reviews of the extensive practice of local partnership have highlighted a number of key issues for consideration.

Chapter 4

Illustrative Examples of Local Partnerships

Introduction

This chapter details a selection of local partnerships which address issues of unemployment and social exclusion. The eight illustrative examples are (see Figure 4.1)[1]:

- PAUL Partnership Limerick

- Tallaght Partnership

- South Kerry Development Partnership

- Dundalk Employment Partnership

- Greater Mallow Area Development Partnership

- Pavee Point

- Greater Blanchardstown Development Project

- Ballymun Task Force

Four fall within the category of local development partnerships and have explicit commitments to partnership and social inclusion. They are primarily supported under the Programme of Integrated Development, though they also have (or had) links with other local partnership programmes: Poverty 3, Leader, ABR and Urban. The other four are local development organisations and reflect a more diverse and less structured approach to partnership

---

[1] The first three are examined in more detail later in the report as case studies.

FIGURE 4.1: ILLUSTRATIVE EXAMPLES OF LOCAL PARTNERSHIPS IN IRELAND

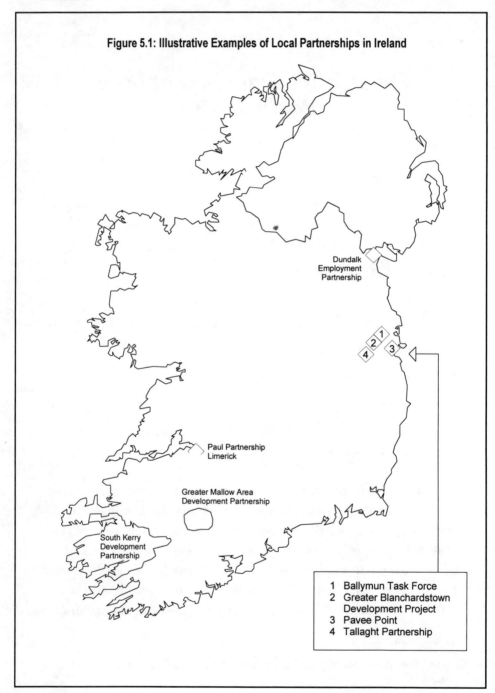

Figure 5.1: Illustrative Examples of Local Partnerships in Ireland

TABLE 4.1: SELECTED CHARACTERISTICS OF ILLUSTRATIVE EXAMPLES OF LOCAL PARTNERSHIPS

	PAUL Partnership Limerick	*Tallaght Partnership*	*South Kerry Development Partnership*	*Dundalk Employment Partnership*	*Greater Mallow Area Development Partnership*	*Pavee Point*	*Greater Blanchardstown Development Project*	*Ballymun Task Force*
Location	urban	urban	rural	urban	urban-rural	urban-rural	urban	urban
Mobilisation	grassroots, Poverty 3	grassroots, government	grassroots, Leader	government	grassroots	grassroots	church	grassroots
Funding	government, EU	government EU, IFI	EU	EU, IFI*	EU	government EU	government;	government, Combat Poverty Agency
Remit	poverty, long-term unemployed	poverty, long-term unemployed	rural dis-advantage, long-term unemployed	long-term unemployed	long-term unemployed	Travellers	poverty	public housing
Partners	local and public authorities, community, voluntary, trade unions, employers	local and public authorities, community, voluntary, trade unions, employers	local and public authorities, community, trade unions, employers	local and public authorities, community, trade unions, employers	local and public authorities, community, employers	community, local and public authorities	community, local and public authorities	politicians, local and public authorities, community

* IFI = International Fund for Ireland

and local development. These have specific sectoral emphases (i.e. enterprise support, housing renewal, Travellers and community development) and incorporate partnership in a variety of manners. Two are community development projects, one is involved in local economic and employment development and the other is a stand-alone urban regeneration partnership. The examples reflect a variety of socio-economic contexts — Dublin, other urban and rural. Only two date from the mid-1980s, the remainder are products of the explosion in local partnership which occurred in Ireland at the start of the 1990s. A further differentiating factor is the funds available to the initiatives, varying from less than £100,000 per annum to £1 million. All projects have sought to document their work, though there is less evidence of on-going evaluation.

PAUL Partnership Limerick

PAUL (people action against unemployment limited) Partnership Limerick (PPL) is based in Limerick city, the third largest city in the country (76,000) and the administrative capital of the midwest region. Limerick's rapid economic transformation from a traditional manufacturing centre and port to a high-technology industry and services location, has resulted in high rates of unemployment. The main casualties are unskilled workers and early school leavers, who find themselves marginalised in a labour market which increasingly requires high educational and skill levels. Those adversely affected by economic change are concentrated in a number of large public housing estates, which were built on the periphery of the city in the 1960s and 1970s. Currently, over 80 per cent of Limerick Corporation tenants rely on social welfare, with two-thirds being out of work.

PPL was formally established in March 1990 at the commencement of the Poverty 3 programme, though its origins can be traced back at least two years to a series of joint initiatives between state agencies and community organisations to address unemployment and related problems in public housing areas. In effect, Poverty 3 proved a timely vehicle for supporting and enabling what was a spontaneous coming together of local interests. PPL was subsequently included in the government's area-based response to long-term unemployment (1991) and also secured funding under the EU global grant and Horizon programmes and a government initiative to tackle indebtedness. Currently, the project's main funding source is the integrated development programme, while additional resources are channelled to affiliated community organisations under the Irish government's community development programme.

The aim of PPL is to support disadvantaged local communities to improve all aspects of their lives. This is pursued through an integrated programme of activities which has as its core a network of "neighbourhood action centres". This work programme has six main components:

1. Employment and economic development;

2. Education and training;

3. Welfare and money advice;

4. Support for families and young people;

5. Environment and housing improvements;

6. Community development.

As well as its local activities, the partnership has addressed issues of national importance in regard to protection for low-income credit consumers, employment provision for the long-term unemployed and access to training and employment initiatives for lone parents. New responsibilities for the partnership include the local employment service, the EU territorial employment pact and a child-care programme combining training and investment in facilities.

PPL has 15 partner agencies who nominate a management committee of 24 (this includes an independent chairperson and a staff representative), a quarter of whom are female. This large membership reflects a compromise between its original Poverty 3 structure (eight community and seven state and voluntary repreitives) and the model proposed under the ABR programme. The partners consist of six state agencies, six community groups, two social partners (employers and trade unions) and two voluntary organisations. Partner agencies nominate between one and three representatives onto the board of the partnership.

The partnership is emerging from a period of consolidation, following the termination of its funding sources under the Poverty 3, ABR and Horizon programmes. This period has been marked by a significant changeover in staff and management personnel, including a new director and chairperson. The partnership continues to be successful in attracting external resources — its budget has almost doubled to £2 million since 1994, despite the termination of the Poverty 3 programme. However, its efforts to generate local partner funds have been much less positive, as has its practical returns from the social partners. There also has been some dissatisfaction among its partner agencies arising from what they see as an increasingly bureaucratic and inward-focused organisation. The partnership is seeking to address these concerns in its new phase of development. Its five-year strategic plan under the Local Development Programme prioritises its support for local communities and also identifies additional local funding sources. Also, it has engaged an external consultant to advise on reform of its management structures and procedures.

Tallaght Partnership

Tallaght Partnership (TP) is located in Tallaght (population 70,000), a "new town" on the western suburb of Dublin. It has experienced rapid population growth in recent years, part of which was due to the location in the area of a number of large local authority housing estates in the 1980s. These estates, as with most newly built public housing in this era, have suffered badly from high levels of unemployment and problems of tenant turnover, culminating in a rapid increase in the number of inhabitants dependent on social welfare. Facilities and services in Tallaght have been slow to develop, through in the last few years some flagship projects have located in the area (e.g. shopping centre, hospital, hotel, technical college).

The origins of TP lie in a growing recognition among community and statutory agencies of the need for an integrated approach to the social and economic problems of Tallaght. This was developed though a number of pilot initiatives, such as the West Tallaght Resource Centre, a community development project in the Second EU Poverty programme, and various state-led employment projects which took place towards the end of the 1980s. A formal partnership structure was established in 1990 representative of community, voluntary and statutory interests to manage a new initiative under the government's community development programme. Later, in 1991, Tallaght was designated as one of the pilot areas in the area based response to long-term unemployment programme and the existing partnership was restructured to take on this task. In 1994, the Tallaght Partnership was included in the local development programme, 1994-99. The project receives funding from a variety of national, EU and international sources and its total budget in 1994 was £800,000.

The remit of the partnership is to address the problems of unemployment and poverty by developing integrated actions to increase employment opportunities and improve the quality of life. Its work programme has four themes:

1. Employment and enterprise;

2. Community development;

3. Education and training;

4. Positive action (focusing on minority groups such as Travellers).

A particular innovation of TP is the Plato programme. Originally devised in Belgium, the programme provides a mentoring and support service for small and medium enterprises. This initiative has since been extended nationwide under the sponsorship of IBEC, the employers' organisation. A feature of the partnership is its emphasis on policy development and it has lobbied successfully for improvements in programmes for the long-term unemployed. The partnership is also one of the promoters of the EU Urban initiative in the Tallaght/Clondalkin area, which is experimenting with a partnership-based model of urban management.

The partnership has 18 partner agencies, comprising six state organisations, two social partners, four voluntary bodies and six community groups. It is managed by a 22-person board of directors (40 per cent female) which comprises, on average, one nominee per partner agency. The partnership has an extensive sub-committee structure which focuses on its key areas of work. It also has a contractual relationship with a number of local organisations which it has taken on to manage and deliver specific projects on its behalf, e.g. enterprise development. For that reason, the staff complement of the partnership has remained relatively modest.

TP has successfully piloted innovative actions in a number of key policy areas, some of which have being mainstreamed by government bodies or the social partners. The partnership has also contributed to the greatly increased economic activity in the area, though ensuring that this benefits economically marginalised communities and groups has proved more difficult. A positive feature of its work is the involvement of local residents in partnership activities, in particular marginalised groups such as women, Travellers and people with a disability. Issues for the future include an explicit commitment from statutory agencies as to their contribution to the partnership, a more formal linkage with local government, in particular with elected members, and stronger mechanisms to target job opportunities to those in greatest need.

South Kerry Development Partnership

South Kerry Development Partnership (SKDP) covers an extensive and predominantly rural area in south Kerry, which includes a network of small and medium sized market towns (population 41,000). The region's traditional reliance on farming for its economic base has been undermined by an on-going decline in the position of small producers. Tourism and small industry are increasingly important components of the local economy. Emigration is an inherent feature of the area's social fabric, resulting in a high population dependency ratio.

SKDP dates from April 1991, when it was formed as an umbrella organisation to administer a Leader programme by two local development federations (Integrated Rural Development South West Kerry and Killorglin and District Resource Development Group). Later that year, the project was restructured as a partnership organisation under the area based response to long-term unemployment programme (then called CRESP — community response for economic and social progress — South West Kerry Partnership). More recently, the partnership has extended its remit to a much larger area and added additional partner agencies under the local development programme, in the process changing its name to SKDP. The project has a multiplicity of funding sources: Leader I and II, Irish government, global grant for local development, local development programme, EU Iris II and Carrefour programmes.

The main objective of SKDP is to improve the economic performance of the area by widening its economic base and improving job opportunities. In this regard, the project has defined its role as an integrator of local initiatives — private, community and statutory — and as a source of additional external resources. Its activities can be grouped under four headings:

1. Education, training and community development;

2. Indigenous resource development;

3. Small enterprise development;

4. Environmental enhancement.

The partnership has placed a lot of emphasis on developing an enterprise culture in its locality. It has also supported the development of agriculture, horticulture, aquaculture, and has provided funds for rural tourism and crafts enterprises. SKDP supports a network of community offices which provide an information outlet for the activities of the partnership, as well as supporting community development activity. SKDP is comprised of state, social and community partners, with 25 people on its management committee (only two of whom are women). The community sector is made up of 29 affiliated local groups which nominate 10 representatives onto the management committee on an area basis. There are 8 state bodies represented on the partnership, including educational and training service providers, development agencies and local authorities. In addition to standard farmer, trade union and employer partners is an international agribusiness company that operates in the region.

SKDP has had considerable success in its assumed role as a rural development agency, especially in supporting local economic development initiatives. It has also succeeded in giving a focus and structure to what were previously isolated and under-funded community initiatives. Its specific achievements in terms of social inclusion are less apparent, though these may emerge over time as the benefits of local economic development filter through. The partnership's distinct local focus to the needs of its area has created concerns about economic displacement and brought it into conflict with statutory service providers who have a wider geographical remit. Better targeting of its activities and a more strategic engagement with its partner agencies would appear to be the partnership's main challenges in the years ahead.

Dundalk Employment Partnership

Dundalk Employment Partnership (DEP) operates in Dundalk, a provincial port town of 26,000 people. The town has been badly affected by the national decline in traditional indigenous industry, a loss of trade to nearby cross-border areas and various problems arising from the conflict in Northern Ireland. Consequently, unemployment in the Dundalk is twice the national average, and is especially concentrated in public housing areas.

DEP was founded in 1991 under the government's area based response to long-term unemployment programme. Unlike other locations, the partnership did evolve from existing local structures. It required six months of intensive consultation and planning before DEP was established in November 1991. Since 1995, the partnership is core funded under the Local Development Programme, with one-off funding for specific initiatives coming from the Enterprise Trust, the International Fund for Ireland, the Peace and Reconciliation Programmes and other sources. Indeed, DEP has proved very successful in tapping additional funding, especially north/south initiatives which it can access as a border town, and now has an annual budget in excess of £1 million. The partnership also operates the Local Employment Service and is one of the three principle partners in the Dundalk Drogheda Territorial Employment Pact. These additional programmes have led to a doubling of the staff complement to sixteen, with additional personnel employed in community outreach centres.

The objective of DEP is to enhance the employment prospects of the long-term unemployed through an integrated programme of community development, education and training, job placement and enterprise creation. Five main areas of activity are pursued:

1. Outreach and counselling with the long-term unemployed;

2. Funding, support and education for small and medium enterprise;

3. Employment projects (temporary and permanent);

4. Community and personal development programmes;

5. Reform of social welfare and taxation policies.

Among the achievements of the partnership are a number of employment projects, notably two commercial small businesses (paper and glass recycling) which provide jobs for the long-term unemployed, along with two social enterprises which provide homecare and draught-proofing services under a government-sponsored temporary employment programme. DEP also has a strong programme of support for self-employment, which includes the development of a £750,000 enterprise centre for small businesses. Uniquely, the partnership has its own premises, part of which is leased for commercial purposes, as well as being used to provide a creche, a community resource centre and a contact point for the local employment service.

DEP has adopted the standard partnership structure of the area-based response to long-term unemployment programme: six statutory partners, six community partners and six social partner nominees. Four of its 18 directors are women. There were initially some difficulties in identifying community representatives, given the limited tradition of community development in the town. Recognising this, the partnership engaged in a community consultation process in order to strengthen its community development activities and to enhance community involvement in the partnership. This has led to the establishment of various community networks (child-care, women, disability, etc), a community resource centre and a community development fund. As well as fostering its own internal partnership structures, DEP has partnered with other agencies, such as Louth County Council and the Bank of Ireland, in specific ventures.

DEP has managed to root itself in the economic life of Dundalk in a relatively short period of time. This reflects a combination of effective management and a focused strategic plan. The partnership has also impacted at national level where it successfully advocated changes in social welfare regulations to enable the long-term unemployed to temporarily retain some of their benefits when taking up work or educational opportunities. The strong focus on employment and enterprise issues resulted in the social/community side of the partnership being considerably underdeveloped. However, it has sought to rectify this imbalance in recent years by re-inforcing its community development remit.

Greater Mallow Area Development Partnership/
Avondhu Development Group

Greater Mallow Area Development Partnership (GMADP) is based in north county Cork, a mixed area comprising the town of Mallow, rural villages and open countryside, with a population of 22,000. The area has a strong local economy centred on agriculture, with dairy farming in the rural areas and food processing plants (milk and sugar) in Mallow. Despite this, unemployment has emerged as a serious and growing problem in the area, which is in turn linked with a high rate of emigration. Unemployment is made worse by the duration of joblessness, averaging between three and four years for over 25s, and the low educational qualifications among the unemployed. In rural areas, the vitality of local communities is under threat, due to a combination of emigration and declining services.

GMADP was formed in the autumn of 1993, following the coalition of two local voluntary development organisations: Integrated Rural Development Mallow (a rural group promoting tourism, small enterprise and community development, based on a national IRD model) and Mallow Enterprise Board (an urban project, sponsored by the Society of St Vincent de Paul, seeking to attract industry to the area). The catalyst for this merger was the availability of funding for local development under ADM. These two groups established a joint management committee comprising representatives of both groups, and included nominees from two local authorities and representatives of an unemployed group and a trade union. GMADP received £95,000 over the period March 1994 to June 1995 for the implementation of a local development strategy and also secured "pre-development" funding under the Leader II programme, with the expectation of additional resources once a business plan is approved. Smaller amounts of money are received from SPEC, an EU initiative which supports employment creation, and a local agribusiness.

The aim of GMADP is to promote economic and social development through a partnership model. Its activities are structured around five themes:

1. Enterprise and job creation;

2. Support for community development;

3. Education and training;

4. Services for the unemployed;

5. Tourism development.

Its main projects have been the establishment of Mallow Area Resource Centre, an information and advice centre for the unemployed which is managed and staffed by local unemployed people, the building of a factory space for small businesses and the commissioning of feasibility studies for various tourism and business products. It has also provided special programmes for women and for early school leavers. GMADP operates an office in Mallow, which is staffed by two people (a business development officer and a community development officer). It also employs 15 people on a temporary employment programme to support the local resource centre and an outreach office in a nearby village.

There are five main partner categories on GMADP: Chamber of Commerce and agribusiness interests; political representatives of two local authorities (Cork County Council and Mallow Urban District Council), including two TDs; community organisations arranged into rural and urban groupings; a local trade union; and the Mallow Area Resource Centre, representing unemployed people. The management committee of the project consists of 17 people (three women), with the largest representation coming from the business sector (six), which also provides both the chairperson and vice-chairperson. While there is no state agency involvement on the board of GMADP, the group has good links with these bodies, getting assistance on specific projects and having representatives on its committee system.

The first stage in GMADP's activities was completed in 1995. The partnership has since successfully collaborated with a development organisation in a nearby town (Fermoy) for a business plan under Leader II. This has necessitated the establishment of a combined management group, including statutory representation, to manage this business plan (called the Blackwater Resource Development Company). GMADP has also linked up with Fermoy on the preparation of a new development plan under the ADM-administered integrated development programme. This has resulted in the creation of a new umbrella organisation — Avondhu Development Group. The combined resources of these two initiatives is substantial: £500,000 per annum under Leader and

£300,000 under the Local Development Programme. It is accepted that the proliferation of development structures between the different towns and programmes requires rationalisation. One outcome is a single chief executive officer with shared office facilities for the Leader and ADM programmes, though still with separate boards due to local factors. Another is the transfer of the activities and personnel of GMADP to the Avondhu Development Group, leading to the winding down of the partnership as a separate entity. Strengthening the membership of the new structures, in particular securing additional representation from disadvantaged groups, is now a priority.

GMADP has successfully negotiated its evolution as a local development agency, though in becoming part of a larger development structure, has now become largely redundant. It initially brought together the considerable energies of various voluntary interests that are concerned about the future development of the locality. In the first year, it refined its organisational structures, with the assistance of an external evaluator, established an office and staff and developed a modest programme of work. Critical issues arose in this period regarding (i) project strategy, in particular how to combine enterprise/economic development and community development activities, and (ii) management, in terms of harnessing rather diverse local interests into an effective organisation and clarifying the contribution of unemployed people. External factors have resulted in the partnership undergoing further consolidation, though this should maximise its impact on employment and community development needs in the Mallow area.

Pavee Point

Pavee Point (PP) is a Dublin-based organisation working with Travellers. Travellers are an ethnic minority group descended from travelling tradespeople. Over time, as their economic status has been progressively undermined, Travellers have become increasingly dependent on social welfare. Travellers' high risk of poverty is greatly compounded by their poor housing and living conditions, resulting in very low life expectancy rates. Their distinctive lifestyle based on nomadism attracts social, cultural and political discrimination. There are an estimated 4,000 Traveller families (c.20,000 people), mainly residing in temporary accommodation adjacent to urban centres. Only a minority of the Traveller population is settled, with most residing in caravan accommodation in temporary halting sites.

PP was founded in the mid-1980s as a voluntary organisation. It consists of Travellers and settled people working in partnership to promote the wellbeing of Travellers at a national level. While many Traveller settlement organisations existed at the time, PP was unique in viewing the issue of Travellers in a human rights context — an ethnic minority experiencing discrimination and racism from the majority population — and in encouraging Travellers to become involved in the management and activities of the organisation. Originally funded as a training agency, over time the group has been able to widen its activities with the support of the Poverty 3 Programme and EU community initiatives. This diversification has been facilitated by secured funding from individual government departments for specific projects and also through its inclusion in the Local Development Programme.

The objectives of PP are set out as follows in its current strategic plan:

1. Promote the needs and aspirations of Travellers as a minority group;

2. Support the social and economic self-determination of Travellers;

3. Encourage solidarity among Travellers and with the settled population;

4. Combat racism and xenophobia against Travellers;

5. Disseminate information on Travellers in the media and other public fora;

6. Advocate policy and societal change in favour of Travellers;

7. Provide support and training for organisations involved with Travellers.

PP is thus a multi-tiered organisation which undertakes a diverse programme of activities focused on the needs of Travellers, ranging from the provision of services (education, training, health, enterprise) to the strengthening of Traveller identity and organisations to the advocacy for policy and attitudinal change at local and national levels. In recent years, PP has become involved with local development initiatives, arising from its work on the Traveller economy, which seeks to identify and support strategies for economic development appropriate to the skills and work ethic of Travellers. As part of the Local Development Programme, PP is funded to support local Traveller groups to identify economic development projects, to advise local partnerships on how Travellers can be included in their programmes and to create a greater awareness of the Traveller economy through research and policy work at national level. It also has access to a development fund which can be used to lever resources from local partnerships.

PP is committed to operating in a partnership context, but not one which is constrained by the model of a formal multi-agency structure. Such a model would be inappropriate given the differences in culture and power between settled people and Travellers. Thus, the group is both itself a partnership of Travellers and settled people and a bridge between Travellers and the settled community for specific initiatives. Partnership thus implies a range of long-term relationships with statutory and other organisations based on agreed agendas, as well as short-term strategic alliances. The informal nature of these linkages is seen as necessary in order to retain the autonomy of PP.

PP has successfully put Traveller issues on the local development agenda. Its brokerage role with local partnerships has increased the understanding of Travellers' diverse needs and facilitated the development of activities targeted at this group. The main achievements to date have been in developing the capacity of local Traveller groups to work with LDPs. Less progress is apparent in integrating Travellers into local development strategies, reflecting in part a lack of know-how and in part the narrow criteria for economic viability, which cannot encapsulate the diverse income-generating aspects of the Traveller economy. This highlights the continuing need to situate the Traveller economy initiative in the wider policy context of the "social economy", which combines economic and social objectives.

Greater Blanchardstown Development Project

Greater Blanchardstown Development Project (GBDP) is situated in Blanchardstown, a new town suburb of Dublin city, which is made up of large, newly developed, public and private housing estates. The area currently has a population of c.70,000, mainly young families. The rapid growth of Blanchardstown has not been matched by the provision of public or private services, including job opportunities, while community and voluntary organisations are also relatively underdeveloped.

GBDP was established in 1984 as an initiative of the Catholic Social Service Conference (CSSC), the social arm of the Catholic Church in the diocese of Dublin. The CSSC assigned two religious sisters to respond to the needs of people living in the area, primarily through the provision of personal and community development courses. Over the first three years, 30 such courses were provided for 500 local people, mainly low income women working in the home. In line with the goal of local ownership of the project, a management structure was developed, initially to include other local professionals and, later, representatives of local residents and course participants. In 1990, the project secured long-term funding under the Community Development Programme. This resulted in the restructuring of the project as a resource centre for community development, under the control of an autonomous local management committee. The project is funded through an annual government subvention of £50,000, which is supplemented by additional resources for educational courses and temporary employment programmes.

The objectives of GBDP are to:

1. Be a resource centre for community development and information;

2. Provide personal development courses;

3. To enable individuals and groups to identify and respond to community needs;

4. Promote awareness of social inequality;

5. Be a catalyst for voluntary and statutory co-operation.

Its main activities to date have included personal development and adult education courses, provision of welfare rights information, support for Travellers groups and promoting awareness of local issues, in particular unemployment. GBDP has also cooperated with the Greater Blanchardstown Partnership on the preparation of an integrated local development plan. The project has also implemented an innovative nutrition programme targeted at low income groups, in conjunction with public health agencies. This peer-led community education initiative seeks to enhance the nutritional health of local people. There is a strong gender dimension to the work of the project in that most of its participants are local women. It has also sought to target the needs of men through the establishment of a men's group.

The GBDP management committee primarily comprises representatives of local community groups, along with two officials from the local authority and the regional health board. Six of the nine members of the committee are women. Linked to the project are local development groups, including a men's group and a welfare rights project. GBDP has four staff: two full-time (co-ordinator and administrator) and two part-time (development worker and secretary). The project receives on-going funding, based on a three year work programme, under the community development programme.

GBDP has successfully evolved as a community-managed project which promotes personal and community development. It has also fostered co-operation between residents and statutory agencies on issues such as welfare provision, educational programmes, administrative support services, health education and local economic development. Though not structured as a formal partnership, it does engage with other agencies on specific activities. It also provides an important vehicle for community involvement in the Blanchardstown local development partnership.

Ballymun Task Force

Ballymun Task Force (BTF) is situated in Ballymun (population 20,000), an exclusively public housing suburb on the northside of Dublin city, which was built in the late 1960s. Ballymun is a unique housing development in that three-fifths of its 4,800 dwellings are in 4, 8 or 15 storey apartment blocks, and it represents the sole Irish experiment in high-rise public housing. A serious decline in housing conditions in Ballymun occurred in the mid 1980s, following an exodus of better-off tenants under a housing surrender scheme: one-in-ten flats became vacant and were frequently vandalised; the proportion of lone parents, single people and homeless families being housed in the area dramatically increased; and, generally, tenant transience became a serious problem. In parallel with this population shift, the physical condition of the estate worsened considerably, reflecting flaws in the original design.

BTF emerged as a community response to this housing crisis. It began as a project of the Ballymun Community Coalition, a broad-based local campaigning group, which sought a forum whereby residents could discuss with the relevant decision-makers (defined as politicians and officials) a new housing policy for Ballymun. Following a positive response from these interests, the idea of a local housing forum (later called a task force) gained further impetus when financial support was secured from the Combat Poverty Agency under its pilot programme for community development. BTF was formally established in 1987 with a specific brief to draw up and get agreement for a new housing policy for the area. It was later reconstituted in 1988 with a wider brief to oversee the implementation of this agreed housing policy and to address other related local needs (e.g. education, job creation).

The principal objective of BTF is to devise and implement a new housing policy for Ballymun with three main components:

housing refurbishment; tenant participation in estate management; and development of community support structures. Refurbishment of housing has been the main focus to date, with the task force making proposals costing £70 million. The first phase of this, a £6 million programme, commenced in 1990 and was completed in 1993. Following a review of this phase, the government decided to demolish the remaining flat complexes and to rebuild Ballymun as a new town. This led to the establishment of Ballymun Renewal, a multi-agency body under the leadership of Dublin Corporation, which is charged with planning and implementing the new Ballymun. BFT is represented on the board of Ballymun Renewal.

A second aspect of the task force's work is estate management. BTF has been instrumental in pioneering innovative management structures for public housing of national importance, following exchanges with the Priority Estates Project in the UK. As a complement to the refurbishment initiative, BTF has sought to develop the community support structures that are considered vital to a programme of housing renewal. For instance, the refurbishment programme was preceded and accompanied by a major exercise in public consultation under the direction of BTF. A community architect was also assigned to the project, which greatly assisted in the process of tenant consultation. Under Ballymun Renewal, BFT has been contracted to manage the community input into the new plan and to develop tenant participation structures in anticipation of a more decentralised housing management policy for the "new" Ballymun. There has also been national recognition for its work in estate management by the inclusion of a representative on a Department of the Environment review group on housing management policy and practice. The task force has also secured assistance from the Ballymun Partnership and the north Dublin Urban programme for its activities.

BTF is comprised of public representatives (4), officials from the different sections of the housing authority (11) and from the health board (1), representatives of the Ballymun Community Coalition (8) and tenants' associations (6), and an independent chairperson. A third of the 33 members are women, with the community sector having the highest female representation. A distinctive feature of BTF is that the community representatives are the *de facto* executive of the organisation, including a local paid worker who acts as secretary to BFT (the staff complement has increased to three in order to meet its additional responsibilities). Their task is to liase with tenants in the estate and to establish a network of people in the blocks undergoing initial refurbishment to act as intermediaries with the builders (the tenants remained on site during the refurbishment). The function of the politicians is to link with central government, a key role given the centralised nature of housing administration.

BTF is pioneering a novel approach to the management of public housing, which is helping to give practical expression to recent national policy aspirations in this regard. Its strengths lie in its bottom-up approach, building relationships between the various partners, having appropriate technical back-up, following a planned approach and, most importantly, giving a voice to the experiences and concerns of the tenants in Ballymun. The fact that BTF is a stand-alone initiative, devoid of the financial and other supports of a government or EU programme, has been its major weakness. Its enhanced role both under Ballymun Renewal and the Urban programme represents an important, albeit localised, break-through in this regard. However, it is still under-resourced in terms of the level of support needed for meaningful tenant participation, especially given the quickening pace of urban regeneration in the area. There is also the need to share its experience of estate management with other local groups and with policy-makers, which is limited by pressure of work and the lack of a national forum on estate management.

Conclusion

This chapter has presented eight examples of local partnerships that were chosen to reflect the diversity of structures that currently exist. A common denominator is their recency, with the most recent dating from the early 1990s. The examples vary, however, in their commitment to partnership and in their scale of operation. The larger and better-funded examples are established as local development partnerships under the Local Development Programme. While having a standardised partnership structure, they differ significantly in the strategies adopted to address social inclusion in a local context, ranging from operating as a general local development agency (South Kerry) to a specific focus on enterprise and employment (Dundalk and Tallaght) to a quite broad community development approach (Limerick). The other examples have a more localised focus (Ballymun, Mallow and Blanchardstown) or, in the case of Pavee Point, has a specific concern with Travellers. The formal role of Pavee Point in the Local Development Programme is an interesting example of how a sectoral organisation can bring added value to the work of local partnerships on a particular issue. The partnership dimension in these four examples is less formalised, both in terms of the number of partners (quantity) and what the partners bring to the project (quality/level of organisational commitment).

Another common denominator in the examples is the innovative nature of their work at the local level. However, the impact of this work is limited by the absence of national structures whereby the local experience can be assimilated with national policy. This problem is especially evident with regard to housing management in Ballymun and micro-enterprise for Travellers, though less so in the Local Development Programme where at least intermediary structures exist for this purpose, though their effectiveness in achieving this exchange is not apparent to-date.

Chapter 5

Views of the Key Actors Involved with Local Partnerships

Introduction

This chapter reflects the views and experiences of the main actors involved with local partnerships. These are grouped as follows:

1. Central government

2. Public agencies (strategy and implementation)

3. Employers and trade unions

4. Voluntary and community groups

5. Researchers and policy analysts.

Their views were elicited through personal interviews with between three or four representatives of each category and a review of relevant documentation. This information is presented around three themes —social exclusion remit, partnership structures and activities, and policy issues emerging. There is also a short account of how the actors engage with local partnerships.

Central Government[1]

Central government has played a crucial role in promoting local partnerships as a policy instrument, as was shown in the previous chapter. Given its widespread advocacy of this model, the views of central government on the rationale for local partnership, its achievements to date, and the outstanding policy issues, carry considerable political weight. The social exclusion aspect of local partnerships receives varying emphases in central government. For some, such as the Department of Agriculture and Food, it is not the key policy concern. Its vision of rural development is primarily about promoting economic objectives and a strategy of "picking winners" under the Leader programme reflects this. Reducing social exclusion is thus a side benefit of a wider policy focus on economic development. The basis for EU support for this policy initiative is similar — to stimulate local enterprise and economic development — which is in accordance with the objectives of the regional funds in particular. However, both acknowledge the value of animation and capacity building as tools for economic development. In contrast, other government departments have social exclusion as the key policy focus, in recognition of the structural nature of long-term unemployment and the knock-on effects it can have on families and communities. This perspective reflects a predominant concern with labour market issues, however. A minority view, held by the Department of Social, Community and Family Affairs, emphasises the importance of empowerment and of a pro-active approach to welfare support. Strategies such as personal and community development are thus emphasised.

---

[1] Interviews were held with the Department of the Taoiseach and the Office of the Tanaiste, which represented the two lead government departments in regard to local partnership policy at the time (since then, this responsibility has been centralised in another government department (Tourism, Sport and Recreation), though many of the same personnel are involved). The views of two line departments were also canvassed (the Department of Agriculture and Food and the Department of Social, Community and Family Affairs), which deliver local partnership programmes and are also represented on the interdepartmental policy committee on local development.

The partnership principle is justified by government as a means of mobilising local initiative in pursuit of local needs. However, different views exist as to the formality of the structures required. One perspective sees partnership as a loose alliance of local interests, bringing together the main actors at the local level, from state agencies, the private sector and community organisations. This pragmatic approach can be contrasted with a more politically inspired model of partnership associated with the Department of the Taoiseach. Here, local partnership structures are designed to reflect the social partnership structures operating at national level between government, employers and trade unions. Another point of difference is as regards the community sector: for some, it specifically refers to disadvantaged groups, while others see it as consisting of generic local development organisations.

The third dimension of local partnerships — the emphasis on the local — is advocated as a complement to existing efforts at economic and social development at national level. Bottom-up and top-down are seen as two sides of the one coin. Local intervention is also viewed as addressing a weakness in the prevailing system of public administration — the limited capacity of local government. Empowerment and subsidiarity are thus seen by central government as particular virtues of local partnership. Central government's assessment of the outcomes, to date, of local partnerships is overwhelmingly positive. Economic gains include more jobs or improved earning opportunities, while social benefits involve strengthening community capacity. Better management of public services and resources is also highlighted, in particular the innovative ability of local partnerships. The negative aspects of local partnerships mainly focus on their occasional support for "parish pump" activities.

The main policy issues identified by government as arising from local partnerships are:

- **Reform of local government structures.** Two discrete issues are highlighted with regard to local government. One concerns the exclusion of local public representatives from involvement in the new partnership structures. Government is conscious of a growing demand via the party political system for this practice to be changed. A second aspect relates to the multiplicity of development bodies in the local sphere and the absence of a structure through which their efforts can be coordinated. As an immediate response to this, "county strategy groups" were instituted to act as a coordinating mechanism for the developmental agencies in a local authority area. These groups consist of the chairpeople of these agencies, under the auspices of the manager of the local authority. With a view to more long-term reform and in order to address both issues, the government, under the Department of the Taoiseach, has established a commission to propose how local authorities could become "the focus" for local partnerships and similar bodies.

- **Interface of local and national.** A unique feature of local partnerships is their policy and funding link with central government. Yet, it is increasingly apparent that government departments do not have the capacity to adequately support local partnerships or to provide a structure whereby good practice can be identified and mainstreamed through the policymaking system. ADM fulfils only an element of this linkage role, given its primary focus on administering funds and its own detachment as an intermediary body from the policy-making process. The interdepartmental policy committee on local development is a more appropriate body for this task, but it lacks a direct engagement with local partnerships. (There is also some concern about the structures for linking with trade unions and employers.)

- **Delivery of public services.** Government departments realise the considerable challenge that local partnerships pose for the traditional centralist and sectoral model of delivering public services. They also accept that local partnerships are a project of central government and that awareness of and commitment to these new structures will take some time to develop. It is for that reason that the current reform of government — referred to as the strategic management initiative

— is highlighted as being an important vehicle for institutionalising support for local partnerships. Three particular issues are noted: coordination at central government level; line management within government departments and affiliated agencies; organisational design at the local level. The recent initiative of a local employment service encapsulates very well the enormity of these challenges, in particular that of organisational design at the local level which is central to this new service.

• **Funding.** The heavy financial dependence on government by local partnerships is another cause of concern. Again, there are two aspects to this. First, the procedures used by local partnerships to administer resources are a cause of worry to government departments, especially in an era which emphasises public accountability and value for money. This issue was graphically highlighted by a report by the Comptroller and Auditor General on the Leader 1 programme, which raised concerns about the funding decisions of local partnerships. Second, given that almost all public funds emanate from the EU, the continuation of this funding in the post-1999 period is of major concern, especially as it is likely at this stage that Ireland will lose its objective one status.

Public Agencies[2]

Public agencies, outside of central government, play important roles in the local partnership experiment. These can be categorised into two: service delivery organisations (e.g. economic, employment, health, education and housing) and policy advice

---

[2] Representatives of four agencies were interviewed: National Economic and Social Council (NESC), Combat Poverty Agency (CPA), ADM and FÁS. Both NESC and CPA played strategic roles in the evolution of the local partnership model as a policy instrument to tackle social exclusion. FÁS is the public service agency most closely associated with local partnerships, while ADM plays a hands-on role in the support and funding of local partnerships. Also, CPA, FÁS and ADM, are all members of the interdepartmental policy group on local development and so have an input into the design and implementation of policy relating to local partnerships.

agencies (such as NESC, NESF and CPA). In addition, there is ADM, an independent agency which implements government policy with regard to local development and related interventions. As expected, the public agencies interviewed had an analytically sophisticated approach to issues of social exclusion, partnership and local development. For example, CPA's arguments for focusing on social exclusion are based on its analysis of the dynamic and multidimensional nature of poverty. Specifically, it sees the need for active measures, involving intended beneficiaries through a community development process, as part of an integrated and area-targeted package. The NESC advocacy of a social exclusion perspective is informed by in-depth analysis of the changing nature of the labour market and of policy responses to unemployment developed in other EU countries. For others, however, social exclusion is more a question of redefining the target group to include non-traditional categories such as Travellers and lone parents and of providing social, as well as economic, supports to assist with labour market participation.

The conceptualisations of partnership are equally well-formulated. To the traditional corporatist rationale for partnership structures is added the qualitative difference of involving excluded groups with the aim of rebalancing traditional power relations. Meanwhile, the disconnectedness of local partnerships from local government and sectoral bodies is seen as being compensated for by a direct link with the senior government department. Aside from these political dimensions, the strategic value of local partnerships in mobilising local efforts is emphasised. Again, public agencies highlight the rationale for this in other countries, e.g. Italy. Also, the view of partnership in Poverty 3 is quoted, where it is promoted as representing the institutional expression of an integrated approach to poverty. A measured understanding of the value of the local dimension is offered by the NESC. Three arguments are put forward: the first notes the importance of an areal level of intervention (e.g. coordination, flexibility), but also incorporating organisational procedures and sectoral strategies; the second suggests the benefits of decentralised policymaking, while retaining strong vertical links to national government; and the third advocates the value of hybrid local structures, through acknowledging the need to link these with an effective system of local government. In essence, local intervention is only worthwhile when accompanied by certain organisational reforms and changes in government structures at local and national levels. Similarly, other public agencies are careful to balance local action with parallel reforms of national policy, e.g. in regard to measures to tackle long-term unemployment.

Generally, the assessment of local partnerships by public agencies is overwhelmingly positive, especially in terms of bringing added value to the efforts of existing bodies. The main benefits are improved coordination and targeting of resources, policy innovation and mobilisation of local energies. The main drawback is the time consuming nature of local partnerships, though this may be primarily a feature of the start-up phase. Public agencies believe that the rapid and rather exhilarating growth in LDPs has not been matched by a review of the policy context in which these new entities function.

The main policy issues relate to institutional issues and development strategy.

- **Institutional issues.** The introduction of a local dimension to development policy in general and anti-poverty strategy in particular has raised many institutional and organisational issues. One of these is the limited capacity for most of the actors in local partnerships to operate at the local level — the traditional remit of state agencies, along with employers and trade unions, was determined at national level. At best, the local arms of these bodies had some administrative powers, at worst they were merely talking shops. There are thus many institutional and cultural patterns to be overcome if local agencies are to fulfil their potential as partners, as distinct from well-meaning individuals, in local partnerships. A second organisational dimension relates to the relationship between local partnerships and local government on one hand and national government on the other. While a realignment of the relationship between LDPs and local government is clearly acknowledged, this should not extend to a take-over of local partnerships by local government. Meanwhile, a strong local/national dynamic is identified as an important aspect of the operation of local partnerships. However, the current mediation of this dynamic via the Department of the Taoiseach is not considered desirable in the longer-term and a more appropriate relationship is required to link bottom-up and top-down.

- **Development strategy.** The development strategy being pursued by local partnerships gives rise to a number of concerns. The first is the role of local development in overall national development policy. It is not enough simply to allow local partnerships to operate to a purely local agenda — many of the issues they seek to address require national, as well as local, action. An example of this is the local employment service, whose successful local delivery will require central government to provide adequate resources and to develop new programmes. The focus of local development strategy, in particular the balance between economic and social goals (enterprise and job creation vs social investment and affirmative action), and between process and outcomes (community development and local networking vs reduced unemployment and more resources), is a second policy issue. Currently, there is a wide divergence across local partnerships and between local partnerships and other local development structures on these issues which should be clarified to ensure maximum effectiveness. Finally, there are the two competing models of partnership operation: service delivery and service planning. There is a concern that the arrival of the global grant has shifted the focus of local partnerships excessively as providers and funders of local activity, thus effectively replicating the work of existing actors. The more challenging aspects of partnership — coordination and monitoring — may not get the attention they require. In the latter regard, local partnerships' recently acquired role in providing the new Local Employment Service should provide a better test of their potential.

Employers and Trade Unions[3]

Employers and trade unions are involved in local partnerships at a macro policy level and through participation in individual local partnerships. The social partners had an important input into the establishment of the ABR initiative and subsequently the Local Development Programme under various national social partnership programmes and are currently involved in monitoring and guiding the programme at two levels: the monitoring committee for the local development programme and the board of ADM. The social partners are also directly involved in local partnerships at an individual and collective basis. An example of collective involvement on the employers' side is the Enterprise Trust, which was established to channel resources and technical support for enterprise development to local partnerships. Its current focus is on the development of local business networks which offer support and advice to new enterprises. Trade unions, meanwhile, have utilised their network of local centres for the unemployed as a mechanism to collaborate with local partnerships. In addition, personnel from both networks have been seconded to the staff of ADM. At the operational level, local employer, trade union and farmer affiliates are represented on the boards of local partnerships. The nature of involvement at this level is very much at the discretion of local nominees given the weak local linkages with social partner organisations. In some instances, Chambers of Commerce or local businesses networks have developed formal relationships with local partnerships, thereby strengthening their involvement in the organisation.

Both employers and trade unions are sceptical of the emphasis in local partnerships on social exclusion. Employers' main interest is in promoting enterprise and creating jobs. This is where they see their expertise and their contribution to local partnerships, though they acknowledge the importance of social-type

---

[3] Three organisations were interviewed in this category: Irish Business and Employers Confederation (IBEC), Irish Congress of Trade Unions (ICTU) and the Enterprise Trust.

programmes to prepare the long-term unemployed for work. Trade unions, meanwhile, are concerned that an emphasis on social exclusion may dilute what they see as the primary motive for local partnerships — to target long-term unemployed males, both those over 35 years and early school leavers. The gender dimension is justified because most new employment is benefiting women. The Enterprise Trust is especially concerned that by having an exclusive focus on the long-term unemployed and similar groups, local partnerships may overlook the potential contribution of local entrepreneurs in stimulating economic development and employment. A wider focus on the whole community is its preferred option, and one on which it feels the EU is in agreement.

Partnership is viewed as a way of working which contains many practical advantages. At the same time, there is a rejection of partnership as some type of bureaucratic formula which is imposed by external forces. The proof of partnership is thus in terms of its ability to cut through state bureaucracy, to be innovative and effective and to mobilise local resources. There is also a realisation of a specific challenge for sectoral groups of local partnership structures, as compared to national partnership where the focus is more on political agreement. In local partnerships, where the focus is more social than political, ways must be found to mobilise and to harness the potential role of constituent members. There is universal support for local development as a way of promoting small and medium enterprise. There is also an awareness of the value of developing the internal dynamic in local economies, and not to be relying exclusively on central government intervention. For some, local development is also about non-state development — a form of communal self-help, whose antecedents can be traced to the co-operative movement of Horace Plunkett. Central to this perspective is the reduction of dependence on the state and promotion of private initiative.

The social partners express a more critical judgement on local partnerships than other interests. While acknowledging the benefits in terms of business start-ups and social cohesion, there are some concerns about the cost of the initiative, especially its reliance on public funding, and the bureaucracy associated with the programme, which is seen as undermining its developmental dynamic. Another concern arises from the rapid extension of local partnerships, both numerically and in terms of the issues they seek to address. This expansion, it is felt, ignores the limited capacity of sectoral groups to contribute to the programme.

Not surprisingly, the policy issues raised by the social partners reflect their more dubious assessment of the operation and benefits of local partnerships.

- **Development strategy.** A greater clarity as to the remit of local partnerships is advocated, in particular the emphasis to be placed on enterprise development. This is not solely a question of balancing the social and the economic; it is also about the role of local partnerships as engines of local development. In this regard, there is a need to review the management culture of local partnerships in order to see how it could be less procedure-driven and more output-oriented. Such a change would have the effect of reducing the gap that currently exists between employers and unions on one hand and state agencies and voluntary bodies on the other.

- **Funding and resource utilisation.** Making local partnerships financially self-sustaining in the longer-term is suggested as a policy priority. The current situation, whereby financial resources are exclusively sourced from the EU, is not seen as viable either in terms of the security of the funding and the ongoing reliance on external support. A scenario whereby public funding is matched by local resources, both community and private, is envisaged. A related issue concerns the management of resources. One proposal is for a cost-benefit assessment of all actions undertaken by local partnerships, to ensure the maximum utilisation of resources. Meanwhile, in order to avoid the danger of diluting the impact of programme funds, more consideration should be given to the optimum number of local partnerships.

- **Local structures.** In common with other actors, social partner representatives point out the need for reform of the institutional context for local partnerships. This is required at two levels: first, developing a linkage with local government, though this would be predicated on the reform of local authorities; second, coordinating local development bodies, especially by addressing a perceived overlap between LDPs and CEBs.

Community and Voluntary Groups[4]

A defining feature of local partnerships is the involvement of local community interests in their management and operation. This reflects the growth of such bodies in disadvantaged areas and groups and the commitment by central government and the EU to having a local input into local partnerships. By contrast, national voluntary bodies, including charitable organisations and service providers, play a marginal role in local partnerships. The input of the community sector occurs at three levels. The first is their involvement in policymaking structures through various national network organisations (unemployed, community development, Travellers, rural groups, lone parents). These networks have supported local development initiatives through policymaking structures at the national level, such as NESF, NESC and specific review groups, e.g. task force on long-term unemployment. Within the programme for integrated development, community groups are represented on the board of ADM and on national and regional monitoring committees. Also, three representatives of community directors in LDPs are on the board of ADM. A second tier of influence is through the involvement of national networks, together with some voluntary organisations, in supporting the activities of local partnerships. Here, their task is to provide advice and support on childcare services, measures to prevent early school leaving, services for homeless people and general community capacity-building measures. Also, a forum of community directors is supported within the programme which shares

---

[4] Representatives of the Irish National Organisation of the Unemployed (INOU), the Community Workers' Co-operative (CWC), the Community Directors Forum (CDF) and Planet, the representative body for local development partnerships, were interviewed.

information with and gives support to community directors in local partnerships. A third input is through the participation of local community groups as partners on local partnerships. While the format of this partnership can vary, e.g. group membership, network organisations, community forums and self-appointed community leaders, community representatives are granted automatic membership on the boards and committees of local partnerships.

Community groups are generally very supportive of the emphasis on social exclusion within the local development programme, though there is disagreement between groups with a community development focus and those emphasising labour market issues. For the former, the collective dimension of social exclusion is paramount. Intrinsic to this is a lack of community participation in existing decision-making structures. Unemployed groups, by contrast, apply the concept of social exclusion in terms of the labour market, highlighting in equal measure issues of income support and of access to employment. Community and voluntary groups view partnership as a useful tool for accessing resources, improving the provision of public services and generating economic development. In particular, it offers an opportunity for dialogue with other interests and for experimenting with new policy responses. They acknowledge the demands it places on the sector, in terms of the capacity of local groups to operate at this level and of the amount of time and resources it demands, as well as weaknesses internal to the model, such as governance procedures. Groups are also concerned about tying themselves too closely to this model of working, at the expense of other strategies such as campaigning, etc. Another worry is the exclusion of minority interests from representation in local partnerships, in particular women and Travellers.

Local development is broadly seen by community groups as providing a means whereby the benefits of economic development can be targeted at socially excluded groups. This equity focus may be complemented by an increase in local control over the development process. For some, though, local development is about securing more resources and jobs for their own area, regardless of the effects this might have in other localities. In assessing the experience to date of local partnerships, community groups emphasise the development of better working methods with the state and other interests rather than concrete gains in terms of jobs or otherwise. The main perceived weakness arises from the voluntary nature of people's commitment to the initiative, with the result that outcomes can vary greatly depending on particular partner agencies and individual local partnerships. Giving statutory recognition to local partnerships is seen as essential to overcome this problem. Another perceived drawback is a growing parochialism, with the result that national policy issues are neglected.

The policy issues identified by community groups are fourfold.

- **Capacity of community sector.** There is some concern about the capacity of community and voluntary groups to engage in local partnerships. While having seats at the decision-making table, the quality of community participation is variable, especially in regard to its ability to represent local interests. The expectations as to what community directors can deliver are excessive and local partnerships themselves must assume more responsibility for some tasks, e.g. consultation. Besides that, additional resources must be invested in enhancing the skills and expertise of the community sector.

- **Accountability of partner agencies.** Another issue is the limited accountability of partner agencies as to their contribution to local partnerships. This reflects the voluntaristic nature of local partnerships, together with the reliance on individuals (directors) to mediate between partners and local partnerships. A more formalised and transparent method of engagement is thus advocated, in order to enhance the institutional commitment to local partnerships among various partner agencies. This would also speed up the process whereby the lessons learned under local partnerships could be transferred into mainstream policy and practice. Such a reform would also strengthen the engagement by voluntary and community organisations with local partnerships.

- **Remit of local partnerships.** The multiple expectations placed on local partnerships and facilitated by their vague remit, is problematic — in the words of one interviewee, "local partnerships are on everyone's wish list". However, agreement on a more restricted remit for local partnerships is not readily apparent.

- **Linkages with government structures.** A final policy concern relates to the lack of connection between local partnerships and government structures, both at the local level and with central government. While the participative nature of local partnerships is welcomed and valued in its own right, it is acknowledged that there is also a role for representative democratic structures in influencing the agenda of local partnerships. At national level, mechanisms for transferring the lessons emanating from local partnerships into mainstream government policy could be improved. In particular, a formal engagement between local partnerships and line government departments is required.

Researchers and Policy Analysts[5]

There has been some involvement of researchers and policy analysts with local partnerships. The two principal areas of contact are evaluation and provision of technical support. For example, during Poverty 3, a two-person research and development unit gave technical support to the projects and helped identify policy issues arising from the programme. In addition, some local partnerships engage consultants to prepare area action plans, to advise on the development of policy issues and to assist in evaluating their activities. Research and policy expertise is sourced from both third-level institutions and private research organi-

---

[5] Interviewed here were evaluators of the Leader, ABR and local development programmes and research/policy analysts involved with the Poverty 3 programme at national and EU levels.

sations. Some colleges have established local development centres as a means of coordinating their links with local partnerships.

Research interests note a widespread confusion over the term social exclusion. Its original analytical basis has been diffused in the process of becoming a "catch-all" term used to broaden the potential target population from a traditional focus on the long-term unemployed. Here, the subjective nature of the phrase has been exploited by applying it to various situations of perceived discrimination and inequality. Social exclusion has also proved difficult to operationalise as a public policy concept, where categories which are easily identifiable and measurable are preferred. Thus, much of the value of the phrase, especially in terms of highlighting the process of impoverishment, has been lost through its incorporation into official jargon. In some sectoral programmes, such as Leader, social exclusion remains outside the policy lexicon as an issue which is primarily a residual welfare concern.

The merits of the partnership approach are widely acknowledged, though its straightjacket application is strongly criticised. The understanding of the term has been dominated by central government, which has formulated the model of partnership to be developed at the local level, as well as specifying the partners. However, this centralist model does not translate easily into the local level for a variety of reasons: different players, limited degrees of autonomy, more fragmented structures and tensions with local government. Researchers feel that partnership has been over-infused with meaning, from its potential as a representational forum to its consensus-building nature. Rather, they emphasise its practical benefit as an organisational structure for mobilising resources, co-ordinating services and encouraging innovation at the local level. In this regard, the quality of board members is of paramount importance, with their institutional allegiance of secondary concern. This is seen as posing a major challenge for community sector representation on local partnerships. The danger of vested interests operating in local partnerships is also highlighted, whether of a sectoral or spatial nature.

The current promotion of local intervention is seen as a response by government and the EU to a wider problem of economic restructuring in urban and rural areas. There are two variants of local development: one is based on the economic development of specific areas, in order to gain a competitive advantage over other similar localities; the other is about fostering a social economy, based on the redistribution of existing and new resources. These two paradigms are reflected in the various strategies adopted by local partnerships: the pump-priming of local entrepreneurs or the capacity-building of individuals and community groups. To date, most of the local dimension in the development strategy pursued by local partnerships has been about the former — channelling external resources into local activities. The assessment of the impact of local partnerships is most positive for the working methods they have developed, in particular the collective mobilisation of partner agencies and the promotion of local strategic planning. Of lesser importance are the number of beneficiaries and the mobilisation of local resources which, while impressive, are of minor significance given the scale of need. The down side of local partnerships is seen as twofold: the time-consuming nature of these organisations and the tendency to cream-off the more capable of the long-term unemployed.

A variety of policy concerns is noted by research experts, though the evolutionary nature of local partnerships limits the preciseness by which policy issues can be defined at this stage.

- **Organisational form.** The appropriateness of existing socio-legal structures to the distinctive goals of local partnerships is queried. To date, the common model of operation is that of a company limited by guarantee. However, this has the effect of privatising its activities, as well as conferring decision-making powers on an elite group of individuals who comprise the board. New models are required to reflect the distinct ethos of local partnerships.

- **Local co-ordination.** There is much concern about the myriad of local partnerships currently in operation. Greater coordination is required to address overlaps and gaps between these bodies. The county strategy team model (see previous chapter) is seen as being too weak to overcome these issues. A stronger coordinating role for local authorities may be the optimum way forward.

- **Transfer of good practice.** The link between local partnerships and the wider policy framework is perceived as haphazard, such that local innovation is seldom transferred into mainstream policy and practice. The one or two examples of where this has occurred are due more to good fortune than planned action. Related to this is a perceived deficiency in the existing systems for monitoring and evaluating local partnerships. The preoccupation with job targets undervalues the work of local partnerships in other, less quantifiable, areas.

- **Vertical co-ordination.** How to co-ordinate the various scales of intervention between the neighbourhood, the county and the region is another policy concern. There is a need for a network of development structures, with local partnerships linked into a county-wide structure which, in turn, would be part of a wider regional structure. In this way, it would be possible to develop a system of partnerships, operating from the local to the national.

Conclusion

This chapter has presented the viewpoints of the main actors involved in the promotion and operation of local partnerships at the national level, though realising that those interviewed represent an elite grouping of officials, activists and other interests. Overall, there is considerable enthusiasm for local partnerships. This is matched by a realisation that the flurry of local partnership activity must yet be matched by reform of structures and policies if their contribution is to be sustained. At the same time, there is scope for an enormous diversity of opinion within the various categories. Trade unions, employers and community groups are broad organisations, with the experience and perception of local partnerships reflecting local and even individual factors. Even with the public sector, there is considerable scope for diversity between the personnel involved in local partnerships. A uniformity between national-level support and the practice on the ground cannot be taken for granted.

Part 2

Case Studies of Local Partnerships

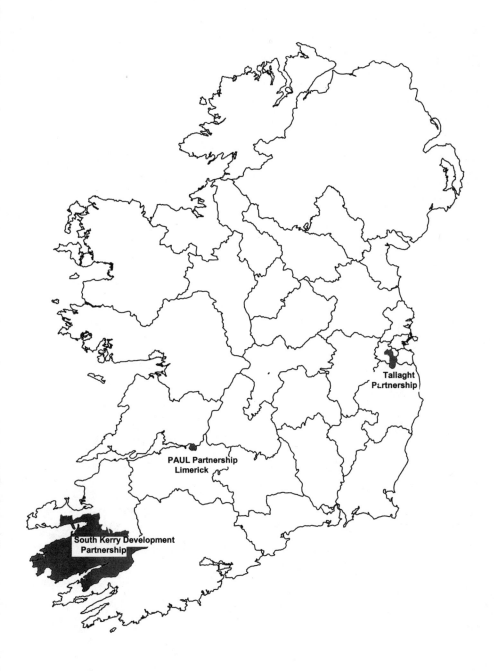

FIGURE 6.0: LOCATION OF THE CASE STUDY
LOCAL DEVELOPMENT PARTNERSHIPS

Chapter 6

Case Study 1:
PAUL Partnership Limerick

Introduction

PAUL (People Action Against Unemployment Limited) Partnership Limerick is located in Limerick city. It was established in 1990 under the EU Poverty 3 programme by a consortium of community, statutory and voluntary organisations, with the aim of addressing the employment and related needs of households in disadvantaged local authority housing estates across the city. Since then, the Partnership has designed and implemented a wide range of innovative anti-poverty measures, supported by partner agencies and funded through various pilot national and European programmes. The Partnership has recently entered a new stage in its operation with the drawing-up of a six-year integrated development strategy to be funded under the joint EU/central government local development programme. This has confirmed the status of the Partnership as a mainstream policy instrument for tackling social exclusion. The Partnership is thus an exemplar for the local development partnership sector in Ireland, with added importance because of its urban context and European influences.

Description of the PAUL Partnership Limerick

Context and Origins

Limerick is the third largest urban area in the Republic of Ireland (population 76,000) and the administrative and commercial capital of the midwest region.[1] Though serving a predominantly rural hinterland, Limerick is part of a growing urban axis incorporating the nearby towns of Shannon and Ennis. Urbanisation reflects the increasing dominance of industry and services in the regional economy, with a strong foreign input especially in the high technology sectors. Limerick is the cockpit of this economic transformation, exemplified by the location of a national technological park (incorporating the University of Limerick) and other large industrial estates. The city has also benefited from an expanding public sector, including two regional hospitals, three national third-level institutions and various local, regional and national government offices. The city's commercial sector is also vibrant, with a ring of suburban shopping centres, a major inner city renewal programme valued at £200 million and a strong tourist industry linked to various historical and cultural attractions. Limerick has a thriving housing market, principally fuelled by an expansion in private home ownership in the suburbs which has resulted in a decline in the population of the inner city.

Like other urban areas, Limerick has experienced some negative consequences of economic and urban change. Notably, these are:

- A collapse in demand for unskilled work, with the result that one in four of the labour force is unemployed, half of whom are without work for one year or more;

- A persistent pattern of early school leaving, leading to increased educational disparities;

- An increase in lone parenthood, especially among mothers with first-time births;

- A residualised public housing sector, catering overwhelmingly for social welfare recipients (86 per cent of tenants) in a small number of low quality housing estates.

---

[1] Limerick city comprises two administrative units: the main part of the city, referred to as Limerick county borough, has a population of 52,000 and is administered by Limerick Corporation; and the city suburbs, with a population of 24,000, administered by Limerick County Council.

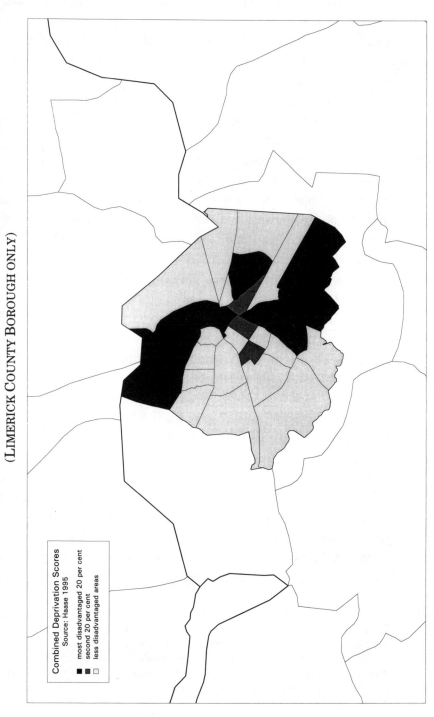

FIGURE 6.1: OVERALL DEPRIVATION SCORES, PAUL PARTNERSHIP LIMERICK ADMINISTRATIVE AREA
(LIMERICK COUNTY BOROUGH ONLY)

Combined Deprivation Scores
Source: Haase 1995

most disadvantaged 20 per cent
second 20 per cent
less disadvantaged areas

These processes are reflected in socio-spatial divisions in the city. Sixteen of the 37 wards in Limerick county borough fall into the most disadvantaged decile in national terms (this represents almost half of the population of the borough).[2] At the other extreme, six wards which rank among the most advantaged decile, account for a fifth of the population. This pattern of affluence extends to the suburbs of Limerick. The spatial distribution of the poorest wards shows a marked north-west to south-east pattern (Figure 6.1), which corresponds to the distribution of local authority housing in the city. The low living standards of residents in these areas are made worse by inferior housing conditions, public stigma, physical isolation, lack of services and weak community structures. Social exclusion is thus deeply entrenched in the social and physical fabric of Limerick, with the many opportunities presented by the city's recent economic development largely bypassing those most in need.

The emerging coincidence of unemployment and local authority housing became of growing public concern in the late 1980s, culminating in a joint application by an informal alliance of public bodies, voluntary organisations and community groups for EU structural funds in 1988. This collective initiative reflected a number of factors, including a tradition of community activism, the experience of inter-agency co-operation, the dissemination of new ideas on an anti-poverty strategy and a concern in key statutory agencies about the uneven development of the city. The structural funds initiative, though unsuccessful, laid the basis for a subsequent and successful application under the EU Poverty 3 programme in 1989. This led, in March 1990, to the establishment of the PAUL project as a "model action project" in the programme. This initiative was made by a consortium of 12 local agencies from

---

[2] This pattern is based on a composite index of deprivation using thirteen surrogate measures of poverty drawn from the census of population [Gamma, (1995), *Limerick City APC Report*, Dublin: ADM and D. McCafferty, (1996) "Urban deprivation in Southill East, Limerick City" paper to Geographical Society of Ireland Annual Conference, "Poor People — Poor Places", Maynooth, September 1996].

the statutory, voluntary and community sectors, with the latter having a key role in formulating the project. The Poverty 3 programme enabled the consortium to establish an organisational structure, to develop a programme of activities and to employ professional staff. The project's aim was, in Poverty 3 language, to promote the social and economic integration of the least privileged in Limerick city. It targeted four discrete public housing areas in the city (defined by parish boundaries), which were characterised by high levels of unemployment and deprivation, for a multi-sectoral programme of interventions.

There followed a rapid evolution of the project, with additional programmes and resources fuelling a major expansion of its role. The first and most important occurred in November 1991, when the project was included in the Irish government programme to tackle long-term unemployment blackspots (ABR). Under this, the project widened its focus to include the long-term unemployed throughout the city and expanded its membership to include employers, trade unions and an additional community organisation. It also gave the project access to additional funding, in particular for enterprise development, through an EU global grant. (The new programme also involved a change in title — the PAUL Partnership Limerick.) Subsequent programmes included an EU Horizon project with lone parents and a Department of Social Welfare-funded money advice initiative. With the termination of three of these programmes in 1994, the Partnership entered a hiatus in its work programme as funds dried up and some staff departed. This time was used by the Partnership to formulate a new strategic plan, following an intensive period of local consultation. This was subsequently approved in late 1995 under the CSF-funded local development programme (integrated development sub-programme), which runs until 1999. During this period, the Partnership also took on responsibility to develop and manage a local employment service as part of a central government initiative. This involves co-ordinating the work of existing training and employment bodies, as well as providing additional services, particularly in adult guidance and job placement. In 1996, the

Partnership also launched a childcare training initiative funded under the NOW programme. Effectively, the Partnership is now back on full steam, with an enhanced status in government policy and an ambitious work programme set out for itself until the end of the decade.

Structure

The Partnership has the legal form of a private company limited by guarantee, without share capital. Its 24 directors are nominated by 16 member organisations (or partners) and reflect a diversity of sectors (see Table 6.1). The partners do not have an equality of representation on the board: state agencies and voluntary organisations have one nominee each; community groups have between one and two nominees; and the social partners have between two and three representatives. A staff representative and an independent chairperson are also included as directors. This complex membership structure arises from the fusion of the original model developed under Poverty 3 and the make-up required under the ABR. Under Poverty 3, a majority of the board represented community groups. In addition, the partnership appointed an independent chairperson, along with a staff nominee. The ABR required two changes to this: the inclusion of social partners and the equal representation of community, statutory and social interests (on a 6–6–6 basis). Representatives of external funding agencies have traditionally had the right to attend board meetings as observers — this is presently confined to ADM. The nomination of representatives on the board is a matter for partner organisations, though there is broad agreement that people of seniority and experience should be appointed.

TABLE 6.1: PARTNER AGENCIES IN THE PAUL PARTNERSHIP, LIMERICK

	Community	Social	Statutory	Voluntary
Local	Moyross Partners; Our Lady of Lourdes Community Services Group; St Mary's Parish Awareness Development Group; Southill Community Services Group; Southill Development Cooperative; St Munchin's Action Centre Committee		Limerick Corporation; Limerick Vocational Educational Committee	Limerick Youth Services; Limerick Centre for the Unemployed[1]
Regional			Shannon Development; Mid-Western Health Board	
National		Irish Business and Employers Confederation; Irish Congress of Trade Unions	Department of Social Community and Family Affairs; FÁS	

[1] Technically, the ICTU representation includes the Limerick Centre for the Unemployed, a voluntary organisation sponsored by the ICTU. In reality, the Centre for the Unemployed can be considered to be a partner agency in its own right for two reasons: it had this status in the Partnership when originally set up under the Poverty 3 programme; its distinctive role as a service provider to and representative of the unemployed.

The Partnership has an intricate management structure. The company's board of directors collectively acts as the management committee to decide overall policy and funding decisions (meetings occur every six weeks for, on average, three hours). Attendance during the period March 1990 to December 1993 averaged 75 per cent, though this hides a decline from 90 per cent in the early stages to 65 per cent. Community representatives were the best attendees during this period (88 per cent), while social partners averaged only 42 per cent. The management committee has three sub-tiers: operational sub-committees, programme development workshops and special project committees.[3] Each tier reports directly to the management committee, and typically has a board member as chairperson and a staff member as facilitator. There are also linkages across sub-structures, e.g. proposals formulated by programme development workshops must get financial approval from the finance sub-committee. Over time, the distinct roles of each sub-structure have become blurred. For example, the economic programme development workshop assumed an assessment role for small enterprise grant applications under the ABR programme. A key motivation for establishing these sub-structures was to deepen (more specialist) and widen (more participative) the involvement of partner agencies in the work of the Partnership. In all, the management structures provide nearly 200 positions, though the actual number of people involved is somewhat less due to multiple membership.

---

[3] Management sub-committees were set up to oversee delegated functions of the board in regard to financial planning, recruitment, research and evaluation and community action centres. The programme development workshops were designed to formulate project activities. Special project committees were established to manage externally-funded programmes, e.g. employment training for lone parents and money advice.

TABLE 6.2: MANAGEMENT STRUCTURE OF THE PAUL PARTNERSHIP LIMERICK

Board of Directors / Management Committee		
Management Committees	*Programme Workshops*	*Special Projects*
Finance	Economic	Money advice debt forum
Recruitment	Education and training	Lone parents task force
Research and evaluation	Housing and environment	Local employment service
Community action centres	Welfare rights	
	Family support	
	Employment services	

The Partnership has acquired a large and relatively stable staff complement, though there was considerable turnover due to the termination of various programmes in 1994. The project director oversees a management team comprising various programme co-ordinators (local employment service, social activities, etc). A third tier is represented by staff working on specific projects, e.g. money advice, education, office support, employment mediation (c.35), while a fourth level comprises staff on temporary employment programmes and work placements (c.30). The latter category mainly assists in welfare rights, money advice and office administration, and most are located in the community action centres. In all, the Partnership employs 70 full- and part-time staff, including a small number of people on secondment from partner agencies. The staff complement in the Partnership evolved rapidly as its activities expanded, despite an initial reluctance to employ more than a minimum number of staff. This reflected an expectation that community expertise could be used to deliver project activities. This was not feasible, however, as the appropriate level of expertise did not exist, either at community level or in Limerick. Over time, an increasing proportion of staff has been recruited locally, including previously unemployed people and seconded staff. This reflects the project's commitment to enhancing local expertise through training and work experience measures.

TABLE 6.3: STAFF STRUCTURE OF THE PAUL PARTNERSHIP LIMERICK

Director
Programme staff (social, economic, employment service and administration)
Project staff (money advice, education, child-care, community, administration)
Temporary staff (money advice, administration)

Objectives and Activities

The Partnership's aim has been very broad from the outset, reflecting both the diversity of needs in its four target areas and the wide parameters for initiating action allowed under Poverty 3, ie social and economic integration. In practice, the project's activities fall into two divisions: measures to improve employment and general living conditions; and initiatives to empower disadvantaged communities and make them more self-reliant. Under its strategic plan, the Partnership has agreed a programme containing 21 discrete activities organised in six broad categories. Some activities were designed and provided by local community groups, while others were managed and delivered by the Partnership. The commitment to community empowerment was primarily reflected in the establishment of a network of community action centres, under local management. An estimated 4,500 people benefited under Poverty 3.

Under the ABR initiative, the Partnership's focus on unemployment was strengthened, especially its enterprise and labour market programmes. The inclusion of the ABR resulted in a growing specialisation within the project between Poverty 3 activities (mainly social) and ABR initiatives (mainly economic). At the same time, the Partnership became more directly involved in service delivery, such as funding job creation ventures in the private sector and co-ordinating initiatives for the long-term unemployed. Similarly, under other funding secured at this time, the Partnership provided services for indebted households (money advice), unemployed adults (guidance and counselling) and lone parents (education and training).

The Partnership re-appraised its aim when formulating its strategic plan 1995-99, with a renewed emphasis on its work in supporting community initiative. This is reflected in the newly stated aim of the Partnership:

> the empowerment and motivation of (disadvantaged) communities to develop their full potential for the betterment of all aspects of their lives, be they economic, social or environmental.

The strategies for achieving this goal highlight the centrality of the community dimension:

- To empower communities to identify their needs;

- To empower communities to develop strategies and tactics to meet those needs;

- To empower communities to resource the plans and action relevant to the attainment of these strategies and tactics;

- To empower communities to manage the implementation of these plans and actions;

- To put in place structures which will enable the mainstreaming of actions and programmes through the participation of communities, the statutory, social and voluntary partners.

The Partnership's work programme has the following components:

- Enterprise and employment development;

- Community development;

- Education and training services;

- Welfare rights and money advice;

- Services for families and young people;

- Environmental development;

- Research, evaluation and appraisal.

Some examples of Partnership activities to date are:

- **Community action centres.** A network of local centres, in each target area, which provide information, services (phone, etc) and support for individuals and community organisations, under local management. The Partnership assists with running costs (c £20,000 per annum), as well as providing central training and support for staff and management.

- **Jobs club.** A community-run employment agency provides technical, guidance and placement services for unemployed people in two target areas of the Partnership. It also operates a short-term jobs placement programme in the Netherlands each year.

- **Early school intervention project.** A five-year project which provides enhanced educational services, in-school and out-of-school, to children at risk of learning failure. The initiative is directed by a local third-level institution, and overseen by a variety of community and statutory interests.

- **Money advice service.** A centrally-organised advice service for indebted households, also available in local outlets, which provides counselling and assistance with debt repayment, liaises with creditors, promotes credit unions and encourages general money management skills.

- **Enterprise support programme.** A Partnership programme which provides advice and grant aid to micro-enterprises, and which assesses applications for a pilot initiative allowing participants to retain their full welfare entitlements for one year.

Resources and Expenditure

A feature of the Partnership is its success in attracting external funding through a variety of national and EU programmes (Table 6.4). It is estimated that the Partnership had a resource base of £3.25 million in the first six years of operation (1990-95). Since then, its funding has continued to grow, reaching almost £2 million in 1997. Its most recent additional external programmes are the Territorial Employment Pact, the local employment service and various child-care initiatives. Partner agencies have made a modest resource contribution to the partnership, through staff redeployment and some small-scale additional funding. For example, the Department of Education (though not a formal partner), Limerick City VEC and the Mid-Western Health Board have allocated staff for various education and child-care projects. Meanwhile, FÁS has paid allowances to participants on various training and employment programmes. Voluntary and community groups have been the main beneficiaries of the Partnership, though they too have contributed by providing volunteers. In general, the contribution of partner agencies has varied considerably and been very much at the discretion of individual agencies, usually negotiated on a case-by-case basis. This situation is intended to change in the current strategic plan where contributions have been agreed in advance. Thus, of a planned expenditure of £18.5 million, less than half (c. £7 million) is to be sourced through external programmes. It is expected that the remainder will be got from a mixture of local and national (i.e. departmental) funds.

The Partnership's Poverty 3 funding was allocated at the discretion of its management committee, within certain broad parameters. Other funding is more restrictive and usually requires prior agreement on proposed activities. With these significant external resources, the Partnership has become a key funder of community and voluntary agencies in the city. For example, during the four years of the Poverty 3 programme, the Partnership allocated £340,000 — half of its activities' funding — to a network of community action centres. A second use of these funds has been to enable the Partnership to directly employ staff to provide services. With the termination of external programmes in 1994, there was a slow down in activities. This has changed again with the coming on stream of the local development and other programmes.

TABLE 6.4: PROGRAMME FUNDING RECEIVED BY THE PAUL PARTNERSHIP LIMERICK, 1990-95

Programme	Time period	Amount (£)
EU Poverty 3	1990-94	1,616,975
ABR	1991-94	286,000
Money Advice	1992-95	125,000
EU Horizon	1992-94	160,300
Enterprise Trust	1992-94	36,600
EU Global grant	1992-94	440,000
Community development	1994-95	50,000
EU Local development	1995	395,547
Local employment service	1995	263,000

Equal Opportunities

The Partnership does not have an explicit equal opportunities focus, though one is implicit in aspects of its work programme. The emphasis on long-term unemployment results in a male bias, due to the traditional measurement of this problem (registration for unemployment benefit). In other project areas, however, the main beneficiaries are women. This reflects the main beneficiaries of actions undertaken by the Partnership, e.g. lone parents, in-debted households, people with learning difficulties, parental in-volvement in children's education and community activities. Indeed, there is some concern that men are under-represented in terms of those who are benefiting from the project and one or two actions have been designed to address this. The Partnership has also initiated a measure targeted specifically at Travellers.

There are six women on the management committee of the Partnership — one of whom is a vice-chairperson — which represents a quarter of the total membership. This figure is considerably below the government-recommended quota of 40 per cent. The low representation is particularly apparent in the social partner and statutory sectors and, to a lesser extent, among community groups. By contrast, both voluntary organisations and the staff are represented by women. The percentage of women on sub-committee structures is considerably higher, averaging over 50 per cent, though this varies depending on the particular group. The staff of the Partnership is overwhelmingly female, though the director and two senior staff are male. (In the initial years of the project, both the chairperson and director were female.) There is no Traveller representation on either the board or staff of the Partnership. Gender or ethnic representation on the board of the Partnership has never been an issue for discussion and largely reflects the composition of partner agencies. Similarly, the gender composition of staff is an indirect outcome of the types of expertise sought by and available to the Partnership.

The PAUL Partnership Limerick in Action

Representation and Power

The line-up of agencies involved in the Partnership arose from a combination of internal and external factors. The original members of the Partnership, under the Poverty 3 programme, reflected local exigencies, in particular the strong community and voluntary involvement in social issues and a marginal involvement of business and trade unions. In addition to seven community and voluntary organisations being included as founding partners, a formula was agreed whereby the community sector had a majority of board members. The membership thus represented a local consensus about who the key actors were and the key role to be played by community groups in the organisation. The down side of this was that only those areas with community representation on the Partnership were included in the work programme, while other potential allies (employers, universities) were left out. Subsequently, this arrangement was changed when the Partnership was included in the ABR programme. Like Poverty 3, the ABR emphasised a partnership approach, but it also specified the composition of the partners and their representation on the management committee. This required a restructuring of the Partnership, expanding to include businesses, trade unions and another community group (representing another local area), and altering representation on the board (on a 6–6–6 basis). A compromise was eventually reached which retained the additional representation by community groups, the positions of independent chairperson and staff representative and the membership by one of the voluntary organisations.

The resultant hybrid structure created a major challenge for the Partnership: how to ensure participation of new interests in the enlarged management structure, while at the same time maintaining the community ethos of the original group? The additional members have necessarily made the management committee more formal and less participative. More than that, the shift from a majority to a minority has had a negative psychological effect on the community representatives, as they feel their input is diluted by other interests. The new structure emphasised the personal competencies of board members to effectively get their views across in a larger and less homogenous forum. This highlighted the lack of experience among community representatives in particular. Equally problematic was the development of common ground among the expanded board. At the time, it was expected that the new interests would simply link in to the existing work programme. However, this had a minimal role for employers and trade unions in particular and it took some time for them to identify a niche for themselves in the project. It also highlighted the personal commitment to the project among its founding members. This transition was reflected in the poor attendance and participation in board meetings by new representatives on one hand and by friction on a number of key issues and decisions on the other.

The representatives of the various partner interests are the key mediators of the partnership relationship, as reflected in their personalised legal status as company directors. The composition and motivation of this small group at the fulcrum of the Partnership is thus critical to its operation. The directors are drawn from a broad social spectrum, though with predominance of professionals/technocrats, a small representation of community activists and an exclusion of political interests. The six state agencies are represented by senior executives with management skills in various fields: adult education, economic development, social work. Similarly, three of the four social partner representatives are senior executives. The community and voluntary sector representatives are a mix of local activists (both unemployed and working on local projects) and church professionals (two nuns and a priest). There has been a high turnover of community representatives, with 20 changes in personnel for nine director positions in a period of five years. There are a number of reasons for this: election to political office or employment on a Partnership-funded project (representatives are obliged to resign in such cases); and personal factors, in particular the demands (time and energy) of being a community representative. The other grouping to exhibit a high turnover is employers.

Marginalised groups are poorly represented on the board, with only 25 per cent women (including two out of nine community representatives) and no Traveller, lone parent, person with a disability or young person. This primarily reflects the exclusively geographic nature of community representation and the absence of sectoral groups. A feature of the board is the status conferred on its chairperson, with the two incumbents to date having a high public profile and being independent of partner agencies. This has been a deliberate strategy in order to forge links between the Partnership and local public opinion (media, politicians, etc.) and also central government. In addition to the external aspect, the chairperson has a key input to the running of the Partnership, on occasions to the extent of being an executive chairperson. This reflects the high demands of the post, especially in the absence of a management executive (though the recent appointment of three vice-chairpeople has addressed this somewhat).

Partner representatives are appointed to the board in two main fashions: nomination and election. Nominated board members mainly come from the statutory and social partner sectors, whereby the chief executive officer identifies a person from amongst his or her staff (state) or membership (business and trade unions) and nominates them onto the board. The two voluntary sector nominees also fall within this category as *ex-officio* appointments. The community sector initially relied on an election procedure to select its representatives, typically at a public meeting hosted by the partner group. More recently, with the turnover of directors, the appointee has been nominated by the executive of a community group. These procedures, however, are more apparent than real and in the majority of cases, both delegated and elected, the appointment of a representative onto the board of the Partnership strongly reflects the personal commitment of the individual concerned. This is clear when analysing the transition from informal grouping to formal structure in the early days of the project, when there was a very clear continuity of personnel across all sectors. Similarly, where directors have had to absent themselves for periods of time from the board, either their places are retained or they relinquish their positions on a temporary basis. Also, there is no precedent for the replacement of a director by a parent organisation, except where this person voluntarily resigns (through there is some suggestion of one or two directors being pressurised to resign). While the company's articles of association specify a three-year tenure cycle for directors, at which point their nomination can be renewed, up until recently this was viewed as a procedural point to be addressed within the board rather than requiring re-affirmation from a nominating body. This individualistic approach to board membership also reflects, first, the legal form through which the Partnership operates (company directors); second, the weak understanding of and commitment to partnership as an inter-institutional arrangement; and, third, the limited pool of people either willing or able to take on the task of being a representative in partner agencies. The latter is particularly acute in the community sector, where community groups have seldom the tradition (inward-looking, participative) or the capacity (structures, resources) to establish and maintain formal linkages with external bodies.

The other side of representation is being accountable to the nominating body. Again, there is a lack of agreed procedures governing these tasks, which are largely at the discretion of individual representatives. Some innovative models of reporting have been devised by representatives in the community sector. For instance, one community organisation restructured itself from a small adult education group to an umbrella organisation for all groups active in their community. Another example is that of Moyross Partners which established a "support group" (in effect a sub-committee) to link with its two representatives on the board. Its specific task is to discuss their involvement with the Partnership, including discussing the agenda of board meetings. Another community group, Southill Community Services Board, has developed links with the Partnership by inviting onto its management committee the project director. This provides the group with a direct contact with the Partnership, in addition to its membership of the board. In the state sector, the VEC representative gives a monthly report to the adult education board, a forum which includes elected representatives and sectoral interests. This is seen as especially important given the dearth of linkage between board directors and the formal political system. Beyond these examples, however, reporting procedures are largely informal and oral, focusing on specific issues of concern. Indeed, even this minimum level is seldom achieved among the social partners due to the absence of links with nominating organisations.

The informality of the relationship between partners and the Partnership has a number of consequences for the organisation. One is the reliance on personal initiative in order to make the project work. The Partnership has been fortunate in this regard because of the exceptional commitment provided by members, often above and beyond what might be acknowledged by the parent organisation (e.g. in terms of hours of work, personal costs, back-up support, etc.). This greatly energised the Partnership in its early days, though is less apparent now with changes in personnel and simply the passing of time. Second, the lack of procedures increases the risk of "freelance" directors, who do not nurture any institutional commitment and who pursue largely personal agendas. This can in turn alienate the Partnership from the partner organisation and *vice-versa*. The image here can be as important as the reality, in that a director who has not got a formal linkage (nomination/reporting) with his or her parent organisation, can find their status within the board undermined. A third issue relates to the continuity of representation where a new member joins or an existing board member is replaced. This was particularly apparent when the social partners joined the Partnership and considerable problems were experienced in securing people who could give the level of personal commitment demanded of directors by the organisation. It is also emerging as a serious issue in the community sector. The Partnership is very vulnerable to personnel changes, with the loss of key people having considerable repercussions for the dynamic of the project and for interpersonal relationships.

The lack of clarity governing selection and reporting arrangements has given rise to increasing frustration among both board members and nominating bodies. Much of this has been directed at the community directors and the extent to which they "represent" community interests. However, rather than discussing this issue and its implications in terms of structures, resources and procedures, it tends to be fudged because of an underlying resistance among community directors to being told what their role is by other sectors. In recent times, the Partnership has sought to address this issue by establishing a sub-committee to review nomination and reporting procedures for board directors, with a view to developing an agreed code of practice. There has also been some discussion about incorporating sectoral groups as part of the community sector representation. This again underlines the absence of a collective understanding of the partnership principle within the organisation.

While there is broad agreement about the strategic remit of the Partnership, there is far less consensus about the role of the various sectors in achieving this. The greatest gap is apparent between community directors and representatives of other partner agencies. Community directors envisage the Partnership as rebalancing power relations between communities and service providers. This commitment to community empowerment is reflected in the original decision to make community directors the majority grouping on the board. Another dimension of this role is channelling Partnership resources to initiatives to meet local needs, notably through the establishment of community action centres. Indeed, in some cases this partisanship goes further as community directors promote the interests of the organisation they represent or are associated with in the community. This arises because of the structure of community representation (geographic and often single-issue community organisations) and the limited capacity of community directors to play a more expansive role given the absence of back-up and resources for community consultation and feedback. Representatives of the two voluntary organisations tend to adopt a similar agency-led approach.

The statutory representatives broadly agree with the community empowerment emphasis of the Partnership. In this, they see the role of the Partnership as co-ordinating and enhancing service delivery for socially excluded groups. There is some variation in the approach of statutory representatives to this, some being proactive by suggesting experimentation and others being passive and only responding when directly asked to provide assistance. Whatever the approach, protecting the sectoral interests and territory of their parent agency remains of paramount importance. The social partners, meanwhile, express no strategic interest in the Partnership. They see their contribution as being altruistic, facilitating what they see as a worthy initiative through personal advice and support. Even then, they have found it difficult to engage with what they see as a rather bureaucratic and obtuse structure. Finally, the independent chairperson and senior staff (the staff representative and the director) make important contributions to the vision of the Partnership. Both the current and former chairperson have strongly supported the community empowerment dimension of the project, an expectation which is also held by the staff representative.

Strategy and Decision-making

The Partnership's strategy, as outlined in its separate work programmes for the Poverty 3 and ABR programmes, was prepared following an extensive planning process. This had two main components: internal discussions at management committee and subcommittee levels and external consultations with interested parties, including submission of proposals. This resulted in the Partnership supporting a broad-ranging list of stand-alone actions, loosely organised according to six themes, e.g. education and training, income support. Most of these actions were supported and delivered by partner organisations, notably those in the community and voluntary sectors. Over time, the planning process has changed perceptibly in two ways: first, the Partnership staff has assumed a more central role in the initiation and design of actions, including preparing two major projects which secured funding under external programmes (Money Advice and Horizon); second, and linked to the previous point, the Partnership has assumed a direct role in the delivery of actions, notably under the ABR initiative where it became involved in the provision of services for the unemployed (e.g. grant-aid scheme for micro-businesses, adult guidance service). The latter resulted in a rapid increase in the staff complement of the organisation.

The drift towards centralisation appears to be reversed in the most recent phase of strategic planning. For this, the Partnership consulted directly with community organisations to seek their views on what actions should be undertaken. This consultation has been reinforced by a decision to encourage the five target communities to formulate their own area action plans. At the heart of these strategies is a neighbourhood development centre (a refashioned community action centre), which is intended to animate and support local initiative. Already, one community has drawn up such a local development plan, which is attracting support from state agencies. This attempt to re-locate the partnership model to a more localised level may prove a major source of contention in the years ahead. There is also a related attempt to move the Partnership away from a delivery role towards one of co-ordination and support for local efforts. There is a crucial issue, then, of the relationship between strategies targeted at particular social groups and the general goal of community development. This relationship is unresolved and the interplay in the next few years between the work programme of the Partnership and the local area action plans will reveal if these agendas can be reconciled.

The multi-faceted nature of the Partnership's strategy is paralleled and facilitated by its complex decision-making procedures. The board follows a business model of operation, with formal agendas, backed-up by detailed position papers, leading to recorded decisions. These meetings are held on a six-weekly basis and take between three and four hours on average, usually on a Monday morning. The setting for these meetings is also rather formal, utilising the boardroom of the regional health board. At these meetings, much of the agenda emanates from the project director and the chairperson. This business model was a deliberate choice of the project and is something which is seen as reflecting both their capacity and intent in tackling social exclusion. In the early days of the project, however, the board meetings had a quite different flavour. At this time, the agenda was more driven by the internal dynamics of the board, as the various representatives sought to establish common ground and trust between one another. There was frequent conflict at these meetings and their duration could often be up to five or six hours. It was realised that such a pattern could not be sustained, either from a time commitment or in terms of the decision-making needs of the project. The shift in procedure, however, went much further than had been anticipated. The extension in the size of the board, together with the change in venue, were further factors in this regard.

There are other aspects of the management committee's *modus operandi* which are relevant here. First, there is the absence of an executive committee with responsibility for on-going management and implementation. This void has been filled by the central role played by the chairperson in the management of the project. This situation has changed somewhat in the last year when a new chairperson was appointed and three posts of vice-chairperson were created. This has created a small network including the project director who consult, in a relatively informal manner, on issues between full board meetings. Second, the Partnership does not use formal voting procedures, preferring to operate on a consensus basis. Nominally, the board is structured on a tripartite basis, with community, statutory and social partner categories. However, this division has little meaning in practice as the various sectors do not operate as cohesive units, with clearly defined positions or views on issues. This can lead to individual powerful representatives being in a position to dictate decision-making.

A third aspect of the management is the use of various sub-committee structures to plan and implement much of the Partnership's activities. These are primarily designed to provide a forum whereby partners can discuss and agree activities relating to various themes. As such, they are meant to compensate for the more formal procedures adopted at board level. Their membership includes board members, other partner agency representatives and representatives of non-partner bodies. Staff are allocated to each workshop where they take on the role of "facilitators". Over time, however, these structures have also become more formalised, following a similar procedure to that of the board. There has also been some disagreement about the decision-making role of these structures and, in particular, how the workshops relate to the specialist committees (e.g. finance, research) and to the board itself. The Partnership's organisational procedures give rise to many negative comments by partner representatives, as if, somehow, a structure has been created which they no longer control. Two issues in particular were highlighted: a lack of co-ordination between the different components of the organisation and an increase in bureaucracy and paper work within the organisation.

Another aspect of the management structure is the staff team. Originally, the Partnership had a clearly articulated policy of having a minimum core staff, whose primary function would be to support internal decision-making procedures rather than to direct them. As the demands on the Partnership increased, the staff complement grew considerably, with over 50 people now employed though this includes over 30 people on a temporary employment programme. This increase in staff has led to a professionalisation of the organisation, which in turn has enhanced the role of the staff in the decision-making procedures of the project quite dramatically. The staff role was also strengthened by the establishment of a number of externally-funded and centrally-managed initiatives, e.g. EU Horizon project with lone parents, Department of Social Welfare project on money advice and a FÁS-funded temporary employment programme. While board sub-structures were set up to manage these projects, they had far greater autonomy within the organisational fabric of the project, with a corresponding greater input from staff. The strengthening of the staff team and the emergence of staff-driven projects have altered considerably the organisational ethos of the Partnership. At the same time, more staff has led to a tension among management, with some directors expressing concern that the expansion of the Partnership has occurred to the detriment of voluntary and community organisations. The increase in staff has also raised issues about reporting relationships and a division of labour.

Resources and Methods

The core financial resources of the Partnership are sourced externally. It was the availability of these under the Poverty 3 programme which acted as the original spur to bring together the partner agencies in the project. Under the ABR initiative, this dependency remained, even though nominally the existing resources of statutory agencies devoted to tackling unemployment were to be scrutinised by the Partnership as to its optimum allocation. In practice, however, this did not happen as budgets were strictly retained within the control of partner agencies. Only relatively small amounts were channelled to the Partnership, almost exclusively to support specific actions initiated by the project, e.g. external training, temporary employment. The dependency on external funding was reinforced under other programmes, as the annual budget approached almost £1 million per annum in 1993/4. The most recent strategic plan endeavours to change this relationship by indicating potential funding allocations from part-ner and other agencies. This plan proposes a total budget of £18 million over a five year period, only a sixth of which (£3 million) is to be sourced from ADM under the local development programme. The remainder is earmarked from central government (£6 million) and partner agencies (£9 million), though in some cases, this money is expected rather than assured. It is also unclear to what extent the £9 million from partner agencies will represent new money, as distinct from resources already committed by partner agencies, but now being assimilated into the budgetary frame-work of the Partnership. Securing resources from partner statu-tory bodies is problematic for a number of reasons: the limited discretionary resources available to statutory agencies at the local level; the long lead-in time required to alter the funding alloca-tions of partner agencies; and the reluctance of partner agencies to cede control over expenditure to the Partnership for fear of the long-term consequences for their own budgets.

Despite its reliance on external funding, the Partnership's re-source base is unique in that its allocation lies largely within the remit of the organisation. This is a significant "carrot" for all partners involved, but in particular for the community sector whose access to resources for development purposes was ex-tremely limited prior to the advent of the Partnership. In the early days of the Partnership, the emphasis was primarily on channelling resources to community and voluntary organisations in order to implement agreed activities. Thus, over the lifetime of Poverty 3, half of all discretionary resources went to fund four community action centres. Under the ABR, this emphasis shifted towards direct funding of Partnership activities, such as support for micro-enterprises or provision of adult guidance. In addition, new external programmes, such as Horizon and Money Advice, enabled the project to engage in activities, principally through the direct recruitment of staff. Consequently, the staff complement of the Partnership grew considerably during this period. However, as resources dried up in 1994/95, the project was increasingly forced to rely on short-term measures to maintain its staff (e.g. temporary employment, student placement and temporary contracts). There are fewer examples of where the Partnership has adopted a broker-age or co-ordinating role. These are mainly confined to initiatives which are funded through external programmes, e.g. to tackle in-debtedness or to prevent early school leaving or, most recently, to reintegrate the long-term unemployed.

As important as the resource base of the Partnership is its ability to mobilise technical and organisational skills. An example of this was the important role played by officials from statutory agencies in drawing up the original submission by the project under Poverty 3. These officials used their technical know-how and organisational expertise to ensure a detailed programme could be drawn up and agreed to by a diversity of interests. The recruitment of the project's chairperson is another example of a targeted attempt to source external expertise for the benefit of the project, in this case identifying someone who had an understand-ing of national policy-making, had considerable political skills and was expert in research and evaluation. The Partnership also suc-cessfully tapped the expertise and resources of local organisations which are not represented on its board. For example, the early school intervention project was animated by the curriculum devel-opment unit of Mary Immaculate College, a local third level insti-tution. The Partnership's research work was also supported by local academics, and its initiative with families with children-in-care was guided by a specialist attached to a voluntary social service agency.

There were some weaknesses in this regard also. Notably, the project failed to mobilise the skills of the local business sector in its strategy to promote enterprise and job creation. There was also a failure to get assistance from established organisations for the financial and administrative aspects of its work. Management skills were also largely neglected. While some representatives had particular skills in this regard, these accounted for only a minority of those involved in the board. The Partnership provided some management training, especially in the early days of the project. However, these tended to be one-off events, rather than part of an on-going programme. In addition, there was no formal induction programme for new directors, in order to brief them on their roles and responsibilities. Not surprisingly, the weak management skills of the Partnership was a frequent criticism raised during the interviews with directors, though recent improvements in the latter are acknowledged.

A huge onus was placed on the staff in order to underpin the management of the project. There was a major deficiency here in the early years of the project, though this was in part rectified by a change in personnel. However, other problems remained, especially in terms of enhancing the skill base of existing staff, most of whom were recruited for specific development tasks, but were later required to take on additional management duties as the number of programmes and staff expanded. Under the Poverty 3 programme, intensive training in project management was provided for four staff. The impact of this intervention was limited because the training occurred rather late in the programme (Autumn 1993) and was not specifically geared towards the needs of staff in the Partnership. A frequent tension in the project is between generalist and specialist staff. Given the scale and resources of the Partnership, there has been great reluctance to recruit a large complement of specialist staff. Most of the staff come from a broad community development background. At the same time, there are a number of rather specialist needs within the organisation: strategic planning, financial accounting, research and evaluation, information and publicity. Meeting these specific needs has proved a constant difficulty, though the project did employ a specialist research and evaluation officer under the Poverty 3 programme. In 1994/5, the project lost some of its more experienced personnel with the termination of its core programmes and had to recruit and train new staff to maintain its operations.

Monitoring and assessment of the work of the Partnership has been an on-going feature of its operation to date. This primarily derives from the Poverty 3 programme, which placed a heavy emphasis on evaluation as a aid to management and a means of learning. Under Poverty 3, responsibility (and funds) for evaluation were devolved to the Partnership itself, which enabled it to employ research expertise (both in-house and consultants) to support its evaluation activities.[4] At a programme level, the Partnership's activities have been included in two external evaluations.[5] Evaluation has not been without its difficulties for the Partnership, especially the chosen model of self-evaluation. The capacity of the organisation to engage in evaluation was limited for various reasons: the number and range of programmes; the lack of clarity around its management structures; the diversity of interests and expectations among the stakeholders; and the experimental nature of the project. Other Partnership programmes also place a considerable emphasis on evaluation, though mostly in the form of gathering information of pre-specified performance indicators (e.g. numbers of clients, jobs created), which are primarily for external consumption.

The Partnership has put considerable resources into training local people, so that they can contribute directly to the work of the project. Training has been provided in research methods, community education, estate management and community development for over 70 people in all. In most cases, this training has been

---

[4] The principal account of the Partnership's activities under the Poverty 3 programme is contained in the *Report on the Implementation of the Third EU Poverty Programme by the PAUL Partnership Limerick*, published by the Partnership in 1994.

[5] Both assessments were conducted by the Combat Poverty Agency, on the Area Based Response to Long-term Unemployment: S. Craig and K. McKeown (1994), *Progress through Partnership*, Dublin: Combat Poverty Agency and on the Poverty 3 programme: Nexus Research Cooperative (1995), "Evaluation of the Poverty 3 programme in Ireland", an unpublished report available from the Combat Poverty Agency.

accredited by professional bodies or local third level institutions. In addition, many short term training programmes were supported in specific skill areas, e.g. computers, financial accounting. A difficulty with much of this training has been to identify a suitable structure whereby these skills can be utilised. The substantial investment in external training contrasts with the limited amount devoted to internal needs.

Linkages and Communication

The Partnership is not an isolated entity — it operates within a local, national and EU framework which greatly influences its ability to promote social cohesion. Significantly, the Partnership has forged strong linkages with national and EU structures as a result of the programmes under which it has been supported. Poverty 3 placed the Limerick initiative in a unique European context, and offered high-level contact with policy-makers in DG V of the European Commission and with European organisations on issues of policy and practice. There was also a strong national dimension to the programme, which was promoted by the national research and development unit and the Combat Poverty Agency. This framework was utilised to disseminate information on the organisational model developed under the programme and on specific anti-poverty policies and practices.[6]

The Partnership's linkage at a national level was further enhanced with the ABR initiative. This provided a direct link with the economic and social policy section of the Department of the Taoiseach and enhanced the potential contribution of the Partnership as a testing ground for policy experimentation and learning. For example, the ABR national connection enabled the Partnership (along with the other partnerships in the programmes) to pilot a number of important policy initiatives aimed at easing the

---

[6] These are reported in P. Commins (ed) *Combating Exclusion in Ireland 1990–1994, a midway report* (1993), B. Harvey *Combating Exclusion, Lessons from the Third EU Poverty Programme in Ireland* 1989–1994 (1994), and B. Harvey and J. Kiernan (eds) *Putting Poverty 3 into Policy*, report of conference (1995).

transition from welfare to work, many of which were subsequently mainstreamed as part of national policy. In addition, both the ABR and Poverty 3 programmes laid the basis for a new national programme of integrated development in designated disadvantaged areas under the EU CSF. Similarly, the Partnership's involvement in delivering the money advice service and employment service has given it formal links to central government departments. This includes membership of a national steering committee whose task was to advise government on policy pertaining to indebtedness and consumer credit. Finally, its initiative with lone parents incorporates a strong policy focus at national level, which is mediated through the Horizon national support agency.

In addition to these programme links, the Partnership initiated contacts with government departments and agencies through various events, such as seminars, submissions, visitations and research reports. For instance, the Partnership published a research report which examined the effectiveness of temporary employment as a labour market programme for the long-term unemployed. This was followed-up by a national conference, co-hosted with the Department of Enterprise and Employment and FÁS, the national training agency, on the role of employment programmes in a changing labour market. Another example was the submission made by the Partnership on draft consumer credit legislation, which recommended a number of changes which were subsequently included in a revised bill and are now in law. The Partnership also contributed to the deliberations of the National Economic and Social Forum on the structure of the social welfare system and the effective delivery of public services. The two chairpeople of the Partnership have been critical in establishing a national profile for the Partnership. Both are well-known in national affairs, one being the president of a third-level institution and the other having been a government minister and MEP. They are thus able to initiate contacts with ministers and senior government officials, often on a one-to-one basis, which has resulted in high-profile visits by national and European figures.

The Partnership's linkages at the local level are also quite extensive, with contacts with local agencies being mediated by their representatives on the board of the Partnership. However, the informal and often selective nature of these links has limited the Partnership's contribution to policy formation. The project has, however, made important contributions to some local initiatives, such as the design and implementation of Limerick Corporation's statement on housing management and tenant participation. Initially, the Partnership worked with community and resident groups to make a submission on this statement. Subsequently, it assisted the residents' group in one area to develop a model for tenant participation, including a public consultation on a redesign strategy for their estate. It also organised a diploma course in estate management, which included officials from the local authority. Similar link-ups on specific issues have also been made with the regional health board (child-care services) and the local VEC (certification and accreditation of adult education), though none have assumed the status of formal agreements.

The Partnership's linkage with community groups has similarly largely depended on individuals. The main area where the Partnership has sought to have a formal programme relationship with community groups is through the network of community action centres. The results here are rather disappointing, with the exception of some co-ordinated work on welfare rights and money advice. Outside of this, there are examples of linkages on specific issues, such as services for lone parents, child-care services, adult education groups, and education and training opportunities. This situation in part reflects the organisational nature of many community groups, whose capacity to enter into strategic agreements with external bodies is quite limited. It also suggests a failure by the Partnership to work with community groups to develop their organisational skills, especially those relating to networking and strategy-building across the community sector. The recent establishment of independent community development projects in each of the five target communities, together with the employment by the Partnership of a community liaison worker, may alter this situation.

The Partnership's recently devised strategy for the implementation of a local employment service may prove to be a new departure in regard to local linkages. Under this government initiative, the Partnership has a key role in co-ordinating the activities of local statutory, voluntary and community agencies with regard to education, training and employment. This framework will be underpinned by a "statement of commitment" from each of the (statutory) partners. Potentially, this initiative may generate formalised linkages between the Partnership and local statutory agencies.

Working with politicians provides a further avenue for linking the Partnership with local and national structures. To date, the policy has been to largely ignore locally-elected politicians, whether local councillors or members of the national or European parliaments. This reflects in part the peripheral role played by politicians in local governance and, in part, a general antagonism towards traditional political structures by the Partnership. (This is especially strong among community partners who see politicians as being part of the established system which contributed to their marginalisation and disempowerment.) The situation has become increasingly untenable as the Partnership has assumed a more mainstream role in government policy at the local level. This has created disquiet among politicians who see the Partnership as excluding them from contributing to an emerging force in local governance. Furthermore, the fact that a number of community representatives have successful sought election to local government has attenuated feelings of rivalry with the Partnership. The Partnership has become increasingly aware of the potential negative outcome of this situation and is committed, in its new strategic plan, to holding regular briefings with public representatives on its work. The fact that the new chairperson is a former politician should help considerably in this task.

The Partnership did not initially cultivate a general public profile of its work in the city. One reason for this was a concern not to exacerbate the negative public image of some areas of the city. Another was the lack of any specialist communications expertise in the project, with a media consultant only being recruited in late 1993. In general, promotion of the Partnership was left to the ingenuity of staff, which necessarily led to a rather hit and miss approach. This deficiency was especially apparent in the project's attempts at producing a regular newsletter and at making a video of the project. Consequently, the Partnership was very dependent on its partners, especially in the community sector, to disseminate information about the project. Given that many community organisations were seeking to establish themselves locally and lacked the resources or skills to undertake this task, the public profile of the Partnership was somewhat haphazard. More recently, the Partnership has sought to rectify this by directly promoting its public image through information material and public seminars.

The Impact of the PAUL Partnership Limerick

Information on the impact of the Partnership can be gleaned from the evaluative material produced by the project and from the interviews with key actors involved in the initiative.

Working Methods

As a method of organisation, the Partnership has achieved a number of tangible gains:

- **Resource mobilisation.** The Partnership has generated additional resources for local initiatives addressing poverty and unemployment. To date, most of this has emanated externally — approximately £3.25 million to the end of 1995 in core funding from central government and the EU. New resources have also been generated locally, mainly from partner agencies, though not to the same extent as externally. The current strategic plan seeks to increase this resource base, with an anticipated budget of £18.5 million. As important as the scale of additional resources is the flexibility by which these resources can be allocated by the Partnership for innovative actions.

This has been critical in enabling the project to support community development activity. The Partnership has also secured mainstream funding for some of its innovative action.

- **Information exchange.** Another practical outcome of the Partnership is the improvements it has achieved in the flow of information and the level of contact between local organisations, both within and across sectors. The most dramatic changes are apparent in the relations between service providers and community groups. This has occurred mainly on a personal basis and marks a significant advance on previous relationships, which were characterised by suspicion and, on occasions, antagonism. In particular, the Partnership has enabled community groups to transcend the traditional clientelist structures whereby users and providers interacted. Institutionalising this information exchange, through changing the practices and attitudes of service providers, has been a much slower process, though there are some positive signs in regard to welfare, housing and adult education services.

- **Community networking.** A particular emphasis of the Partnership is the strengthening of community-based networks, which bring together individuals and groups operating in specific sectors across the city. One of the most successful here is a network involving lone parents which provides a forum for discussing issues of common concern and for offering personal support and information. Another network-type intervention brings together parents and other family members whose children are in care, with the aims of mutual support and collective representation. At a community level, the Partnership developed community action centres to support and co-ordinate local activity, though with a limited impact. At a city-wide level, the Partnership has improved links between community groups, though these have not been formalised through the establishment of a community forum, for example.

- **Capacity-building.** Another benefit of the Partnership is in enhancing the capacity and know-how of local agencies to tackle poverty issues. The various strategic planning exercises, together with participation in a multi-tiered management structure, have provided important learning experiences for partner agencies. Important gains have been achieved in regard to research and, to a lesser extent, evaluation. The Partnership's in-house research expertise was complemented by external experts from local universities and local people trained in social research (though much of this has been lost with the termination of Poverty 3). The Partnership has also operated as a key resource for the design and delivery of anti-poverty programmes. In particular, its know-how on client participation and on community-based delivery has shaped new service initiatives, e.g. a local employment service and local estate management. The Partnership's capacity-building role is hindered, however, by the bureaucratic nature of its management structures, which sometimes makes partner and other bodies reluctant to engage with the organisation.

Social Inclusion

The Partnership's impact in promoting social inclusion can be analysed at two levels: first, the extent to which unemployment has been reduced and general living conditions enhanced and, second, the degree to which groups and communities have been empowered.

- **Employment.** The principle measures of the Partnership's success in tackling employment include participation in education and training programmes, placement in jobs and new business start-ups. The achievements of the project here are decidedly modest, especially when the "added" value of the Partnership is calculated, as distinct from the activities of mainstream service providers. Its achievements can be quantified as over 2,000 participants on employment-related courses, approximately 180 people placed in (full-time and temporary) jobs and 124 new jobs, mostly self-employed.

- **Educational attainment.** Significant gains in educational attainment can be recorded under the Partnership, though most of these are at the soft end of the spectrum: literacy, adult and community education and personal development. It has proved more difficult to develop an accreditation framework whereby these gains can be translated into recognised qualifications. By contrast, potential career benefits are indicated for the 80 children undergoing a four-year early intervention programme.

- **Income support.** The project's impact on households' income levels is impossible to quantify in the absence of detailed information on increases in benefit take-up, though some credit can be claimed in terms of a national increase in the payment rate of school-related costs. Indirect benefits are also hard to measure, such as a reduction in the social costs of welfare dependency due to improved delivery of services and less stress and worry associated with household budgeting due to the provision of money advice services.

- **Services for families.** Services for vulnerable families have been considerably improved. The most tangible gain is for the parents of the 150 children who receive some degree of childcare every week. The benefits for lone parents and for families with children in care are less amenable to measurement, though potentially of great significance, being primarily to do with enhancing self-esteem and improving personal relationships.

- **Housing and the environment.** The work of the Partnership here has been largely confined to one-off activities, whose long-term impact must be considered to be minimal. The one exception is the on-going initiative on tenant participation, though the time required to see some improvements in individual or collective housing conditions is quite long-term.

An overall comment is that the Partnership has developed actions (and applied its resources) across a wide range of issues, reaching over 4,000 beneficiaries. This approach has been justified by its multidimensional remit and facilitated by its diverse partner composition. Consequently, the degree of intervention (and scale of resources) on any one issue is rather limited, with a predominance of short-term and single-dimension measures, to the detriment of long-term and multi-faceted activities. The main exception to this is the Moyross school project, where the duration of the intervention, the complexity of its actions and the level of resources and skills are in marked contrast to other Partnership activities. Even in the employment category, where more strategic measures might be expected given both its nature and its priority, the actions remain low quality, with the modest "cost-per-job" of £2,000 raising some questions about the quality and life-expectancy of this employment.

Assessing the extent to which the community sector has been enabled to contribute to the development process is a difficult task. Generally, it is accepted that there have been some gains, in that some groups are now more informed of services and development issues and that their access to decision-makers has been improved. Equally, the Partnership has undoubtedly provided a unique voice for community groups with local decision makers. However, at a local level, the impact of the Partnership has been rather hit-and-miss, with a failure to initiate an indigenous and self-sustaining process of community development. In this regard, the network of community action centres established under Poverty 3 has proved rather ineffective and a revised strategy is being implemented under the Department of Social, Community and Family Affairs funded Community Development Programme. This will focus on enhancing the software of community development, engaging with people more than providing services.

Policy

An outstanding feature of the Partnership has been its focus on policy development. This reflects the pilot nature of the programmes under which it has been funded to date, with their emphasis on pioneering new approaches to problems of unemployment and social exclusion. Issues on which the Partnership has made a policy impact can be grouped as follows:

- **Social solidarity.** At a general level, the Partnership has improved awareness of social exclusion in Limerick city and encouraged social solidarity. Having an organisation dedicated to social exclusion has encouraged partner agencies and other interests to be more conscious of the issue. The Partnership's research programme has also heightened local and indeed national awareness of particular issues pertaining to social exclusion (e.g. educational costs, labour market measures, welfare disincentives). The Partnership has provided a means of disseminating know-how and good practice on strategies to tackle social exclusion, principally with the support of the Poverty 3 programme. The Partnership has also acted as a medium whereby the commitment of individuals and agencies to social solidarity has been animated. This applies not just to the community and voluntary sectors, but also to professionals in state agencies, private businesses, trade unions and other bodies (e.g. universities, schools).

- **Enhanced service delivery.** The delivery of services has improved under the auspices of the Partnership, notably in regard to social welfare, child-care and labour market programmes. Important gains such as improved public awareness, easier access to services and altered assessment procedures have all arisen from the work of the Partnership. The Partnership has also sponsored many innovations in services for the unemployed, while new services were pioneered in regard to money advice, child-care, adult education and job placement. Greater co-ordination is also apparent under the auspices of the Partnership, notably in the early school intervention project. Here, the Partnership has worked with a variety of interests (education providers, parents and experts in curriculum development) to provide multi-faceted actions to enhance school-based learning. A similar-type project is currently being developed with regard to measures for the long-term unemployed, in order to ensure a planned programme of progression, culminating in employment.

- **National policy reform.** A major focus of the Partnership has been to influence policy and programmes at national level. Various studies initiated by the Partnership highlighted the limited impact of temporary employment schemes on the work chances of the long-term unemployed and the financial difficulties associated with participation in such schemes. This work was influential in encouraging the government to introduce a new programme, as well as improving the financial incentive to participate in labour market programmes. The Partnership was also influential in the drafting of new legislation governing the control of moneylenders, a largely unregulated and high cost form of consumer credit used primarily by low-income households. A third policy issue promoted by the Partnership is an integrated approach to the problems of distressed urban areas, based on a partnership model. Through its involvement in two pilot national and EU initiatives, the project actively contributed to the design of the national programme for integrated development, funded under the EU CSF. The Partnership has specifically promoted the urban dimensions of local development, such as the management of public housing and the physical and economic renewal of local estates.

Conclusion

The Partnership has evolved in a relatively short period of time to become a significant force in tackling social exclusion in Limerick city. After just six years in existence, it has a well-established organisational structure, which is supported by the main statutory and non-governmental agencies in the city. The Partnership is embedded in a range of central government initiatives, which gives it a key role in the design and implementation of public policy in distressed urban areas. Arising from this, the Partnership has been able to attract significant resources from a variety of national and EU programmes to the city, with an annual budget of almost £2 million and a staff team of almost 40 full-time and 30 part-time people.

A review of the Partnership reveals a strong personal commitment to the organisation, which has sustained its operation while structures and staff were being developed and financial resources being mobilised. However, the institutional linkages between Partnership and partners are underdeveloped, with the absence of formal mechanisms of feedback and accountability a notable weakness. While the Partnership has made considerable efforts to develop a participative decision-making process, it has been at the cost of diluting the coherence of the organisation and of its work programme. The ability to mobilise external funding has been a defining feature of the Partnership, though more from external sources than among partner agencies. Its main methods of allocating these resources have been to either channel support to existing local agencies or to deliver new initiatives and services. Only in one or two areas has it adopted a co-ordinating role in regard to existing services, though the new employment service initiative may enhance this practice. Finally, the Partnership's success in influencing mainstream programmes at the national level has not been matched at the local level where its profile has been less well developed, both among its target population and local bodies.

The rapidity of the Partnership's development and its enlarged scale of operation have brought new challenges. It would appear that those aspects of the Partnership which were critical in its formative days — personal commitment, open structure, access to external funds, national profile — are no longer sufficient to sustain its operations as it moves into the mid-stage of its lifecycle. Key issues for the organisation in sustaining its partnership ethos involve deepening the involvement and commitment of its many and diverse stakeholders, improving the functioning of its management structures, optimising the utilisation of its considerable financial and staff resources and, finally, ensuring the systematic monitoring and assessment of its multi-faceted work programme.

Perhaps the most critical issue is redefining the position of the Partnership in regard to its various constituencies — local people, community groups, state bodies, etc. To some participants, the Partnership has lost its direction, spreading its limited resources and expertise in too many directions and gravely over-extending itself in the process. This fragmentation reflects the multiplicity of internal demands on the organisation, initially facilitated under the broad remit of Poverty 3 and later extended under the ABR programme. With its new local development role, there is a severe danger that the Partnership is being overloaded by responsibility for tackling the many dimensions of social exclusion in Limerick city. A further criticism relates to the growth of the Partnership as an organisation in its own right, with its complex decision-making machinery and its large staff. As more programmes have been tapped into, new tiers of decision-making introduced and more services directly provided, the central role of the Partnership has greatly increased. With these tendencies toward fragmentation and centralisation, there is a feeling that the organisation has developed a momentum of its own which its originators find difficult now to rein in.

The current strategic plan is an attempt to redirect the focus of the Partnership towards the empowerment of disadvantaged communities. In seeking to develop local community plans, with community organisations being the main movers in designing and implementing these plans, the Partnership is hoping to return to its original motivation. Yet, the evidence to date has been that the Partnership may not be the appropriate body to undertake this task. The Partnership is necessarily too centralised and bureaucratic an organisation to be able to respond to individual community needs. Its niche may be one step removed from the hands-on nature of community development — a meeting point between the sectoral focus of specialist agencies and the multi-faceted needs of individuals and communities. Indeed, this is the role suggested for the Partnership in the detail of its new work plan. The ability to reconcile the endeavours of community-based organisations which encourage self-help and empowerment with the services and resources of state and other external bodies will determine the extent and duration of the Partnership's impact on unemployment and social exclusion in Limerick.

Chapter 7

Case Study 2: Tallaght Partnership

Introduction

This case study examines the development and operation of the Tallaght Partnership. It focuses on the period from 1991 to the present but also includes some of the history of the Partnership's inception. The interviews for the case study were completed in July 1995. Since then developments have taken place within the Partnership. Consequently, the information from the interviews represents a snap-shot overview of the Partnership work. The Partnership dates from 1990 and has been part of major national and EU initiatives. Its main focus is on tackling long-term unemployment and on community development.

Description of the Tallaght Partnership

Context and Origins

Tallaght is located on the western periphery of Dublin at the foothills of the Dublin Mountains. Tallaght was developed as part of the 1972 County Development Plan which proposed the establishment of three new towns west of Dublin to cater for a projected population increase. In thirty years Tallaght was transformed from a small quiet village to one of the largest urban centres in Ireland. Population currently stands at 70,819. The rapid expansion of Tallaght's population was not accompanied by the social, economic, environmental and cultural infrastructure and support services required by such a large popula-tion. There has been a serious time-lag in the provision of adequate facilities. Also, there is an excessive degree of social polarisation between public and private housing estates. Furthermore, families from inner city communities were relocated to areas of public housing and no attempt was made to integrate them with people already living in the area.

The development of a local infrastructure of public service delivery in Tallaght has taken place very slowly since 1972. Many reports have indicated that the primary cause for this was the lack of a local development agency with overall responsibility for Tallaght. However, some developments have taken place in recent years. The Square, a major shopping centre, was opened in 1990, a regional technical college was established in 1992 and a new hospital was opened in 1998. In addition, a new Social Welfare Services Office was opened to cater for the people of Tallaght and the IDA have developed a high-quality industrial park in West Tallaght. Notwithstanding these developments, the problems of unemployment, poverty and social exclusion are still very much in existence in the Tallaght area.

A number of features distinguish Tallaght from other areas in the country. These include:

- A growth in population of 13.2 per cent between 1981 and 1991;

- A significantly young population (38.5 per cent are aged 14 years and under);

- Severe educational disadvantage (43 per cent left school at age 15 or under);

- An unemployment rate of 22.9 per cent, one-third higher than the national average.

FIGURE 7.1: OVERALL DEPRIVATION SCORES, TALLAGHT PARTNERSHIP ADMINISTRATIVE AREA

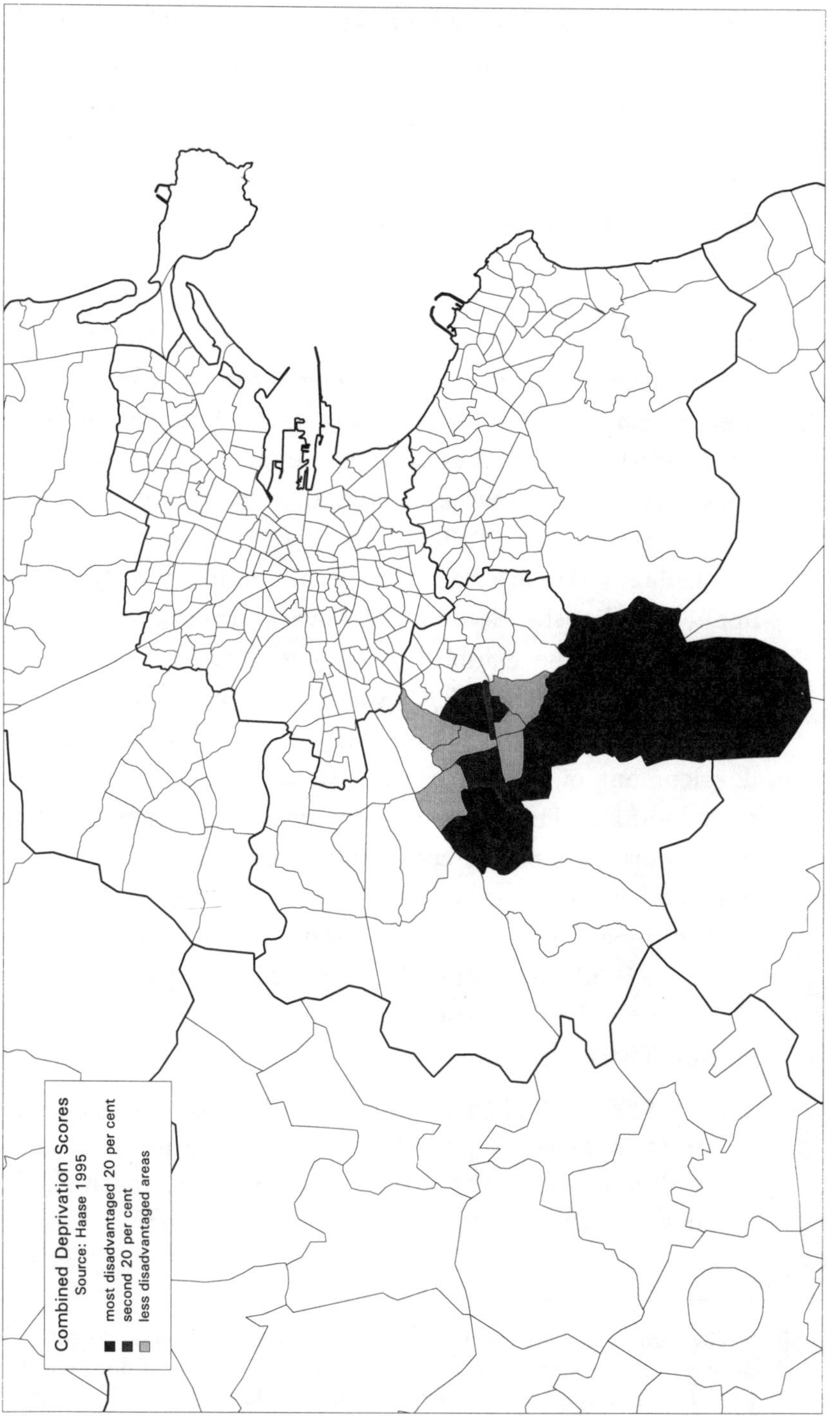

Combined Deprivation Scores
Source: Haase 1995

most disadvantaged 20 per cent
second 20 per cent
less disadvantaged areas

Figure 7.1 shows the overall deprivation factor score in Tallaght in 1991.[1] Of the 15 electoral areas contained within the Partnership area, almost half (7) have been classified into the most disadvantaged decile in national terms showing high levels of deprivation for the area. A key feature in Tallaght is the extent of local authority housing, which accounts for between 35-45 per cent of all housing. Large concentrations of local authority housing are clustered in particular areas such as Fettercairn, Jobstown and Killinarden and the absence of facilities in these communities remains a major problem for the people living in the area. In some areas like Jobstown, over 30 per cent of households are headed by a lone parent (the equivalent national figure is 10.8 per cent) and this creates additional economic and social needs.

The origins of the Tallaght Partnership date back to 1985 when the Tallaght Welfare Society, a local voluntary body, successfully applied under the Second EU Poverty Programme (cf. national overview) for the establishment of the West Tallaght Resource Centre (WTRC). The WTRC was a community development project which devised and implemented an integrated approach to the development of a number of local authority housing estates in west Tallaght. This project incorporated a partnership dimension in its work, where the community sector identified the need for itself and state agencies to work together to tackle disadvantage.

A number of integrated partnership type arrangements followed on from this initial structure. Some of these were initiated by statutory bodies, others were the joint actions of community groups. These initiatives include:

- COMTEC (1986-87), a pilot initiative of the Youth Employment Agency to provide a local planning and monitoring mechanism for all services funded from the youth employment levy (cf national overview).

---

[1]The deprivation score is calculated using thirteen surrogate measures drawn from the Census of Population in which electoral divisions have been classified. For more detailed explanation, see footnote 2 in PAUL Partnership Limerick case study (chapter 6).

- Tallaght Integrated Development Programme, a FÁS initiative initially targeting the generation of extra employment, enterprise and local employment initiatives and laterally focusing on measures to tackle long-term unemployment.

- Publication of *Agenda for Integration* report in 1989 which contained the ideas and views of four of the larger community groups in Tallaght. This document proposed an area-based development strategy for Tallaght and comparable communities, an idea later taken up and developed in the ABR initiative.

- Application in 1989 for funding from Poverty 3 by local community and voluntary groups and statutory bodies, which led to the establishment of a formal partnership arrangement in Tallaght which has continued to develop since then.

In 1990, the WTRC along with two other Tallaght-based projects was funded under the Department of Social Welfare's Community Development Programme. A management committee — the Tallaght Partnership — representative of community, voluntary and statutory interests was established to manage this wider initiative. In 1991, Tallaght was designated as one of twelve pilot areas in the government's area-based response to long-term unemployment programme (ABR). The existing partnership was maintained but expanded to take on this initiative. The role of the pilot partnership structures was to look at the problem of long-term unemployment in their areas and to devise and implement recommendations to tackle the problem. In 1994, the Tallaght Partnership was included in the integrated development strand of the local development programme under the CSF (1994-99), which focuses on disadvantaged areas (cf. national overview).

Partnership Structure

The Partnership is managed by a board of directors which consists of representatives of 22 partner agencies, comprising 6 state organisations, 6 social partners, 2 local social partners, 6 community groups and 2 voluntary bodies. Table 7.1 outlines the social category and scale of the agencies involved in the Partnership.

TABLE 7.1: PARTNER AGENCIES IN THE TALLAGHT PARTNERSHIP

	Community	Social	Statutory	Voluntary
Local	West Tallaght Resource Centre; Disability Interests Forum; Women's Forum; Youth Forum; Community Initiatives Tallaght; Get Tallaght Working	Tallaght Centre for the Unemployed; Tallaght Chamber of Commerce	South Dublin County Council; South Dublin Vocational Educational Committee	Tallaght Welfare Society
Regional			Eastern Health Board	
National		Irish Business and Employers Confederation; Irish Congress of Trade Unions	Department of Social, Community and Family Affairs; FÁS (training and employment agency); Forbairt (industrial development authority)	Barnardos

The Partnership is formally constituted as a company limited by guarantee and without share capital. The initial blueprint for the make-up of the board as defined by the ABR initiative was a tri-partite partnership model consisting of representation from the community, statutory and social partner sectors. The Partnership did not originally have any trade union or employer representation at board level but when Tallaght was designated for inclusion in the ABR, one of the requirements was that the structure would reflect the partnership that exists at national level between employers and trade unions. The partnership structure was expanded to include this dimension.

In addition to the board of management, the Partnership comprises sub-committees on education and training, community development and enterprise (see Table 7.2). These sub-committees are made up of board members, staff and others who live and/or work in the Tallaght area. The role of the sub-committees is to progress actions from the Partnership's plan. An executive steering group also exists which deals with all aspects of the work. It consists of the chairperson, manager and a number of partners — representative of each of the three sectors. In addition, a number of working groups meet around specific actions or programmes of the partnership. Together, the sub-board structures have a responsibility to develop and manage the partnership's programme of work. Board meetings take place every six to eight weeks. The main areas for meetings to address are setting policy, overseeing projects and decision-making concerning funding.

TABLE 7.2: MANAGEMENT STRUCTURE OF THE TALLAGHT
PARTNERSHIP

Sub-Committees	Working Groups	Special Projects	Special Interest Groups
Steering Committee; Education and Training;* Enterprise;** Community development	Core staff; Community employment staff	Tallaght Local Employment Service; WTRC; Jobstown Integrated Development Project; Tallaght Centre for Unemployed; Springboard	Travellers; Disability

* Responsible for child-care initiative

** Responsible for Plato programme

The core staff of the Partnership (see Table 7.3) consists of a manager and a number of administrators. In addition, some staff were seconded from the Tallaght Centre for the Unemployed and the education and training authorities to work with the Partnership on an information and advice programme for the long-term unemployed under the ABR. Most of these staff members now work with the local employment service. A community links worker was employed by the WTRC and funded by the Partnership to carry out the community development dimension of the Partnership's Plan. In 1995, an additional community links worker was employed. The role played by the manager is central to the work of the partnership as she co-ordinates and facilitates the development of the work across the range of issues with which the partnership deals. Because a considerable amount of the Partnership's work is sub-contracted to local groups the main tasks are to ensure that work is integrated across the range of measures undertaken.

TABLE 7.3: STAFF STRUCTURE OF THE TALLAGHT PARTNERSHIP

Manager
Education Co-ordinator   Local Employment Services Staff
Community Links Workers
Administrative Staff

Objectives and Activities

The initial remit of the Partnership was to address the problem of unemployment and poverty by developing integrated actions to increase employment opportunities and improve the quality of life. The Partnership identified five primary functions for itself. These were :

- To promote additional employment in Tallaght;

- To develop an improved and integrated delivery of public and community services designed to meet the needs of those communities and individuals experiencing poverty and deprivation;

- To empower disadvantaged communities to combat problems of poverty and deprivation through the development and resourcing of personal and community programmes;

- To identify and implement more effective uses of training/educational resources and services to the benefit of people who are long-term unemployed or at risk of becoming long-term unemployed;

- To encourage the development of effective partnership between all members of the company and their respective agencies and to encourage active participation by those most affected by poverty and deprivation in all aspects of the Partnership's work.

Although the emphasis of the government programme was on unemployment, the Tallaght Partnership consistently argued that both economic and social development should be part of any over-all strategy of local development and that community development and capacity-building should play a major part.

The Partnership's initial work plan (1991-93) covered the pilot phase of the initiative and had four themes. These and some examples of various activities undertaken are outlined now:

- **Employment and enterprise.** The Partnership contracted a local enterprise agency, Get Tallaght Working, to deliver its enterprise development activity. A number of problems were identified in the Tallaght area which were seen to influence the ability of local people to become involved in enterprise creation. These included the non-availability of space, the shortage of seed-capital and the lack of support/advice for business ideas. Get Tallaght Working agreed to provide support and information services and to identify additional work space units on behalf of the Partnership. This work is ongoing and has had considerable success. Part of the responsibility for enterprise includes the management of the operation of the Plato Programme.[2]

- **Community development.** The Partnership implements its community development strategy through a number of community development projects and their community links workers. This work has also sought to develop user participation in service delivery, in particular in housing management. This included the establishment of a forum involving the local authority and residents to develop new models of tenant participation in decision making.

- **Education and training.** The work of the Partnership in this area concentrates on the redirection of opportunities in education and training for the long-term unemployed. A considerable amount of the work concerns itself with co-ordination and integration of the work of existing training and development agencies in the area and with piloting of

---

[2] The Plato programme was originally developed in Belgium. Its aim is to facilitate economic development in Tallaght through support for small and medium-sized enterprises.

new, flexible approaches for the re-integration of long-term unemployed people.

- **Positive action.** The Partnership is committed to the inclusion in its development strategy of groups such as people with disabilities, Travellers and lone parents. Actions include strategies to assist these groups to participate in, and to gain access to, mainstream actions as well as improvement of services to the groups.

The Tallaght Partnership has developed a further strategic plan for 1994-99 as part of its involvement in the sub-programme of the local development programme. The Plan continues the development of the work undertaken previously and builds on three main approaches:

1. Development of/participation in a small number of pilot actions/projects;

2. Co-ordination, linkage and influencing of statutory sector activity to ensure its optimum relevance and impact on the Tallaght community;

3. Policy development and analysis.

The new plan identifies eight action areas for the Partnership to address in the coming years. These actions are outlined in Table 7.4 below.

TABLE 7.4: ACTION AREAS IN THE TALLAGHT PARTNERSHIP'S STRATEGIC PLAN, 1994-99

Action Area 1	Creating and developing enterprise and employment
Action Area 2	Accessing employment
Action Area 3	Developing young people
Action Area 4	Developing the community
Action Area 5	Positive action
Action Area 6	Information
Action Area 7	Co-ordination and linkage
Action Area 8	Administration and programme support

The emphasis of the new planning phase is not only on the development of local actions but also on linking these actions to a national strategy for local development. The Partnership recognises that matters such as adequacy of social welfare income and the development of the infrastructure cannot be resolved at local level but that close operational links between local, regional and national levels will influence how development takes place. Another important boost for the Partnership has been its involvement in securing funding under the EU Urban programme for the regeneration of local authority estates in West Tallaght and North Clondalkin. TP is one of five partners in this initiative, involving South Dublin County Council, the Clondalkin Partnership, the Tallaght Institute of Technology and the South Dublin County Enterprise Board. Urban will provide £5 million over four years for an integrated programme of measures across four themes: enterprise and employment, training and education (with a specific youth focus), environment, and community infrastructure. As well as having a direct input into the implementation of the programme, TP has been contracted as delivery agent for a number of actions. The Urban initiative obviously complements the strategic work plan of TP under the Local Development Programme.

Resources and Expenditure

Since its establishment the Partnership has had access to a number of funding sources (see Table 7.5) some of which provide resources directly for project work identified in the Action Plan while other resources are ear-marked for specific activity. The main funding for the partnership is the EU global grant for local development, amounting to £1.3 million over the years 1991-96. Government funding also accounts for a significant part of the Partnership's budget, for example, the Department of Social, Community and Family Affairs' Community Development Programme provides funding for the three community development projects in the Partnership area (though this is since being provided directly) and the Department of Enterprise, Trade and

Employment provides the budget for the local employment service. In addition, EU initiatives like NOW provides resources for particular projects being co-ordinated by the Partnership.

TABLE 7.5: RESOURCES OF THE TALLAGHT PARTNERSHIP, 1991-96

Source	1991-93 £000	1994-96 £000	Total £000
Exchequer Funding[1]	£240	£120	£360
EU Global Grant	£450	£920	£1,370
Community Dev. Programme	£200	£220	£420
Local Employment Service[2]	—	£100	£100
EU Now (child-care)	£85	£195	£280
Total			£2,530

[1] Department of the Taoiseach funding for the ABR.

[2] Funding from Department of Enterprise, Trade and Employment specifically for the Local Employment Service.

Because of the emphasis on co-ordination rather than delivery, the Partnership does not spend all the resources available for project work. Instead, it uses this money to lever additional resources into locally based initiatives and spends considerable time lobbying for European funding for some of its projects. The Partnership's budget under the local development programme for the five-year period up to 1999 is estimated at £2 million. Further funding will be forthcoming in relation to the Local Employment Service, NOW and Urban.

Equal Opportunities

In the establishment of the Tallaght Partnership the involvement of women was a central feature as there were women particularly in the community sector who had been working at grassroots level in preceding years and who were skilled to participate in partnership. Under the local development programme, a government stipulation on gender balance (a minimum of 40 per cent of each gender) has raised discussion about gender representation across sectors and has become a factor in selecting a replacement for retiring board members.

In the current board structure nine of the 22 directors are women representing 41 per cent of the total and within sub-committees women are represented. Both the chairperson and manager of the Partnership are women. The existence of a network of women's groups and its representation on the board ensures that issues of gender and equality are raised. Particular concern about equality issues is also reflected in the work of the disability interest group whose role is to work for the inclusion of disabled people in decisions about local job opportunities, access, etc. For example, people with disabilities were actively involved in the planning and implementation of the EU Horizon programme that operates in the area. This group has continued to meet regularly with support from the Partnership and has contributed to the Partnership's understanding of "access" and "integration". Recognition of gender issues is apparent in the work that the Partnership has undertaken. For example, in 1993, the Tallaght Partnership supported a project on men's participation in adult education and training to examine the reasons why men who are long-term unemployed were not participating in community and educational activities. In addition, the Partnership supported a project funded by the NOW programme which assisted women who were involved in child-minding duties.

Among those interviewed, particularly those who were women, it was stressed that gender balance at the board level of the Partnership should be achieved within each sector rather than on the board as a whole. However, the lack of participation of women at senior management level in statutory agencies, trade unions and within industry was highlighted as a significant obstacle in achieving this balance. It was suggested that the achievement of this balance in future depends on how seriously the Partnership regards the gender equality guidelines proposed by ADM as well as a commitment by individual agencies in this regard.

The Tallaght Partnership in Action

Representation and Power

As with the other ABR partnerships, there was a strong central government input into the categories of partners in TP. However, given the pre-existence of a partnership structure in Tallaght, there was agreement that this structure should be built upon and so the process of establishment did not conform with that laid down by Government for the other pilot areas. Statutory and social partner representation was considered at central Government level and agreement was reached in co-operation with the Partnership. As outlined previously, the suggested 6–6–6 format was not implemented in Tallaght as there was a strong feeling within the community sector that six places would not be sufficient to represent its interests.

With the evolution of the partnership concept, there have been attempts to refine selection of representation across the sectors. Initially, the social partnership of trade unions and employers was considered as one sector for representation but over time, the Partnership has begun to regard them as separate constituencies. There is also a distinction between local and national interests in the social partner representation. Most of the statutory agencies represented were involved at the early stages of the partnership's formation and would have been partners because of interest and involvement in the Tallaght area. In this sense their selection differed somewhat from the other ABR partnerships. With the commencement of the local development programme there is a greater awareness of the partnership approach. Statutory agencies are now increasingly more enthusiastic about their participation in partnership and with the broader objectives of the partnership there are more agencies who would like to be considered as potential partners. The main avenue through which the Partnership engages these agencies is through its working groups.

Nomination for the employer sector comes from the national employer organisation, IBEC. The individual employers on the Partnership board were identified by the Department of the

Taoiseach in conjunction with IBEC. There is a general consensus that if partnerships are to address enterprise and economic development that it is important for employers to be partners. They can also play a key role in the development of links between, for example, education and enterprise and enterprise and employment. Potentially, they can also build the links at local level that have been forged at national level through the national partnership arrangements, though this has not yet happened to any significant extent. The experience of those interviewed is that employers have played a key role in the development of the enterprise aspects of the Partnership's work and, in particular, the securing and running of the Plato programme. However, there is a difficulty around centrally nominated representation as individuals tend not to have links with the local experience.

Trade union representation on the partnership comes from ICTU which represents trade union issues nationally. The role of trade union representation in the Partnership is regarded by a number of the partners interviewed as reactive rather than proactive. For example, it was suggested that they could play a role in bringing forward issues relating to low pay, work conditions etc. but that they do not consider this type of role for themselves in the Partnership. The Centre for the Unemployed in the area also has representation at board level as a local social partner and plays an important role in the provision of services for unemployed people through its jobs club. However, the lack of liaison between it and its parent body ICTU has lessened the likelihood of developing local/central links. The view of some of the directors of the Partnership is that individual partners provide a useful contribution but that there is a greater need for emphasis on a sector-based approach to the work. This would mean that partners adopt a collective approach to addressing the problems posed for the Partnership rather than acting as individuals. This has also been the experience of a number of other partnerships in the ABR programme. In 1995, the Partnership underwent a number of changes in its representation as it moved from a pilot ABR phase to being part of the local development programme. Changes have included the inclusion of *local* social partner interests[3] to strengthen the local dimension of their contribution and to overcome the lack of connection between local and national issues.

Over the past number of years the Partnership has undertaken considerable work in the development of the community sector and in addressing community development issues generally. The appointment of a community links worker greatly facilitated this process. At an early stage in the Partnership's formation, a number of difficulties revolved around community dissatisfaction that the partnership represented a "golden circle" in which a small number of organisations and individuals had access to funding; the partnership was perceived as "a closed shop". An internal review of community representation recommended that there be three individual nominating bodies, the West Tallaght Resource Centre, Get Tallaght Working and the Tallaght Welfare Society. The remaining five places are rotated among the other organisations and networks who are members of the Community Development Sub-Group. The sub-group now operates as a mechanism for selection. The sub-group provides a wider representation because of the strengthening of existing networks around key interest groups such as women, young people and people with disabilities. The community partners play a lead role in the identification of issues for consideration by the Partnership.

Feedback from board members to their own constituencies or parent organisations varies across sectors. At an early stage in the development of the Partnership, statutory agencies did not have formal feedback mechanisms but over time there is an increasing onus on partners to provide parent agencies with reports and information. This improves the likelihood that parent agencies will respond to issues emerging from the Partnership. Feedback to the local community is directed through the community development sub-group. The community links worker plays an active part in this process. The network approach has facili-

---

[3] Local partners include the Chamber of Commerce and the ICTU Centre for the Unemployed.

tated the dissemination of information to increasingly more organisations.

The partnership approach is viewed by several partners to be
still in a developmental phase. It represents a structure whereby
voices that went hitherto unheard are now being listened to. The
community sector represents a strong lobby since they present the
local perspective on issues pertaining to the area. The statutory
agency partners for the large part act as individual interests
rather than as a public service voice of the Partnership. One of the
difficulties for the Partnership is in getting pilot work mainstreamed. As a result, Partnerships are often left holding on to
projects which should have been passed on to be funded by the
relevant statutory agency. This is partly due to the highly
compartmentalised nature of the public service that does not allow for flexibility in taking on new projects.

Strategy and Decision-making

The development of a common view about the main problems to be
tackled in the Tallaght area has taken place through the Partnership's work on agreeing a strategic local development plan for the
area. The Partnership accepts that each partner brings different
expertise and experience to its work. It does not, therefore, insist
that there is total consensus before the Partnership can decide a
certain line of action. Instead, there is a recognition that each
partner is committed to development in the Tallaght area. Inevitably tensions arise, particularly, in the debate on whether economic
or social development is more appropriate. The division is usually
on a sectoral basis, with social partners and industrial development
agencies most concerned with economic issues. However, there is a
recognition among partners that, to date, the Partnership has
greatly educated all sectors about issues of social exclusion.

The decision-making process centres around the sub-
committees in which most of the detailed discussions take place
about actions contained within the plan. Sub-committees also
have responsibility for designing that part of the plan which
relates to their work. The plan represents a blueprint for action by

the Partnership for the five years to 1999. It also acts as the mechanism whereby the Partnership draws down funding from ADM, the intermediary body responsible for funding local development. The Partnership has just completed a rigorous planning phase in which considerable consultation took place with the community and with key actors in the Tallaght area. The plan includes, in addition to the local actions identified, a number of activities and actions that are prescribed for the Partnership as it is part of a national programme. For example, the new national Local Employment Service is to be coordinated by the Partnership for the Tallaght area.

One of the problems identified is the difficulty of planning in the absence of information about the extent of funding available for local development. In 1994, a transition period following the end of the previous global grant phase (1991-93) and the beginning of the next, resulted in a lack of clarity about the timescale for availability of resources. This indicates the importance of clear and continued budget lines for partnerships if they are to act efficiently. Staff members play an important role in the planning process since they have responsibility for compiling ways of implementing the area action plan in their own areas of work. They are involved in sub-committees and process decisions which emerge from meetings. In this way the sub-committees play a valuable role in progressing the overall functions of the Partnership.

Each sector brings a different perspective to bear on the partnership. The community partners provide an understanding and experience of disadvantage and social exclusion. Employers provide an insight into issues relating to the current labour market and provide expertise on funding issues. The trade unions, through their Centres for the Unemployed, provide a direct link with the long-term unemployed. The statutory agencies bring an understanding of the public service approach and how the system operates. In discussions with board members a number of difficulties relating to participation were highlighted. These include:

- **The language of partnership.** A particular language and terminology develops within the Partnership which in itself excludes those who are not familiar with it. Use of jargon becomes a way of working.

- **Paperwork and partnership.** The Partnership produces a considerable amount of documentation which partners are required to read. This can present an "information over-load". The newsletter, which is produced by the Partnership on a quarterly basis, is a valuable means of summarising information in an accessible way.

Resources and Methods

The role that the Tallaght Partnership plays is one of brokerage between the range of actors and activities that fall within its remit. This means that the Partnership does not undertake the delivery of services or programmes directly but instead acts as a facilitator for public agencies and community-based organisations. Because the partnership does not engage in service delivery *per se*, it avoids the creation of an additional layer of bureaucracy for users and groups. To implement its actions the partnership negotiates funding or resources from partners on the basis of their contribution to the work. The Partnership may then supplement this with global grant monies etc. This means that partner agencies carry out the work but the Partnership contracts out and facilitates the process.

The Partnership has always ensured a key role for both research and evaluation as part of its strategy for action. Research on unemployment, poverty and social exclusion has created a better understanding of issues and has improved planning. For example, research on fuel poverty paved the way for the HEAT project which highlighted the difficulties experienced by low income families in affording adequate heat in their homes and attempted to effect change in government energy policy. It also proposed the establishment of a community business around heating and insulation of housing for low-income families.

Self-evaluation has helped the Partnership to be clearer about its role and responsibilities and about which strategies need to be designed to combat social exclusion. Although some of the evaluation sessions were poorly attended by partners, the process ensured that the Partnership is more aware of its role in Tallaght and individual partners recognise their own particular contribution. The Partnership's recognition of the need for evaluation is also exemplified in its commissioning of a report on the expenditure of the global grant.

Linkages and Communication

Because the Partnership is part of a government initiative, its proximity to the policy-making environment is high. Responsibility for exchange of information among partnerships and between partnerships and central administration rests with ADM. ADM staff attend meetings of the board of the Partnership. This provides an opportunity for ADM to learn first-hand about the issues that face the partnership and what is needed at the policy-making level for progress to be made around some of these issues. This link has not, however, been fully realised as a mechanism for ensuring that local experience is translated to the policy level. The Partnership, with the other eleven pilot ABR local partnerships, frequently lobby government around issues relating to long-term unemployment. One example where this was effective was in the area allowances initiative which was implemented by the Department of Social Welfare during the pilot phase of the partnerships. Area allowances allowed long-term unemployed people living in the partnership areas to undertake education and training courses or to set up their own business without losing social welfare income or secondary benefits, such as free medical services, for the period of one year. This was implemented in response to partnerships who had identified the disincentive effects involved in taking up training and employment opportunities. The area allowance concept has since been mainstreamed as the Back-to-Work Allowance scheme, which is now available on a nation-wide basis.

Local politicians were excluded from participation in partnerships but the Tallaght Partnership has consistently argued that they should be included in any consultation about local development and that their exclusion from partnerships represents a devaluing of elected democracy. As a result, the Tallaght Partnership has frequently engaged in discussion with locally elected representatives about local development issues in Tallaght. The involvement of South Dublin local authority officials in the partnership has also influenced the allocation of the EU Urban programme which will be jointly implemented by the local authority along with the Tallaght Partnership and other local groups. In addition, the manager of the Partnership is represented on the South County Dublin Enterprise Board and is also a member of the county strategy group established to co-ordinate the local development programme.

Outcomes of the Partnership's Work

Partnership as a Working Method

The Partnership has been successful in building a good relationship between each of the sectoral interests represented at board level. Partnership requires an attitudinal change to the ways of working that partners bring to the process. This has been slow to develop but partners are of the opinion that some progress has been made. The Partnership has allowed informed decision-making because it involves an exchange of perspective and co-ordination of the work. To date, the Partnership has exposed partners to the different cultures in which each operates. It has given partners an experience of shared decision-making and allowed them to work in a co-operative manner that has improved their ability to get things done. Also, because state agencies have come together there is greater potential for the exchange of ideas and information about what each agency does as well as a wider appreciation of the inter-agency liaison necessary at local level.

Because the Partnership brings together the collectivity of interests in the Tallaght area, there is increased interest in the range of actions taking place at local level. The increase in circulation of information can probably account for the Partnership's success in accessing resources and programmes (see below). The shared approach has also improved the level of co-ordination at both state agency and community levels. A number of the partners represented on the Tallaght Partnership have been attending meetings since 1990 when the Partnership was established. The contribution required by the individuals has been significant when one considers the amount of time involved not only in attending meetings but in reading documentation and in ensuring follow-up with parent organisations and agencies.

The Partnership has been successful in identifying and mobilising resources for addressing the range of problems that exist in the Tallaght area. Four examples illustrate this:

- **Plato:** the Partnership through its links with the employer partners, secured the operation of the Plato programme which has provided a support facility for the development of small and medium sized businesses;

- **Global grant for local development:** this funding enabled the Partnership to lever additional funding from other partners for their work;

- **EU Urban programme:** this is implemented by the Partnership in conjunction with other local groups and the local authority. This is the first opportunity for a partnership to operate in co-operation with a local authority on such a programme;

- **EU NOW child-care initiative:** a pilot child-care initiative was established and implemented which provided accredited training for local women.

Support for pilot projects and actions is a key contribution of the Partnership. For some pilot work, it is intended that on the basis of a pilot phase, lessons learnt might be picked up and acted upon by relevant agencies. This need to influence and effect change is a primary function of the Partnership. Equally as important as access to monies, is a recognition that all the main players in education, training, employment, enterprise are involved and that together they can encourage positive change in the Tallaght area. For example, the development of a positive relationship with the regional office of FÁS has given the Partnership access to additional training provision that may not have happened otherwise. The Partnership has also had an impact on the development of alternative methods to planning. The promotion of an integrated approach to local planning is being adopted by other local bodies.

Impact on Social Exclusion

The impact of the Tallaght Partnership's work on social exclusion to date has been relatively small. A number of partners attribute this to the need to tackle the infrastructural causes of social exclusion that are outside the scope of the Partnership. However, the Partnership does have an advocacy role regarding the critique of existing strategies to tackle disadvantage and can facilitate a local response to local issues. It also provides, through its community development work, an enabling role and capacity building for local communities. One outcome of this approach is the initiative for developing greater tenant participation in estate management. A number of partners noted that because of the long-term nature of this approach it is premature to claim that success has been achieved in tackling social exclusion.

The Partnership has succeeded in addressing a number of issues relating to labour market policy. For example, the Partnership has identified the crucial importance of providing unemployed people with a continuum of opportunity to enable them to break out of the closed circuit of unemployment. The education and training sub-group of the Partnership has, therefore, been looking at the development of linked actions that will lead to employment. The potential of this approach is that mainstream initiatives will emerge from the Partnership's pilot projects and that these initiatives will outlive the Partnership as unique mechanisms for addressing social exclusion.

One of the weaknesses of the Partnership has been the lack of emphasis on measuring the impact of its work on social exclusion. Most of the evaluative exercises undertaken by the Partnership concentrated on the organisational and operational issues which a partnership approach emphasises.[4] This lessens the likelihood of focusing on social exclusion. The consultation process undertaken by the Partnership for its planning work through a series of public meetings and fora for discussion has however, allowed for feedback from the community about its work and perceptions of the impact of this work. Similarly, evaluation of the Partnership's work at the national level (Craig and McKeown, 1994) and the global grant evaluation undertaken for ADM and the European Commission (Hasse *et al*, 1996), did not adequately measure the impact of the Partnership on social exclusion. However, in the local development programme the Partnership is required to establish performance indicators that will allow it to monitor progress over time.

In general, the Partnership has provided a greater local understanding of the multi-dimensional nature of social exclusion. It has also identified the factors that contribute to social exclusion: unemployment, poor educational levels, inadequate housing, lack of facilities, lack of training and inadequate access to public services.

Altering Practices and Policies

It is difficult to show that the Partnership alone has been responsible for particular policy changes since its establishment. However, the Partnership has been used frequently as a sounding board for development of new services and alteration of existing services, e.g. the Partnership piloted a temporary employment programme that is now in the mainstream. With its eleven counterparts in the ABR initiative, the Partnership developed a voice at the policy-making level as evidenced, for example, in its work on Area Allowances.

---

[4] One exception is the evaluation the Partnership commissioned on its use of the global grant funding.

Because the Irish administrative system is highly compartmentalised and centralised it has been difficult for the Partnership to influence its direction. However, work undertaken in the pilot phase highlighted the need for a mechanism for transferring local experience to the policy level which resulted in the establishment of an interdepartmental policy committee on local development. In addition, the manager of the Partnership is a member of the Local Government Devolution Commission which is advising government on reform of local government and is chairperson of the Combat Poverty Agency. Other partners are members of ADM's board of management and are involved in, for example, its sub-committee on community development. This involvement increases the Partnership's potential to impact on policy at the central level.

Conclusion

The Partnership continues to play a significant role as a catalyst in the development of the Tallaght area. Through its involvement at the local level it has contributed to the addressing of issues around long-term unemployment and community development. Through its negotiation with other agencies and organisations at local, regional and national levels it has secured a position of influence on decision-making around the economic and social development of the area. The global grant monies allocated to the Partnership gave it the resources to undertake work in the areas of enterprise creation through Get Tallaght Working and in capacity building of the local communities. Although the budget was small by comparison with state agency budgets the Partnership was still able to invest money in pilot work. The Partnership also succeeded in generating considerable interest in the development of the area. This has helped to ensure that local initiatives are generated and that there is a greater degree of interest in their success.

A weakness of the Partnership has been its failure to date in addressing issues of educational disadvantage and in understanding the obstacles that exist to participation in education and training programmes for unemployed people. The difficulty is in convincing state agencies of the need for innovation in recruiting long-term unemployed people for its courses. The work of the local employment service may help to ensure an increasing interest in innovative approaches as well as progression routes for long-term unemployed people. Because the emphasis of the Partnership has remained on community capacity building, the work undertaken in community development has been of particular significance. The decision to channel resources into the appointment of community links workers to co-ordinate the activities taking place at community level has been a very positive one. The work of the Partnership has been strategically planned and implemented. There is an increasing awareness in the Partnership of the need for longer-term consideration and review of its work including the period after the end of the local development programme in 1999. In addition, the Partnership is wholly realistic about what can be achieved in local development without recourse to regional and national policies that affect the local situation.

Chapter 8

Case Study 3:
South Kerry Development Partnership

Introduction

The South Kerry Development Partnership was originally constituted as CRESP, (Community Response for Economic and Social
Progress) the South-West Kerry Partnership. The latter organisation was established in 1991 to administer the government ABR
initiative and the EU Leader I programme in the Iveragh peninsula of County Kerry. Since then, the Partnership has undergone
considerable expansion, both in terms of the number of
programmes administered, and in terms of the population and
area served. This increase in scale has also entailed some restructuring and refocusing of the Partnership as it entered a new phase
of operation between 1995 and 1999. This case study, which concentrates on the Partnership during its initial phase of operation,
highlights the particular challenges faced by partnerships in
remote rural areas, and illustrates the difficulty of focusing on
social exclusion in an area which is itself disadvantaged.

Description of the South Kerry Development Partnership

Context and Origins

The area administered by the South Kerry Partnership (Figure 8.1)
currently covers some 2,444 square kilometres and contained a
population in 1991 of 41,305 persons. The area includes the Iveragh

Gaeltacht,[1] which contained a 1991 population of 2,050, but for the purpose of Leader the Gaeltacht part of the region (approximately 300 square kilometres) is administered by Meitheal Forbartha na Gaeltachta, the designated Gaeltacht Leader group. The population density of 16.9 persons per square kilometre is just 65 per cent of the average population density for County Kerry as a whole and 33 per cent of the national figure, reflecting the fact that much of the land is sparsely populated hill and mountain terrain.

Agriculture and tourism constitute the economic base. Agriculture is the single most important industry in terms of employment, accounting for almost one quarter of the labour force in 1991, but it is characterised by a high level of under-employment, with many small unproductive farms which are incapable of generating adequate family incomes. The result has been an on-going decline in the farming population with an estimated 100 farmers per annum leaving agriculture. Among those who remain in farming there is a high degree of dependence on off-farm part-time employment and/or social welfare payments. The tourism industry too suffers from structural problems. It is highly seasonal, based on an eight weeks mid-summer peak, and both employment and revenue generated are very unevenly spread geographically, with a particular concentration in Killarney, and, to a lesser extent, Kenmare.

The lack of full-time jobs outside agriculture has resulted in a long tradition of out-migration from the area, particularly of the younger and more highly educated sectors of the population. As a result, the age structure of the population is weighted towards the older age groups, with those aged 65 years and over accounting for 15.5 per cent of the area's population as compared to 11.4 per cent nationally. In fact only 7 out of 66 district electoral divisions (census districts) recorded percentages of older persons below the national average. The immediate demographic implication of the

---

[1] The Gaeltacht is the officially designated area in which Irish (Gaeilge) is the dominant everyday language.

FIGURE 8.1: SOUTH KERRY DEVELOPMENT PARTNERSHIP ADMINISTRATIVE AREA

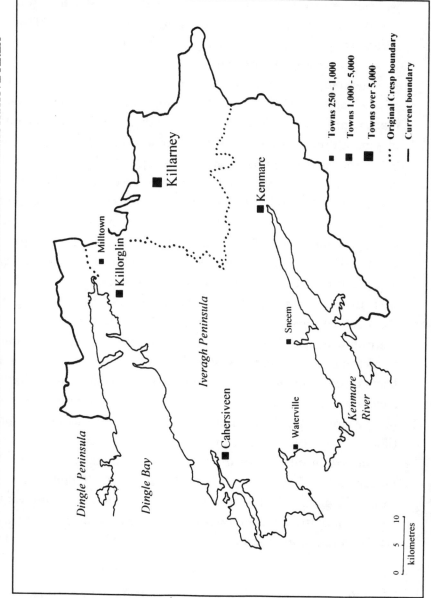

older age structure is that natural decrease prevails over much of the area,[2] and this combined with out-migration resulted in a population decline of 1.6 per cent between 1986 and 1991. Decline was widespread throughout the area, with over 70 per cent of census districts experiencing population loss. The rate of decline across these districts was 6.3 per cent, and 9 districts recorded losses in excess of 10 per cent.

Unemployment is not a major problem in the area as a whole, partly because of the role of out-migration in relieving labour market pressures. Hence, in 1991, both the male rate of unemployment (16.1 per cent) and the female rate (12.9 per cent) were below the corresponding national averages (18.4 per cent and 14.1 per cent respectively). Much higher levels of unemployment are encountered locally, but the districts affected tend to be among the least populous, so that their problems remain hidden within the aggregate data. This trend carries over into the pattern exhibited by the more general concept of relative deprivation, with a tendency for the highest levels of deprivation to be associated with the more remote and sparsely populated districts, mainly in the western part of the area (Figure 8.2).[3] Thus, while almost 23 per cent of census districts fall into the most disadvantaged quintile in national terms (i.e. those with decile scores of 9 or 10), these districts contain under 20 per cent of the area's population. What this suggests is that deprivation in the south Kerry area is, in a sense, more a problem of areas than of people. This, in turn, has implications for the nature of developmental activity in the locality.

The urban infrastructure of the area is weak. Other than Killarney, which has a population of just under 10,000 and is the second largest town in the county, there were only three centres with a population of over 1,000 — Kenmare, Killorglin and Cahersiveen. Population decline threatens the viability of a wide range

---

[2] In 1990 the birth rate was estimated at 11.8 per 1000 population compared to a death rate of 13.5 per 1000.

[3] See footnote 2 in the PAUL Partnership Limerick case study for an explanation of the measure of relative deprivation.

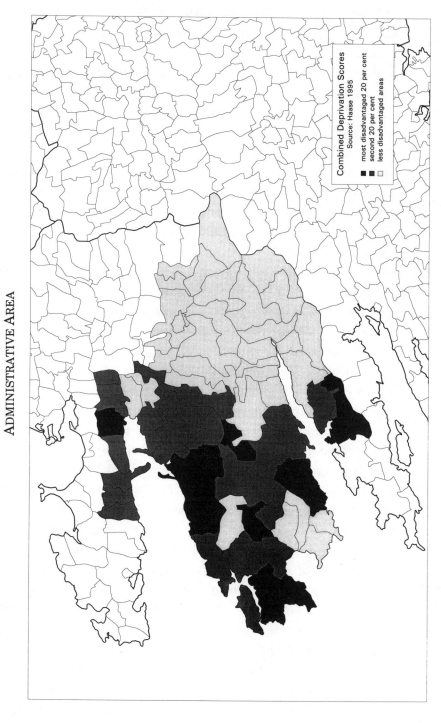

FIGURE 8.2: OVERALL DEPRIVATION SCORES, SOUTH KERRY DEVELOPMENT PARTNERSHIP
ADMINISTRATIVE AREA

of both private and public services in these centres, especially as the latter are increasingly required to operate on the basis of a commercial mandate. As a result, access to essential services, such as basic health care, is severely restricted for those living in the western part of the peninsula. The problems of trying to sustain commercial services in the area are compounded by the extremely poor state of the local road network. This has the effect of imposing high travel costs, thereby increasing the delivered prices of goods and services, and further dampening demand in the rural hinterlands of service centres. Car ownership is somewhat below the national average, and those districts which show the highest levels of households without a car tend also to be located in the most remote part of the area. Even in car-owning families, isolation is a problem when the main breadwinner uses the family car to travel to work, leaving spouses (usually women) without access to transportation throughout the day. A vestigial public transportation service does little to overcome the problem of isolation experienced by remote households.

Faced with the problems outlined above, the south Kerry area has generated a large number of developmental organisations and initiatives. Many of these have overlapped and intertwined, especially in terms of the personnel involved, but it is possible to discern two distinct traditions which eventually coalesced in the establishment of CRESP. With both traditions there is a clear line of progression over time from small scale community based activity to larger scale partnership based activity. The first of these antecedents — essentially a community development tradition — can be dated from the 1940s and the establishment in south Kerry of a number of parish councils affiliated to Muintir na Tíre (cf. national overview). Much of the activity of these councils was focused on the improvement of local infrastructure. In the 1970s this tradition found expression on a larger scale with the establishment of the South-West Kerry Development Organisation (SWKDO) which campaigned on infrastructural issues and against the rationalisation and closure of local public services throughout the region. In the early 1980s SWKDO put together an integrated development plan for the area, based on the then novel idea of partnership between state agencies and local communities. Partly through the lobbying of SWKDO, south-west Kerry was included in the Pilot Programme for Integrated Rural Development administered by the Department of Agriculture and Food between 1988 and 1990 (cf. national overview). In the two years when the programme ran, a wide range of projects was undertaken, many of them involving the development or upgrading of community social and cultural resources.

The second tradition in local development initiatives is a more business and enterprise focused approach. This is represented for example by the co-operative movement which was strong in the Gaeltacht area, and by the establishment in the 1980s of a number of resource development groups (cf. national overview). In 1990, two umbrella organisations representing between them 15 such local development groups were formed: Integrated Resource Development South-West Kerry Limited (IRDSWK), and Killorglin and District Resource Development Group. Both organisations employed a full-time manager, raising the necessary funding locally with, in the case of IRDSWK, additional support coming through the Department of Social Welfare-funded Community Development Programme. In late 1990 the latter organisation became actively involved in the preparation of a bid for Leader funding, but it was recognised that the small population base served by the organisation (17,600) would militate against a successful application. As a result, the Federation of South Kerry Communities was formed early in 1991 as an alliance between IRDSWK and Killorglin and District Resource Development Group for the purpose of facilitating a south Kerry Leader submission. In addition to the full-time management of the two constituent bodies, the Federation drew on the expertise of the Kerry County Development Team and the co-ordinator of the local IRD core group in preparing its Leader submission. Following the designation of south Kerry under the pilot ABR programme in May 1991, the Federation was renamed as CRESP and restructured as a local partnership between community, statutory and social partner interests. Meanwhile, the Partnership had assumed responsibility for the south Kerry Leader application and was confirmed as a Leader group in November 1991.

Since its establishment the Partnership has taken on a number of new programmes in areas related to its role as a local development organisation. This programme expansion has entailed designation as a Rural *Carrefour* or Centre for European Information (1994–), administration of a model project within the EU Iris II network which promotes and supports vocational training for women (1994–) , and delivery of the EU Youthstart programme (1995–97) which provides vocational training for early school leavers. In 1995 the Partnership entered a new phase in its development when it was designated under the Irish Government's Local Development Programme (sub-programme 2). This programme, which is part of the EU Community Support Framework 1994–99, represents an extension and elaboration of the ABR initiative. Also, in 1995, the Partnership was confirmed as a Leader II group.

The number of community groups affiliated to the Partnership increased from 15 to 21 in 1993 and to 29 in 1995, paralleling the expansion of its functional remit. The latter expansion was as a result of a central government decision in February 1994, under which the area administered by the Partnership was extended northwards to include part of the Dingle peninsula, and eastwards to include the area around Killarney (see Figure 8.1). To accommodate this expansion the company was restructured in 1995 and renamed the South Kerry Development Partnership.

Structure and Operation

The South Kerry Development Partnership is legally constituted as a company limited by guarantee and without share capital. Following the standard model for partnership companies established under the ABR, the board of the company has a tri-partite structure consisting of representatives of community organisations, social partners and statutory organisations (Table 8.1). The community directors are elected to the board by affiliated community organisations which are grouped into four area-based con-stituencies, with each constituency nominating either two or three directors. The social partner and statutory sector directors are nominated by designated partner organisations which have one or two representatives each. Initially each of the three sectors had six representatives in total, but following the area extension of 1995 the community representation was increased to 10. Three co-opted directors were also added to the Board at this time, two representing state agencies and one a private sector company (see Table 8.1 for profile of organisations).

TABLE 8.1: PARTNER AGENCIES IN THE SOUTH KERRY DEVELOPMENT PARTNERSHIP

	Community	*Social*	*Statutory*
Local	Cahirciveen community groups; Kenmare community groups; Killarney community groups; Mid-Kerry community groups		Kerry County Council; Kerry County Vocational Education Committee
Regional		Kerry Group plc*	Udarás na Gaeltachta*
National		Irish Congress of Trade Unions; Irish Business and Employers Confederation; Irish Farmers Association; Macra na Feirme	Bord Fáilte; Forbairt; FÁS; Teagasc; Bord Iascaigh Mhara*

* Denotes co-opted organisation

The day-to-day work of the Partnership is undertaken by the gen-eral manager and staff. The professional staff consists of an assis-tant manager, a global grant administrator, a Leader programme manager and assistant manager, and a number of officers who for the most part are sectorally deployed with responsibilities in areas such as horticulture, mariculture and tourism (Table 8.2). Staff are supported through programme funding and through secondment from partner organisations. The staffing level as of May 1995 (including the general manager but excluding clerical staff) stood at sixteen, fourteen of whom were full-time. The two part-time staff members, and two of the full-time staff were secondees.

TABLE 8.2: STAFF STRUCTURE OF THE SOUTH KERRY DEVELOPMENT PARTNERSHIP

	General Manager	
Leader Administrator	Assistant Manager	Global Grant Administrator
	Project Staff	
	Clerical Staff	

Staff and directors come together in a working relationship through the Partnership's system of sub-committees. Since 1993 a two-tier committee system has been in existence (Table 8.3). First tier committees have been established for each of the main operational areas of the Partnership, namely: employment services, education and training, and community services. In addition, there is a Leader administration committee and a "ways and means" committee that deals with funding and operational matters. The primary function of first tier committees is to consider matters of policy and the development of new projects, and to report to the board on same. Membership is drawn mainly from the board but there is some staff input also. Second tier or management committees have been established for most of the areas to which a sectoral officer has been appointed. These committees are responsible for the agreement, implementation and financial control of the work plans of the officers. In addition to the sectoral officer concerned they include one or more board members. Both types of committees include individuals from organisations that are not represented at Board level. In this way the committees are used to increase the expertise available to the Partnership and to extend involvement in the work of the Partnership.

TABLE 8.3: MANAGEMENT STRUCTURE OF THE SOUTH KERRY DEVELOPMENT PARTNERSHIP

Board of Management				
First-tier Operational Committees:				
Ways and Means	Employment Services	Education and Training	Community Services	Leader
Second-tier Sectoral Committees:				
Mariculture	Horticulture	Tourism	Culture	Enterprise Education

Objectives and Activities

CRESP had a dual mandate from the outset as a Leader group and an ABR partnership company. While the ABR initiative placed the focus on the problem of long-term unemployment, Leader gave to the company a broader concern for rural development. The Partnership has attempted to integrate these twin concerns by analysing the problem of long-term unemployment as arising primarily from the underdevelopment of the local economy. The chairman's inaugural statement of June 1991 (before the Leader I programme) set out seven objectives for the company, the first of which was "to stimulate the level of economic activity in South Kerry". This remains the Partnership's primary objective, and it views itself as essentially an integrator of initiatives geared towards the goal of rural development. The Partnership recognises that sustainable local development requires a multi-sectoral, multi-dimensional approach and that many of the core resources that are required have to come from state or EU programmes. However, to maximise the synergy and hence the impact of these programmes, a high degree of complementarity is required and the Partnership aims to provide this, not just through the integration of measures at the implementation stage but also by influencing programme design.

The activities of the Partnership have been wide ranging, reflecting again the nature and scope of the programmes that have been implemented. Leader I was essentially a grant aid mechanism whereby individuals and groups in the locality could be financially assisted with eligible projects that would contribute to local development. Activities could be assisted up to a limit of 50 per cent of total investment under six headings. These, and examples of projects funded under each heading, are as follows:

- **Technical support for rural development.** Feasibility studies on the establishment of a health spa in Sneem and of a sports and leisure centre in Cahersiveen; employment of a consultant to develop a waste management programme for a pig co-operative at Kilgarvan.

- **Vocational training and assistance for recruitment.** Provision of tour guide training programme for 24 participants. Successful participants were awarded Bord Fáilte certification.

- **Rural tourism.** Grants for the establishment and upgrading of bed and breakfast accommodation, self-catering accommodation, restaurants and other tourist facilities.

- **Assistance to small firms, crafts and local services.** Conversion of old vocational school in Killorglin into an enterprise centre for the support of start-up businesses; assistance to a blade and knife manufacturing firm to develop and market a new product range and to meet quality standards.

- **Development and marketing of farm, fishery and forest products.** Employment of mariculture development officer to work with local fishermen's co-operatives to develop mariculture potential of the area; assistance to a local co-operative for the development of bogs and of turf harvesting equipment.

- **Other measures.** Grants towards the refurbishment of passenger boats for tourist day trips; hosting of international seminar on rural development.

Unlike Leader, the ABR programme was not designed as a grant aid mechanism. Instead, the emphasis was on the co-ordination, integration and targeting of activities undertaken by existing agencies. However the introduction of a global grant for local development in 1992 allowed the Partnership to directly fund activities related to its ABR strategy.[4] The global grant was allocated to four main themes: education and training; community capacity building; minor infrastructural works; and cultural development, with the greatest shares of funding going to projects in the first two categories. The following are some examples of projects supported through the global grant:

- **Community resource centre assistance programme.** Grants were provided for the development of office facilities at the community centres in Killorglin, Cahersiveen, Waterville and Kenmare which form the main hubs and service points in the Partnership's network.

- **Community leadership training programme.** Eight part-time community animators were trained and employed for twenty weeks to work with the affiliated community groups in order to facilitate the preparation of resource audits and the production of local development strategies within the overall planning framework of the Partnership.

- **Schools enterprise programme.** A teacher was employed to run an extra-curricular course in enterprise education in local second level schools. Through the mechanism of schools-based mini-companies, students acquired practical skills in product design, market research, marketing and production.

- **Cultural development programme.** A cultural development officer was employed to support existing cultural activity and to initiate new events, in particular those involving the performing arts, throughout the area. In addition to preparing

---

[4] The global grant for local development was established by the European Commission in 1992 to support the development of indigenous potential at local level. The grant was allocated to the Partnerships established under the ABR and to local community organisations.

a comprehensive audit of cultural resources, the officer facilitates training in the arts.

Resources and Expenditure

The most significant source of funding for the Partnership during the first phase of its operation, 1991-94, was the Leader I Programme, under which a total of £1.9 million of EU and government assistance was received, including funding for set-up and administration costs. Altogether some £2.3 million of matching private funding was raised locally, bringing total expenditure under the programme to £4.2 million. Leader had a strong business and enterprise orientation: over half of all grant assistance went to rural tourism projects, and a further one-third of project funding was roughly equally divided between measures to support the development of local produce and support for small firms (Table 8.4). Within the rural tourism category the most common type of project funded was the development of tourist accommodation by private individuals. The comparatively low level of funding for education and training measures and for community projects was due mainly to difficulty in raising the required 50 per cent matching funding in the case of such projects, a problem which was compounded by the short time span — effectively two years — over which monies had to be allocated by the Partnership.[5]

Core funding for administration costs in relation to the ABR programme was provided by the Department of the Taoiseach. The global grant for local development provided £350,000, and this was followed by two tranches of interim exchequer funding amounting to £189,000 to April 1995. The latter resourcing was designed to allow the Partnership to continue its activities until the local development programme came on stream. The projects supported by the interim global grant funding tended to be social

---

[5] In the course of the programme's implementation the matching expenditure requirement was reduced to 25 per cent, which in the case of community projects could include voluntary labour.

in nature, complementing the more business and enterprise focused Leader activities.

TABLE 8.4: DISTRIBUTION OF LEADER GRANT AID BY SOUTH KERRY DEVELOPMENT PARTNERSHIP TO DECEMBER 1994

Category	Number of Projects	Total Assistance (£)	Per cent of Total	Average per Project (£)
Technical Support	47	72,169	4.30%	1,535.51
Vocational Training	30	76,172	4.54%	2,539.07
Rural Tourism	61	891,389	53.16%	14,612.93
SMEs	32	277,587	16.55%	8,674.59
Primary Produce	18	284,077	16.94%	15,782.06
Other Measures	25	75,518	4.50%	3,020.72
Total	213	1,676,912	100.00%	7,872.83

Source: CRESP Progress Report 1994

Currently, the main external funding instruments available to the Partnership are the local development programme, and the Leader II programme. Under the Local Development Programme, the Partnership has been allocated £2.6 million for the period 1995-99, while Leader II has committed £1.67 million. The resources provided by the other programmes are more modest. The Youthstart programme has a budget of £250,000, while the Rural *Carrefour* initiative provides part of the salary of the Partnership's European Information Officer. Iris II does not provide finance for the Partnership's training programme for women, aside from assistance with publicity, funding for attendance of trainers at a summer school, and assistance for international exchanges.

After a period of some uncertainty following the expiry of the Leader I programme, the Partnership's financial resource base has now been secured until the end of the decade. It is also evident that the resource base has undergone some restructuring, with a substantial reduction in per capita funding from Leader II, and hence a decline in the relative importance of this source. Partly because of the relatively high level of resourcing which it provided, Leader I had a major influence on the priorities and work programme of the Partnership during its first phase of operation. It seems likely that, with the restructuring of the funding base, there may now be some refocusing of activities towards more socially-based projects.

Equal Opportunities

The gender composition of the board has been imbalanced from the outset, with just three women directors out of 18 initially, and two out of 25 currently. Both of the current women directors represent organisations in the social partners sector. The prevailing view in the Partnership is that the gender imbalance, while undesirable, will be difficult to rectify in the short term since it is not directly within the control of the Partnership itself. The tendency of the state agencies to nominate representatives on an *ex-officio* basis, and at as senior a level as possible, is part of the difficulty here because of the under-representation of women at senior management levels in these organisations. The absence of any women from the community sector is more surprising, as this is the sector which tends to provide most women directors across partnership companies in general. Part of the explanation may lie in the fact that the South Kerry Partnership grew out of a tradition of local *economic* development, a sphere of voluntary activity which has traditionally been male dominated. Interestingly, one of the women directors felt that her nomination to the Board, at the time of inception of the ABR programme, derived from a perception within her nominating organisation that the social focus of the latter programme placed it within the domain of women's issues. In addition to this factor, a number of directors felt that the lack of female community representatives reflected the huge commitment required of community directors in general, and the fact that women found it more difficult to make this commitment largely because of the burden of home duties such as child-care and elder-care which is disproportionately borne by them.

The under-representation of women at board level is compensated for, to some extent, by their greater representation among the staff, which is predominantly female both at managerial and officer level. As of May 1995, 11 of the 16 staff were women. More significantly, the activities of the Partnership have been strongly geared towards meeting the needs of rural women, especially in areas such as education and personal development, and most of the beneficiaries of the Partnership have been women. This is true even of the Leader programme, where women constituted the majority of project promoters. The development of women's groups through capacity building and training provision has been one of the successes of the Partnership, and the hope is that, in the longer term, a better gender balance at board level will ensue from the efforts to affiliate a wider range of organisations, including women's groups, to the Partnership (see below).

There is no member of the Travelling community on either the Board or the staff, and none of the activities of the Partnership during its initial phase of operation were specifically geared towards meeting the needs of this group. This was a reflection of the fact that Travellers were not prevalent in the local area. However, with the area extension in 1995 and the incorporation of Killarney, this is no longer true, and there is now a recognition among the directors that greater consideration will have to be given by the Partnership to Travellers' issues. There is an active Travellers support group in Killarney, with whom one of the community directors is closely involved, while another director serves on the Board of the Kerry Travellers Development Group based in Tralee.

The Partnership in Action

Representation and Power

Even though CRESP evolved from pre-existing local organisations, there was nevertheless a strong degree of central government input into the construction of the Partnership. In particular, the Department of the Taoiseach, which initially administered the ABR programme, decided on the statutory and social partner organisations to be represented at Board level. Within the Partnership there is a feeling that, while the balance of the Board as between the three sectors is about right, the selection of statutory organisations in particular could have been better attuned to the needs of the area. For example, there was initially no place allocated to Bord Iascaigh Mhara (the state agency with responsibility for the fishing industry), despite the considerable developmental and job creation potential of the fishing industry in the area. This omission had to be rectified by the Partnership itself through the mechanism of co-option.

Representatives were nominated by the state agencies and social partners to the Partnership board largely on the basis of the individual's function within the organisation and of a central recommendation that representation should be at the most senior level possible within the region/locality. However the application of this principle has meant that few of the statutory sector representatives reside within the Partnership's area, a fact which is considered by some to have been detrimental to the Partnership's efforts to engage this sector fully. Because of the large area served by the Partnership, the expansion of this area over time, and the fact that levels of community development vary considerably throughout the area, community representation has been a difficult and sensitive issue for the Partnership. Since the first agm in 1993, the community directors have been elected by the affiliated community groups. For electoral purposes these are grouped into geographically defined constituencies, in which each organisation has one vote. All the affiliated organisations are locally-based, and most of them have an enterprise/economic development focus rather than a social focus. However, the area expansion has meant that a wider and more complex range of social problems is now encountered, and there has been a growing awareness of the need to involve issue-based voluntary organisations and self-help groups within the Partnership. As a result, the basis of community representation is currently being reviewed, and the possibility of developing a community forum for this purpose, consisting of a wide range of both area- and issue-based groups, is being examined. The development of some such structure(s) would also facilitate reporting back by community representatives which at present is hampered by the lack of coherent structures within the constituencies.

Another issue in relation to community representation has been the allocation of seats at board level to different sub-areas, and in particular the question of whether community representation should be on the basis of sub-area populations or not. At present, community representation is not on a per capita basis, and the adoption of such a system would entail a relative increase in the number of seats allocated to the eastern part of the area. However such a change would be difficult to implement for a number of reasons. First there is the historical legacy, and the fact that the Partnership had its origins in the western part of the area. This in turn arose out of the high level of community activity in that sub-area, which continues to bestow on it an entitlement to strong representation on the grounds of capacity. Second there is the argument that problems such as peripherality and inadequate infrastructure are more severe in the western area. Finally, it has been argued that the greater number of statutory and social partner directors based in the eastern part of the area goes some way to rebalancing any perceived imbalance on the community side. In part it was the difficulties surrounding this issue of area representation which led to the decision to increase the number of community directors significantly at the time of expansion, rather than attempting to reallocate the existing seats. However, in the opinion of some, this has now created an unwieldy board.

No one dominant partner organisation can be readily identified, in part because the range of activities undertaken has been so wide that partner organisations have tended to become involved mainly in relation to areas that impinge on their own interests/remit. However the community sector as a whole played a very strong role in the first years of the Partnership's operation. This was due in part to the high calibre of the community representatives who had strong backgrounds in community activism, and the fact that the impetus which brought both Leader and the ABR programme to the area came initially from the community sector. In part too, it was due to the fact that the Leader programme, because of its larger budget, tended to dominate other Partnership activities. This was significant in two ways. First it meant that the state agencies were not called upon to perform as central a role as they might have been if the ABR programme — with its greater emphasis on directing the activities of the state sector — had occupied a more prominent place on the agenda. Second, because Leader introduced an unprecedented element into local development activity — the ability of a locally-based group to determine the allocation of significant project funding — it created a very high degree of interest among the community at large, and expectations on the part of the community of their directors. Significantly all of the community representatives were on the Leader committee which was responsible for agreeing funding for projects.[6]

Strategy and Decision-making

From the outset, there has been a strong degree of agreement among the partner representatives that the key issue for the communities of south Kerry is that of on-going population decline, fuelled by the out-migration of the younger age groups. This out-migration is a result of a lack of local employment opportunities arising from the weak economic base of the area. The solution therefore is seen as the economic development of the area, and, as noted above, this has been the primary aim of the Partnership since its inception. The Partnership's analysis of the problem of unemployment similarly emphasises demand deficiencies in the local labour market, rather than supply-side factors such as lack of education or skills. This analysis underpins the Partnership's

---

[6] Financial assistance up to a level of £10,000 could be approved by the Leader committee. All expenditure above this level had to be approved by the board.

basic strategy as an integrator of initiatives, in that supply-side measures such as education and training are seen as necessary but insufficient on their own to solve the area's unemployment problem. Training, for jobs that do not exist locally, is only likely to lead to further out-migration, thereby compounding the social and economic problems caused by depopulation. Instead the need is for complementary enterprise and training measures which the Partnership seeks to delivery through its various local development funding. This also explains the Partnership's strong commitment to enterprise education.

This analysis is widely subscribed to among the directors, including the community representatives. The result has been a high level of agreement about the aims and activities of the Partnership, and no significant inter-sectoral divisions. Where tensions have arisen within the Partnership these have tended to be on an intra-sectoral basis. Within the statutory sector for example there have been some tensions arising out of the "territoriality" of particular agencies with regard to their functional remits. Among the community representatives also there was a degree of mutual distrust at the outset, in particular between those from different sub-areas. This was due in large part to the size of the area covered by the Partnership and the diverse backgrounds and level of development of the various community organisations affiliated to the Partnership. Also significant in this respect was the fact that, as noted earlier, working together at inter-community level in the way required by Leader, i.e. to decide on the distribution of significant project finance, was an entirely new experience for community representatives.

However, while such tensions may have been evident at the outset, a high degree of consensus has since been established at board level both between and within the various sectors. This consensus has been built up over time, and the role of the current chairman (elected from amongst the directors in 1993) is widely regarded as having been vital in this respect. The result is that most board decisions are now made without the need for a vote. Decision-making in general is described as relatively informal.

The general manager and staff play a crucial role in the Partnership because of their function in planning, developing new ideas and implementing the decisions of the board. The preparation of plans is undertaken by the staff in the first instance and by the general manager in particular, with all plans subject to formal ratification by the board. In order to facilitate the directors to make an input in this area, a series of policy and planning days has been organised on an on-going basis. However, the amount of business that can be transacted at board meetings is limited by a number of factors. Most importantly perhaps, the frequency and duration of board meetings is restricted by the fact that directors are widely dispersed not just within the region but also beyond it, and that travel within the area itself is difficult.[7] This problem is exacerbated by the large size of the board, which, following the restructuring of 1995, considerably exceeds the norm for partnership companies. As a result, a lot of work has to be done through the sub-committee system, and much of this falls to the staff. The management committees provide staff officers with an opportunity to work with the relevant sectoral partner representatives, and to develop proposals that are likely to gain the approval of the board. Decisions in relation to the implementation details of activities are usually left to the general manager who enjoys a high level of delegated decision-making power.

Resources and Methods

The Partnership has engaged intensively in detailed local research and planning as the basis of its various activities. All research has been undertaken in-house, mainly by the general manager, and this represents one of the major skills assets of the Partnership. Much of the formal planning has been programme related: Leader required the preparation of a business plan and the global grant was allocated on the basis of an area action plan submitted by the Partnership. However, in striving to fulfill its

---

[7] The board has scheduled meetings of two hours duration approximately every 5 to 6 weeks on average.

role as an integrator of initiatives the Partnership has also engaged in on-going strategic planning. This involves the identification of complementarities between programmes so that gaps in provision under one initiative can be met by resources provided by other programmes. To date there has been less consideration given to the evaluation of programmes or initiatives, partly because the rather compressed timescale for programme implementation allowed little opportunity for this. However the need for an officer with responsibility for evaluation is now acknowledged by the Partnership.

The community sector is acknowledged as having made a major contribution to the Partnership, mainly in the form of expert knowledge of the area and its needs. Given that most of the state sector representatives are based outside of the Partnership's area this input is obviously vital. In the implementation of the Leader programme, the community representatives also played an animation role in informing potential applicants about the programme and its regulations, and in encouraging the development of proposals by project promoters. The Partnership estimates that altogether the time input by the community directors in servicing the Leader committee (which met on average once per fortnight) exceeded 1,000 person hours, and that a similar amount of time was expended promoting and supporting the initiative at community level. Initially there was a tendency for the community directors to lobby on behalf of individual promoters, especially those from their own areas, but a more unified and corporate approach developed over time as inter-community fears and suspicions were allayed.

The main resources contributed to the Partnership by the state agency and social partner representatives are sectoral expertise and seconded staff. The expertise of the state agencies in particular was important to the Partnership in the vetting of Leader proposals, and this was also one of the areas where the presence of directors from different agencies on the board was of most benefit to the Partnership. One of the key roles played by statutory body representatives was in filtering out applications for Leader funding that could be supported by existing grant mechanisms (e.g. Department of Agriculture grants in the area of agri-tourism), thereby helping to ensure the additionality of the projects that were supported by Leader.

Apart from the input of their representatives on the board, the most significant resource contribution by statutory and social partner organisations has been made by way of staff secondments. Seconded staff have been provided in the areas of agricultural research and development, education and training, and services to the unemployed. In addition to the financial resource transfer involved, these secondments provide the Partnership with a level of sectoral expertise and agency knowledge that would be difficult to obtain through other recruitment mechanisms such as direct contract employment. However, there have also been a number of drawbacks associated with the use of secondment as a staffing mechanism. First, and in general, staff cohesion and morale within the Partnership have not been served by the fact that salary and conditions of employment for secondees are determined by their parent organisations and, therefore, vary considerably. Second, the implementation of secondments in some cases has reduced the net benefit to the Partnership, such as when the secondee has remained based in the office of the parent organisation. In one case all office support and travel expenses for the secondee — which because of the nature of the work involved were considerable — were paid for by the Partnership. The specific work programme undertaken was central to the concerns of the parent agency, and in the view of several directors would have been undertaken by it anyway. On completion of the project in question the secondee was withdrawn by the agency, leaving these directors with the impression that the agency had gained more from the secondment than the Partnership.

Partly because of experiences such as the above, there is a fairly widespread feeling that the Partnership has not secured sufficient funding from the state agencies operating in the area. However, it can be argued that this was never the role expected of the agencies under the ABR programme: the more significant point is that the model of partnership operation envisaged under that programme has not been followed. This model entails the Partnership operating in a brokerage role whereby it seeks mainly to influence and redirect the delivery of services by statutory organisations and other service providers without itself becoming directly involved either in the funding or delivery of services. The Partnership has not adopted such a role but instead has tended to pursue both direct delivery and "agency" working methods. The latter entails the Partnership identifying particular service needs and providing the funding for third party agencies to deliver those services. This method of working is most evident in relation to the education and training activities of the Partnership, where typically the Partnership has provided funding through for example the ADM global grant mechanism for organisations such as the VEC and FÁS to deliver courses. The attraction of this approach for the Partnership was that it allowed it to accomplish a lot in a short time and thereby establish a profile in the area. There is also a strong view within the Partnership that the brokerage role envisaged under the ABR programme is inoperable in a profoundly rural context because of the lack of resident service providers.

Besides the geographical context, the working methods of the Partnership have also been influenced by the nature of the programmes implemented. This is evident in relation to Leader which dominated the work programme of the Partnership in the first two years of its existence. One of the major problems encountered in relation to Leader was the 50 per cent co-funding requirement, which together with the short time scale over which monies had to be committed and expended, meant that it was almost impossible to fund community development activities. Thus in implementing its business plan under Leader the Partnership was restricted to a reactive decision-making mode in the sense that it was dependent to a large extent on project promoters coming forward with the required matching finance, and, while ineligible or unsuitable projects could be turned down, there was limited scope for the Partnership to generate its own projects.

Linkages and Visibility

As the Partnership has strived to establish itself and to develop
its structures and procedures, attention has been focused more on
communications within the Partnership itself than on the organisation's public profile. Internal communications, for example between staff and directors, are generally described as very good,
and a high level of information about programmes and activities
is made available at all times to board members. However, there
is general acceptance of the need to further develop and improve
the Partnership's visibility in the area. The Partnership relates to
its constituent organisations mainly through their representatives
at the board. A number of other linkages also exist, the most important of which are via partner representatives (other than directors) on the sub-committees and contact directly between the
general manager and chairperson of the Partnership and the
CEOs or other relevant officers of the various organisations. The
latter channels of communication are also used in the case of organisations not formally included in the Partnership. A further
linkage in the case of state and social partner representatives is
provided by seconded staff.

Notwithstanding the existence of these varied linkages, there
is a feeling that the relationship between the Partnership and the
partner bodies, in particular the statutory bodies, needs to be
broadened further. It has been generally acknowledged that one of
the weaknesses of the way in which partnership has been opera-
tionalised in the ABR partnership companies is the over-reliance
on individuals, and on the relationship between the chairperson
and general manager and the partner representatives. In the case
of the South Kerry Development Partnership there is the added
problem that most of the state agency representatives — especially the more senior (CEO level) representatives — are not
based within the Partnership's area and, for some of these, attendance at board and committee meetings has been difficult. Those
representatives who are based locally tend to be in less senior positions within their organisations and, hence, to have fewer delegated decision-making powers. This trade-off between seniority

and commitment/input is yet another of the many dilemmas which arises from the geographical context.

The Partnership participates in the networks established under the various programmes it delivers. In particular, it has been an active member of both the Leader national network and the network of ABR partnerships, and it was instrumental in establishing Fiontar Faoin d'Tuaith (Rural Enterprise Network) together with three other rural partnerships. These programme networks give the Partnership access on an on-going basis to both central government and EU bodies. In addition, the Partnership has bi-lateral links both with funding agencies (ADM and the Department of Agriculture, Food and Forestry) and with other development organisations. A representative of ADM has observer status on the board of the Partnership, while the Department of Agriculture maintains close contact through its monitoring role in the Leader programme. The Partnership has sought to develop links with other multi-functional development organisations, and in particular has established a close working relationship with the Welsh Development Agency.

Because of the size of the area served and the poor road network, the organisation has supported the development of offices in each of the four main centres of population within the original administrative area, Kenmare, Cahersiveen, Killorglin and Waterville. The Partnership has links with its affiliated organisations through an organisational model whereby these sub-area offices act as "hubs" from which "spokes" radiate out to the local communities. This hub and spoke system is used for both the delivery of services and the dissemination of information. A monthly newsletter as well as a series of information sheets is distributed to community organisations which enhances the visibility of the Partnership among these local groups. However the profile of the Partnership among the public at large is somewhat less, with the possible exception of the Cahersiveen area where the head office is located. However, recent improvements have been made in this regard, and in particular the Partnership's function as a rural *carrefour* has helped indirectly to raise its profile both within and beyond the south Kerry area.

The partnership model introduced under the ABR initiative did not allow for the inclusion of political representatives on boards of management, and the Partnership has not developed any links with the political system. In fact, the Partnership has had a difficult relationship with local politicians whose attitude appears to have changed from initial indifference to growing antagonism as the public profile of the Partnership has developed. Given the strongly clientilist political culture of the area, it is not surprising that the disbursement of public funding by the Partnership might have been resented and indeed interpreted as a threat by political representatives. Several members of both the staff and the board of the Partnership view local politicians as having failed to adequately represent the area, and they blame the party system in particular for this in so far as it has prevented the development of territorial politics. Some directors however are of the opinion that the Partnership needs to develop links with political representatives in order to increase its influence with central government.

The Impact of the Partnership

Assessment of the impact of the Partnership is difficult for a number of reasons. First, there is the fact that the Partnership has been in operation for a relatively short period of time, during which it has been continually evolving. Second, and as noted earlier, the Partnership has not engaged intensively in the kind of formal evaluative research that would provide a basis for impact assessment.

Impact on Working Methods

The Partnership has generated a number of major benefits for the south Kerry area in terms of local development activity. First, it has brought a professional approach to what previously was largely a voluntary activity, combining a high level of management skills and sectoral expertise with the enthusiasm and detailed knowledge of local people. Second, it has undoubtedly improved relations between the organisations which are represented within the Partnership, particularly at board level, as mutual knowledge and understanding have been built up over time. For the community sector, where perhaps there were the greatest divisions, trust has been built and parochialism has declined as a greater awareness of the problems of the area as a whole has emerged. There is now an appreciation of the need to work on a larger scale and in a more professional manner if government and EU funding is to be attracted to the area.

A third and perhaps the most significant beneficial effect of the Partnership has been the impact on the level of community and voluntary activity in the area. The experience of partnership working in the implementation of major government and EU programmes has demonstrated that there can be meaningful and successful local involvement in decision-making about local development. While the exercise of decision-making has not been without its difficulties for local community representatives, the general feeling is that it is infinitely preferable to the remote decision-making which has shaped the fortunes of the area in the past. Both the confidence and sense of responsibility of the communities have been boosted and this has led to a greatly increased level of activity. A number of new community groups has been set up, and established groups that were inactive have been revitalised as a result of the general stimulus that the Partnership has provided. As a result, the capacity of the area to engage in development activity has been enhanced.

Through its administration of both Leader and the global grant for local development, the Partnership has injected a significant amount of funding into the area. This external funding has been matched by a high level of funding levered from the community with, for example, a ratio of Leader to matching funding of 1:1.21 (excluding administration costs). For rural tourism measures the ratio was 1:1.37. As indicated earlier, the Partnership has had rather less success in securing extra resources from the statutory sector. In part this is due to the fact that state agencies were precluded by government from contributing to Leader-funded projects, on the grounds that such funding already included a state contribution. More generally though, the state agencies have been inclined to plead a lack of discretionary funding within budgets.

The area expansion of 1995, arising from a decision of central government bodies administering Leader and the local development programme rather than organic growth, have posed considerable challenges for the Partnership and its working methods. In some respects the area expansion has been beneficial. From the point of view of tourism development, for example, the inclusion of Killarney, which is the main base for tourists to the Iveragh peninsula, should allow for more coherent planning. On the other hand, a new set of urban-based social problems has been introduced which may call for a different strategic approach from that which has been pursued in the western area. Also the expansion has undoubtedly created a huge burden on the administration and organisational structures of the Partnership which, at the time of writing, were still in the process of adapting.

Impact on Social Exclusion

The impact of the Partnership on social exclusion is difficult to assess owing to the fact that the Partnership has not been focused specifically on this issue, but rather on the development problems of the area as a whole. Many of the partner representatives are somewhat dubious as to the impact on excluded groups, but feel that this was more a reflection of the nature of social exclusion in the area, rather than of any shortcomings of the Partnership itself. Clearly, exclusion in a peripheral and sparsely populated rural area is qualitatively different from that encountered in urban areas. The excluded groups which have been identified by the Partnership include the long-term unemployed, the elderly living alone, and women in remote households. These and other groups are scattered at low density throughout the area, with no significant concentration in any one locality. The link between unemployment and income poverty tends to be more tenuous in rural settings because of the greater opportunities to engage in informal activities such as part-time fishing and farming. The combination of welfare-dependency and informal black economy employment is seen as part of the culture of the area. Groups such as the elderly living alone often find it difficult to express a need for, or to avail of, assistance, due in large part to a sense of pride and spirit of self-reliance.

Notwithstanding these difficulties in focusing on social exclusion, various initiatives targeted at the long-term unemployed are regarded as successful. These include training courses which have sought to develop manual skills, and supports that have been provided to those availing of the area allowance (a social welfare incentive to long-term unemployed persons to start their own business). The latter initiative involved the use of global grant funding to establish a revolving loan fund that could be used by those availing of the area allowance in order to fund start-up capital costs. These costs, which acted as a major deterrent to those interested in availing of the allowance, had threatened the viability of the scheme. The ability of the Partnership to find a way of overcoming this obstacle is an example of successful and innovative integration of initiatives.

Against these gains, there is a view that some of the activities of the Partnership may have been counter-productive in relation to the problem of inequality. In particular, a number of directors felt that the Leader programme may have increased the disparity between haves and have nots — again owing mainly to the very short time scale for the programme and the 50 per cent matching funding requirement. Together these features of Leader resulted in a concentration of funding on existing businesses, where it was used to finance expansion, rather than on the development of new enterprise. One point of view that was expressed was that Leader mainly benefitted the established business community. While accepting that Leader was focused largely on established enterprise, the Partnership points out that by concentrating on businesses where high levels of initial investment had already been made, and where long-term viability was more certain, job creation under the programme was maximised (see Table 8.5). In this respect the operation of Leader can be seen to have been subject to a classical trade-off between equity and efficiency gains.

TABLE 8.5: ESTIMATED JOB CREATION BY SOUTH KERRY DEVELOPMENT PARTNERSHIP UNDER LEADER

Employment Type	Number of Jobs	Full-Time Equivalent*
Full-time year round	48	48
Part-time year round	20	10
Full-time seasonal	76	38
Part-time seasonal	96	24
Total	240	120

*Part-time employment and seasonal employment were weighted as 0.5 FTE
Source: CRESP Progress Report 1994

Policy Impact

It is difficult to identify policy changes that can be attributed specifically and exclusively to the experience and activities of the Partnership. This is because of the centrally co-ordinated nature of both the ABR and the Leader programmes. Implementational problems experienced by the local groups were fed back to the relevant central agencies which were then charged with offering advice and finding solutions. While this has led to improvements in both the community employment programme (the main labour market measure targeted at the long-term unemployed) and also in the Leader programme, these improvements have resulted from the common experience of several of the local groups and cannot be attributed to any one.

Notwithstanding this observation, however, the Partnership has been particularly active in lobbying for policy changes where elements of programmes have been seen as difficult to implement in its area. The Partnership has fought for the flexibility to deliver programmes in ways that are responsive to local needs and has generally been innovative in programme delivery. Examples here would include the schools enterprise project and the cultural development project, both of which were global grant funded.

However, while there has been improved targeting of, and responsiveness to, local needs in the activities of the Partnership itself, there has been less success in relation to the programmes administered by the state agencies. While there is general agreement that the statutory bodies are now more aware of the problems and needs of the area, and also of the local impact of their programmes, probably the biggest single criticism of the partnership process has been that these agencies have shown an inflexibility in relation to the implementation of programmes in the area, and an unwillingness or inability to adapt to local requirements. For example, the supply of education and training by the relevant state agencies has been characterised by both underprovision (lack of locally based courses) and inappropriate provision (courses mounted at unsuitable times, inappropriate course content). Part of the problem here is the insistence on minimum enrolment levels which are not feasible given the low population density of the area. One result has been the involvement of the Partnership in service delivery, as noted earlier, as it attempts to fill the gap.

With regard to the related issue of co-ordination and integration between the state agencies the general feeling is that while there has been some improvement at the operational (programme implementation) level, this has not yet carried over into improved co-operation at programme design level. There is a widespread feeling that for there to be improvement in this area there will first have to be a change in the culture of the statutory bodies, and that this can only come about as the result of central government pressure.

Conclusion

The Partnership has been mainly involved in the administration of the government's ABR initiative and the Leader I programme. While the two programmes were quite different in scope — Leader focused on the economic aspects of rural development and ABR on the social problem of long-term unemployment — the Partnership has attempted, with some success, to implement the two in an integrated fashion. The Partnership sees itself as a rural development agency, attempting to help both the unemployed and the underemployed on low incomes by widening the local economic base and generally improving the economic vitality of the area. The Partnership's view is that the lack of job opportunities in the area as a whole supercedes the problem of unemployment within the area, in that the latter cannot be tackled in isolation from the former problem. To attempt to do so, for example by stand-alone education or training measures, would in all likelihood exacerbate the demographic problems of the area, with long term deleterious consequences in social as well as economic terms. Thus the economic agenda has tended to take precedence, as was reflected in the fact that Leader dominated the Partnership's work programme during the first three and a half years of its existence.

Given the remoteness of the region, and the difficulty of travel between it and major external employment centres, the above analysis of its problems seems to be well grounded. It is also true that the Leader programme had major beneficial effects in the area. There has been a marked improvement in the morale of those active in development in the local communities, and a feeling that locally led development based on the exploitation of local resources can be successful. Leader has enabled the Partnership to establish a profile in the area, and to fill the vacuum that existed due to the fact that there were no resident service providers. Most importantly, Leader made local decision-making a reality for the first time in south-west Kerry.

Nevertheless, there has been some concern expressed about the fact that during its initial phase of operation the Partnership had little explicit focus on the problem of social exclusion, and that the Leader project funding had little progressive impact in this regard. The latter criticism probably applies more to the programme itself than to the Partnership's operation of it, and indeed the Partnership lobbied intensively for changes to the programme. Also, there have undoubtedly been considerable difficulties involved in developing a focus on social exclusion due to the lower visibility of the problem in the area, which is itself a consequence of the dispersed population. However, the expansion in the Partnership's administrative area to include the urban centre of Killarney has changed the context radically in this regard, and clearly poses a major challenge to the Partnership.

Finally, geography has had a major bearing also on the working methods of the Partnership. It has tended in general to adopt a delivery mode of operation, either providing services directly to the client population, or funding other agencies to do so. Clearly, there are dangers in the adoption of delivery approaches by an organisation working on the local (sub-county) scale: in particular there is the possibility of displacement effects in economic activity. Furthermore, the adoption of this role has created a tension between the Partnership and some of the main statutory bodies, as well as with local politicians. As against these considerations however, the experience of the South Kerry Development Partnership suggests that there are major problems in attempting to apply brokerage methods of partnership operation in remote rural areas. Many of the major service providers do not have a base in the area, and are difficult to engage fully in the partnership process as a result. More significantly, there is the fact that state agencies engaged in service provision are increasingly being required to work to a commercial mandate. In this context the prospects for service delivery by mainstream agencies in sparsely populated rural areas are not good, and there is a clear role for local partnerships acting in a delivery capacity.

Chapter 9

Overview, Conclusions and Recommendations

Introduction

This chapter presents the report's main findings, conclusions and recommendations on the role of local partnerships in promoting social inclusion. As the preceding sections have indicated, there is a rich vein of experience on this subject in this country. Reports under individual programmes, e.g. Poverty 3, ABR, have highlighted specific aspects of this experience. Some wider lessons arising from the Irish experimentation with local partnerships have also been identified in recent OECD and EU reports (OECD, 1996, Department of the Taoiseach, 1996). This study under the auspices of the European Foundation adds to this analysis of local partnership structures in Ireland in three important ways. First, it examines in detail the programmes and structures of local partnership and how these relate to central and local government, the social partners and community/voluntary organisations. Second, it explores the evolution, practice and impact of local partnership though three indepth case studies. Third, it situates the Irish experience of local partnerships in a wider European policy context of strategies to promote social inclusion. (This aspect is further developed in the European synthesis report on the research — Geddes, 1998.)

The chapter has three sections: part one presents the main findings of the study in terms of the policy and practice of local partnerships; part two draws some conclusions about local partnerships as an organisational form, focusing on issues of motivation, structure, process and strategy; and part three outlines some policy implications of local partnerships for the various actors involved.

Main Findings

Local partnership has been successfully rooted as an innovative aspect of Irish public administration. The apex of this is the support for local partnerships under the EU-supported local development programme, though local partnership is also a favoured model in other policy arenas. The main findings arising from this review of local partnerships are:

- Local partnerships are the primary conduit for a radical new localism in public policy, reversing a longstanding hegemony of government centralism. This localism is based on three pillars: the concentrated incidence of unemployment and social exclusion in certain localities; official recognition of the contribution of local self-help in achieving public policy goals; and the development of social partnership as a framework for the design and implementation of welfare and employment policy. The EU plays a crucial role in this new departure through its political and financial support for innovative local employment initiatives based on a partnership model.

- At the heart of this new localism is a major contradiction: local partnerships are primarily a project of central government, which defines the parameters of these initiatives and their location and controls their main supply of funding. In a perverse way, local partnerships are instruments of national policy — a means of circumventing traditional local organs of public administration, including local government, to address difficult social problems at the local level. The tradition of strong central direction of policy is thus combined with the local delivery of policy through partnership structures, a position reinforced by the continued failure of government to devolve powers and resources to non-national tiers of public administration, including the structural funds. This local-national nexus, without parallel institutional reform, leaves local partnerships in a highly dependent position.

- At the core of this new localism is the establishment of local partnerships: autonomous structures which mobilise a variety of organisational interests in support of an agreed local strategy. Local partnerships can coalesce around different strategic policy issues, including local development, enterprise/job creation, service provision, community development or urban regeneration. The common ingredients in local partnerships are multi-agency involvement, local (bottom-up) planning, integration of activities, innovation, capacity-building and community participation. While administratively autonomous, local partnerships are supported by an extensive network of central and local institutions. At the apex is the Department of Tourism, Sport and Recreation, supported by a government committee of other relevant departments. Intermediary funding bodies play a key role in channelling EU and government resources directly to local partnerships, though local government has a rather peripheral involvement. The social partners, together with voluntary and community groups, are also involved in the support structure for local partnerships.

- Local partnerships represent an innovative form of local governance, involving state agencies, social partners and, uniquely, community groups. Local partnerships exercise a considerable degree of influence over local policy issues, as well as having local discretion over a relatively significant pool of resources, which can be used to lever additional local and national funds. At the same time, local partnerships rival rather than complement the existing system of local government, with a minimal input from elected local representatives. This separation has persisted despite numerous attempts to reconcile these two structures. Local partnerships have also overcome other administrative anomalies such as their non-governmental legal structure as independent private companies and their lack of formal agreements with partner organisations on their resource input.

- Promoting social inclusion is a core aspect of local partnerships, reflecting growing public policy concerns about the structural nature of unemployment and poverty. The designation of certain urban and rural areas as sites for local partnerships is complimented by further local targeting of disadvantaged groups. There have been very tangible achievements by local partnerships in terms of jobs, education and training, family services and community development. The involvement of representatives of these groups in local partnerships strengthens the social inclusion focus by giving these groups a unique input into decision-making. These gains are still rather marginal in terms of the scale of unemployment and poverty. A key weakness is the detachment between these local inclusion initiatives and mainstream policy which still exerts the major impact on disadvantaged areas, such as social housing, urban renewal, agricultural and industrial development and public services.

- There are concerns as to the sustainability of the present experimentation with local partnerships. The diversity of central government and EU local partnership programmes has resulted in an *ad-hoc* proliferation of such structures, which is ripe for rationalisation. This problem is compounded by an almost total dependency by local partnerships on EU-provided central government funds, which are due to run out in 1999. Another difficulty arises from the resource-intensive management structures in local partnerships, which primarily rely on individual goodwill.

- Equal opportunities are a subsidiary emphasis in local partnerships. There are government stipulations as to the gender balance of the membership of local partnerships, along with guidelines on gender-proofing their activities. Important measures have also been taken by some local partnerships with regard to women and Travellers. By contrast, disability and other minority issues have received little attention. Despite a general awareness of equal opportunities, there remain significant barriers to the participation of women and minority groups in decision-making procedures of local partnerships and in particular activities, e.g. enterprise.

- Local partnerships, even where funded under the same programme, are in practice a heterogeneous grouping. This derives from differences in decision-making structures, operating methods, involvement of partners and management style, in particular the roles of the chairperson and the manager. There has been little attempt to document and evaluate these differing approaches to local partnerships, so as to tease out their benefits and drawbacks. Consequently, there is very little formal transfer of know-how and good practice in the operation of local partnerships.

- National government continues to exert a huge influence on the operations of local partnerships. This occurs in two ways: directly through the administration and funding of local programmes; and indirectly through the continued dominance of various central government departments in framing local policy. In order to strengthen the policy milieu for local partnerships, the Taoiseach's Department has established an interdepartmental committee on local development. However, the linkages between this structure and the local experience have not been formalised.

Local partnerships remain a form of local policy intervention about which we are still only learning. Their novel composition, rapid growth, penchant for self-promotion and lack of rigorous evaluation, have hindered objective analysis of the value of local partnerships as a policy response to unemployment and social exclusion. This initial enthusiasm for local partnerships is slowly giving way to a more critical analysis of their achievements, strengths and weaknesses. Arising from the extensive research undertaken for this study, the report now identifies organisational and policy issues which influence the effectiveness of local partnerships as an instrument for social inclusion. The discussion begins, however, by considering the underlying dynamic of local partnerships.

Understanding the Dynamic of Local Partnerships

At the core of local partnership as a policy concept is the belief that by combining diverse and often conflicting interests, this can generate added value or synergy for those involved. This synergy represents the underlying dynamic in local partnerships and justifies the "unnatural" combining of diverse forces. Public understanding of this rationale for the local partnership model is still underdeveloped, with a preponderance of descriptive definitions, such as the one adopted for this research report. However, to fully comprehend the potential impact of local partnerships as a policy instrument in tackling social exclusion, it is critical that the different forms that this synergy can take are adequately conceptualised. In attempting this task, the analysis relies on an earlier framework developed by Mackintosh (1992), which is adapted to fit the Irish situation.

First, synergy can arise through the local partnership enhancing the resources available in a particular area. This is achieved, in the first instance, by attracting in external resources either through direct programme support or by securing additional resources from other non-local sources. Budget enlargement can also occur through leveraging local resources as matching funding for specific projects. These resources can be levered from the public sector, private entrepreneurs and their financial backers and from voluntary and community groups in terms of personnel and goodwill. This approach is exemplified by the South Kerry Development Partnership, which defines its role as an integrator of indigenous and external resources in support of rural development. This attribute of local partnerships is set to become more important as structural funds are reduced and the financial role of the private sector is expanded. The challenge, however, is in maintaining a strategic view of how additional resources are spent, and not to simply become an accumulator and consumer of scarce resources. Even if well used, such resources may only represent a small fraction of the overall public/private expenditure pool. Thus, it may not impact on mainstream investment in public infrastructure or, in the case of private funds, be unable to stem the haemorrhage of resources from disadvantaged areas, e.g. the flow of capital from rural areas into urban renewal tax relief schemes.

A second form of synergy associated with local partnership is through the more effective and efficient delivery of services, be it in terms of improved take-up, greater co-ordination, better targeting or enhanced responsiveness to local needs. The crucial ingredients here are the knowledge, skills and methods of the different partners, which the local partnership can bring together. For example, the Tallaght Partnership has used the Plato model to harness the business expertise of the private sector to support local micro-entrepreneurs. No amount of training or resources could compensate for this hands-on involvement. Similarly, in Limerick, the local partnership was able to improve the take-up of welfare benefits by facilitating a dialogue between beneficiaries and the health board, and also by involving national authorities in this discussion. The downside of this approach is the time and effort required to overcome the cultural and sectoral differences between partners, whether between users and providers or between rival providers. It is also interesting to note that services provided by the private sector, outside of jobs, have not formed part of the discussion in local partnerships, especially in crucial areas such as financial services, shopping and leisure facilities and affordable housing.

Local partnerships can give rise to a third added value through generating new investment opportunities, whether in terms of property development or markets for goods or services which have a social payback (referred to as "social capitalism"). In this model, local partnerships can facilitate the creation of new assets that have a commercial and a social value. Surprisingly, this aspect of the partnership remit has been rather under-exploited, which reflects the weak commercial remit of local partnerships and the limited role of the private sector. For instance, local partnerships have not to date engaged with the private sector on joint property development ventures under the urban renewal scheme. Even where local partnerships have worked directly with the private sector, it has been to jointly promote micro-businesses, not to enter a strategic relationship requiring the investment of private resources. Similarly, local partnerships have been slow to explore the potential of the social economy, though the Tallaght Partnership, for one, has recently established a unit to focus on this, while

Pavee Point has also done some work on this. There are some examples where commercial joint ventures have emerged. In peripheral rural areas such as South Kerry, the local partnerships have worked with small producers (farmers and fishermen) and the private sector to develop new markets for local produce. The Dundalk Employment Partnership has developed an enterprise/ retail/office centre and also established business arrangements with the private sector to create local employment opportunities. These are exceptions which point to a general lack of "developmentalism" among local partnerships, a pattern that is all the more surprising given that this was a key driving force for their emergence. It also highlights their almost total dependence on public funds, a situation that may have to change quite dramatically post-1999.

A fourth source of synergy in local partnerships is through dialogue, consensus-building and shared decision-making. Local partnerships are designed as arenas for negotiation between sectors that are normally opposed to one another, and can be seen as oscillating between positions of conflict and consensus, inequality and parity. The involvement of otherwise disenfranchised groups in local partnerships is the key factor here. Traditionally, this group has not had an input in local decision-making and their involvement poses huge challenges for themselves and for service providers. The difficulties in achieving this can be enormous: in the case of the PAUL Partnership Limerick, the project spent much of its formative period in breaking down years of mistrust. Yet, this was seen as crucial if the local partnership was to become an effective force for change in disadvantaged areas of the city. Bridging traditional gaps between the public and private sectors is also part of this equation, though less so as between the often conflicting interests of business and trade unions. A key focus of the private-public-community sector dialogue in local partnerships is around the role of enterprise as a response to social exclusion on one hand, and the responsibilities of employers to recruit the long-term unemployed on the other. Unfortunately, this dialogue has not developed very far in the majority of local partnerships. Also, while local partnerships can broaden the policymaking circle to include previously excluded groups, this may be achieved only on an individual basis or through the co-option of weaker partners. Thus, community representatives in local partnerships may become part of a new policymaking elite that is un-accountable to the wider community and on which they have very little input. The exclusion of elected representatives in local partnerships is an example of how one group's gain can be another's loss.

Local partnerships often seek to incorporate these different dimensions at the one time, though usually with a dominance of some over others. This adds to the intricacy and challenge of local partnerships as a policy construct. Local partnerships are thus subject to a variety of pressures and expectations, with on-going struggles over resources, services, benefits and values. Local partnerships are thus at the cutting-edge of wider policy debates about the creation and distribution of wealth and power in society. Often these internal struggles are affected by external factors. Thus, success in securing external funding may reduce internal pressures for some partners to provide resources. Equally, the new urban renewal scheme strengthens the opportunity for local partnerships to engage with the private sector in joint property ventures, as a way of securing community gains for disadvantaged areas in terms of facilities and housing.

Organisational Issues

We now turn to how the contribution of local partnerships in tackling social exclusion can be supported. This question can be addressed at two levels: improving the organisational features of local partnerships and enhancing the roles of the main actors involved in these ventures. Organisational issues are analysed under three headings: structure, process and strategy.

Structure

The kernel of local partnerships is their hybrid organisational structure based on the principle of social corporatism. They are established as independent entities and take the legal form of private companies, limited by guarantee. It is clear that the local partnership structure has brought a new positive dynamic to localities. It creates a new awareness of social exclusion among local actors and gives new energy and focus to their efforts to tackle this issue. There are, nonetheless, some difficulties in relation to the choice of local partners and the role played by their representatives on local partnerships.

It is clear that greater flexibility is required in deciding the membership of local partnerships. Currently, membership is a mix of national prescription and local selection. The application of a standard formula for partnerships, while ensuring national uniformity, undermines the principle of "bottom-up" development. A further consideration is that pre-defined partnerships can become closed to new members or be reluctant to dispense with members who cannot make a meaningful contribution. The weak relationships with local government, in particular with local politicians, are also a cause for concern. Meanwhile, the composition of community representation can be unbalanced, in that the preference for area-based organisations can result in the interests of sectoral groups, e.g. Travellers, lone parents, being ignored.

The lack of a formal relationship between partners who make up a local partnership is another problematic area. The current model of local partnership emphasises the quantity of partners rather than the quality of the engagement, i.e. what partners can bring to a local partnership. Ideally, local partnerships should be underpinned by an institutional commitment on behalf of all partners in the form of a written statement of commitment, which would be subject to the approval of the other partners. This could also be used to assess the contribution of partner organisations at the end of the year.

The lynchpin of local partnerships is their board of directors nominated by partner agencies. This heterogeneous grouping, consisting of between 18 and 25 people, is the conduit between the partnership and the partners. At the moment, there are no guidelines on the personal and social skills required for the type of collaborative working envisaged in a local partnership. The tendency to choose someone of seniority should be balanced with other factors, such as commitment to the partnership ideal, and familiarity with the needs of an area or social group.

Another issue relates to the relationship between directors and their parent organisations. In many cases, even in the statutory sector, this role is unclear and is heavily dependent on individual discretion. Not surprisingly, then, there is a poor quality of reporting procedures between directors and partner organisations. Ensuring accountability is especially problematic for community directors given the underdeveloped nature of representative structures for disadvantaged groups and communities. There is, in particular, confusion as between the participation of individual community activists in a local partnership and the collective involvement of the community as a formal partner.

Recommendations

- There should be greater flexibility in the structuring and composition of local partnerships, with more local input in the determination of same. Ideally, broad criteria should be set out by central government, with the actual composition being decided at local level.

- The exclusion of politicians from local partnerships should be reviewed. A procedure whereby the chairperson of the local authority was included as a director would ensure a link with traditional forms of representative democracy, while at the same time not altering the apolitical ethos of partnerships.

- Partners should set out a formal statement of their commitment to a local partnership, which should be the subject of agreement from the other partners.

- Guidelines are needed on the choice of partner representative. While seniority is important, other factors to be taken into account should be their commitment to the partnership and their capacity to engage and work with other interests.

- Partner representatives should forge on-going links between their parent organisations and the partnership and the individualistic legal understanding of a director's role should be complemented by a protocol on their duties and obligations.

Process

Local partnerships are designed to involve the traditional social partners, along with voluntary and community groups, in processes of public policymaking and implementation at the local level. They are also expected to exert a strong influence over the recruitment practices of local employers and the work of other non-statutory partners. It is through the directors and staff that local partnership is transformed from a formal architecture to a dynamic engagement. What is required to ensure that this partnering process happens?

Local partnerships have developed quite sophisticated internal structures, whose main features include: a broad-based board of directors which is responsible for overall policy; sub-committees which formulate and implement specific programmes of work; professional staff with a diversity of competencies; and chairpeople who are expected to take on a strong leadership role. The hidden determinant as to whether all this works is the quality of management in local partnerships. Too often, local partnerships do not invest adequately enough in enhancing their collective management skills. Action is needed to identify weaknesses in the management capacity of local partnerships and to develop measures which address these, e.g. through the provision of training programmes or by recruiting personnel with particular expertise in partner organisations. Another aspect is the need for clarity as to the respective roles of management and staff, in particular, a willingness to delegate appropriate tasks to professional staff as a local partnership matures.

A key consideration for local partnerships is to maximise opportunities for participation in decision-making through sub-management structures. These can also tap the personal energy and enthusiasm of a larger number of individuals in partner agencies. However, the objective of participation needs to be balanced with the requirement for effective decision-making. Problems especially arise when there is a lack of co-ordination between internal decision-making tiers, where structures that were originally designed for consultative purposes are later used to implement actions, and where an excessive number of committees are involved in decision-making. This can give the impression that local partnerships are overly bureaucratic bodies whose lines of decision-making are not transparent, with a resultant loss in the sense of ownership of the endeavour among partner agencies, especially community groups. In particular, it is essential that the administrative practices of local partnerships are different to those that have traditionally operated in the public sector.

The capacity of organisations to engage in a local partnership varies considerably. This unevenness is to be expected given the difference in status between partners, e.g. service providers and users and those at work and the unemployed. These differences should be acknowledged from the outset and procedures put in place to enhance the capacity of weaker groups. In particular, the rhetoric attached to the involvement of poor communities and groups in local partnerships masks a great diversity in terms of local practice. In some cases, community participation rarely extends beyond token consultation due to the limited capacity of community groups to participate effectively. This highlights the necessity to provide resources and support to animate the contribution of community groups and ensure real leverage over strategy. One example of this by some local partnerships is the employment of community liaison workers who support the involvement of community groups in the partnership. Another is to rebalance the representation on the board, though this appears less effective. A more practical issue relates to the high costs of participation in a partnership, both for the individuals chosen as community directors and for their nominating organisations who may "lose" the time and skills of key members.

Seemingly open management structures may also mask more fundamental power relations in local partnerships. This highlights the importance of the governance procedures in local partnerships, i.e. patterns of participation and styles of management which determine the way in which agendas are framed, strategies decided upon and projects delivered. Given the hybrid nature of local partnerships, there is scope for choosing different governance practices. All too often, however, local partnerships have adopted a business model of organisation that appears in keeping with the legal structure of a private company limited by guarantee. Such a model may not be conducive to the diversity of skills and outlooks that is represented on a partnership board of management. It is also one that is predominantly hierarchical and male-oriented.

Recommendations

- Management structures in partnerships should be given careful consideration, in particular during the set-up stage, so as to maximise opportunities for participation.

- Local partnerships should prioritise measures to enhance their management capacity.

- As local partnerships mature, management procedures should be revised and streamlined as fewer management levels and less frequent meetings may be required. Special efforts should be made to ensure the transparency of local partnerships.

- Partnerships should reflect on the style and culture of management within their organisations and identify those aspects which inhibit participation. A programme of positive discrimination should also be drawn up in favour of women and other marginalised groups.

- A strategy should be put in place to enhance the capacity of partners. This would include resourcing community groups to better research and represent local needs.

Strategy

The integrative function of local partnerships is a key element of their operational remit: having a comprehensive overview of local needs; linking the skills and resources of different service providers; combining economic, social and environmental measures; and providing a channel of communication between local initiatives and national policies. This is an ambitious remit that is fraught with a number of difficulties. A main one is the danger of local partnerships dispersing their energies and resources over too broad a range of issues. While the scale and complexity of needs among the target population of local partnerships are undeniable, there are also limits to their capacity to respond in a way that will ensure lasting benefits. It is important, therefore, that the broad remit of local partnerships is used selectively, so as to prioritise issues on which they can make meaningful interventions. Also, there is a danger with area-based strategies that the needs of specific groups are neglected.

At a technical level, the planning, research and monitoring capacity of local partnerships needs further development. Local strategic plans are not easy to formulate and are prone to becoming simply shopping-lists of actions desired by individual partners. Another extreme is where there is also an over-reliance on external consultants to prescribe a strategy. A related challenge is to better understand the local processes that contribute to the ghettoisation of the unemployed and other groups in particular localities, which is a key dimension of the local partnership approach.

An underdeveloped aspect of local partnerships is the key role they can play in integrating policy interventions at different levels: national, regional, local and community. In particular, local partnerships are uniquely placed to link sectoral initiatives with community provision. This model is being used in the development of the Local Employment Service. There is also scope for integration in other policy arenas, e.g. providing one-stop-shops for all public services, developing new management structures to accompany new physical resources, and enhancing public transport systems in order to access jobs and services.

While many local partnerships operate within a development framework, their main emphasis is on enhancing local services or supporting private enterprise. By contrast, there has been inadequate attention to the physical regeneration of rundown neighbourhoods through housing and other types of infrastructural projects. Indeed, the lack of connection between the government urban renewal scheme and the work of local partnerships is a missed opportunity to utilise a major programme of public and private investment to achieve social goals. This raises a related issue: the potential role of local partnerships in initiating joint economic ventures with other interests, public or private. Such a "developmental" model of local partnership is, at the moment, largely unexplored.

Recommendations

- Partnerships should avoid the temptation to develop catch-all strategies which seek to ameliorate the many aspects of poverty but focus instead on a small number of integrated initiatives which can make a lasting impact on social exclusion. The needs of particularly vulnerable groups should also be included in such strategies.

- More resources are required to develop the technical capacity of local partnerships in the key management functions of research, planning and evaluation.

- Local partnerships should be more aware of the many different levels at which they can enhance the work of their partner agencies, and seek to develop a balance between short-term gains (more resources, better services), and long-term impact (better inter-agency co-ordination, community input into local decision-making).

- Local partnerships should examine the scope to directly engage in market-based actions which promote the physical and commercial renewal of disadvantaged areas and investigate new instruments of regeneration which combine economic and social dimensions, e.g. social enterprises and community co-operatives.

Policy Implications for Government and Other Actors

Local partnerships involve a wide range of actors – how can their contribution be enhanced? The main actors in Ireland are central government and the EU, which have played a critical role in the rapid development of local partnerships. But there are also implications for the various partner agencies involved in local partnerships: local government, employers and trade unions, state agencies and the community and voluntary sector.

Central Government and the EU

Local partnerships currently operate apart from the traditional local administrative framework: their legal structure is that of a private company and their main sponsor is central government. The autonomy of local partnerships from existing administrative structures, together with their own resource base sourced from central government, positions them to respond in a flexible and innovative way to local needs and opportunities. However, the sustainability of this situation in the longer term is unlikely and there are also drawbacks to the anomalous institutional status of local partnerships, which can undermine their legitimacy in the eyes of public agencies, politicians and other interests. It should be possible to regularise their position, without compromising their current independence and flexibility. This would include clarification of the linkages between partnerships and elected local representatives, in order to enhance local democracy and accountability.

There exists considerable confusion and potential for overlap due to the multitude of local partnerships under various government and EU programmes — up to 200, with 6-8 per county. There also continues to be a tension between traditional sectoral economic and social programmes and local development initiatives. What is needed is a strategic framework under which both top-down and bottom-up initiatives could co-ordinate their efforts and resources, linking the local, regional and national levels. This should include a definition of the remit of local development and how it interacts with more conventional approaches. Linked to this should be a rationalisation of local partnership structures.

A defining feature of the local partnership model is the vertical links between partnerships and central government. These links are critical given the centralised nature of the Irish state. At the moment, vertical links are informal, focused on one institution (the Taoiseach's office) and largely nationally driven. A mechanism is required to link local practices and insights with the national policy agenda. In addition, local partnerships have not gained access to the range of national partnership mechanisms for policy making (e.g. NESC, NESF). Acknowledging local partnerships as a new sector in society and deepening their relationships with national policy fora is thus required.

The lifeblood of local partnerships is access to discretionary resources to energise their work. Realistically, this is only possible through external funding from central government. Current funding under the structural funds is due to expire in 1999. With Ireland about to lose all or part of its objective 1 status, it is important that an alternative mechanism is found to channel EU funds into local partnerships. Also, external funding must continue to be flexible and responsive to local needs. The existing model of a dedicated intermediary body to distribute such funding should be retained. At the same time, local partnerships should be encouraged to source additional funds, in particular from the private sector through joint ventures.

Local partnerships represent a novel departure in public administrative practice. They are both organisationally unique, reflecting the principles of partnership and participation, and strategically innovative, pursuing an integrated and area-targeted approach. What is required to underpin these new approaches is a whole battery of management and technical skills — planning, research, evaluation and capacity-building. Currently, the provision of such skills is largely left to the initiative of individual partnerships, some of which contract with outside consultants to provide training and support. This is a rather haphazard approach. Furthermore, given that much of the work of partnerships is based on learning-by-doing, a mechanism is needed to assist in the transfer of know-how and good practice between partnerships, as was provided in the Poverty 3 Programme. Also, local anti-poverty initiatives, no less than any other aspect of policy, require adequate information for them to be effective. Yet, local partnerships operate in an information vacuum — local statistics on poverty and unemployment are very sparse and their ability to commission research in order to identify needs or opportunities is limited. Meanwhile, at a national level, information is needed as to the processes creating areas of disadvantage and which of these are amenable (and how) to local intervention.

How government integrated local partnerships into its broader policy remit is also important. To date, government has tended to off-load responsibility for difficult socio-economic issues to local partnerships. There is a danger that local partnerships may be seen to assume exclusive responsibility for government action to tackle poverty and social exclusion in certain locations, and that the broader policy issues, which also impact on poverty, are neglected. Local partnerships have a role to play in tackling social exclusion, but need a supportive national policy framework to maximise their effectiveness. A potential model for this is the national anti-poverty strategy prepared by the Irish Government arising from the recent UN social summit. This strategy seeks to provide coherence to anti-poverty goals at all levels. Similar frameworks should also be prepared as to how local partnerships fit into both wider area-based policies (at regional, rural and urban levels) and local sectoral policies, such as education, housing, etc

There have been some important goverment and EU initiatives to promote equal opportunities in local partnerships, notably the requirement for a minimum gender balance. However, in other areas, action has relied on the publication of guidelines and the holding of seminars. A more forceful intervention is probably required to ensure that such measures are successful. This could include, for example, having equal opportunities as one of the key criteria for deciding to approve the action plans of local partnerships. Reserving a portion of funds specifically for equal opportunity measures would be another option.

Recommendations

- Give institutional recognition to local partnerships, including a role for elected representatives, while not compromising their flexibility and responsiveness.

- Set out a strategic framework for local development, which would include a co-ordination and rationalisation of existing local partnership structures.

- Central government should develop a mechanism for identifying and transferring good practice from local partnerships into public policy.

- Local partnerships should be recognised as a new sector in society, with access to national-level government advisory institutions.

- A secure and independent national funding structure for local partnerships should be established, while at the same time encouraging local private funding sources.

- Support structures for local partnerships should be further developed, especially in regard to local and national research on the geography of social exclusion.

- The work of local partnerships in tackling social exclusion should be recognised and supported by mainstream government policies, e.g. urban policy, housing policy.

- The legal and financial framework underpinning equal opportunities policy in local partnerships should be strengthened.

Other Actors

Local Government

Local government has a crucial role to play in the work of local partnerships. Yet, to date, they have been one of the weakest statutory partners. Part of this reflects concerns about the status of local partnerships and the exclusion of local elected representatives. Part of the explanation is also the division between physical development (the traditional remit of local government) and social development (seen as the remit of local partnerships). This is a false dichotomy, especially as a strong determinant on the living conditions of disadvantaged groups is the quality of their housing and environment. Interestingly, this connection is recognised in the EU Urban programme. This initiative could be used as a springboard for a stronger alliance between local partnerships and local government on local physical development.

State Agencies

The impact of local partnerships is strongly influenced by the level of commitment by state agencies. At the moment, the involvement of local state bodies in partnerships is primarily mediated by individuals. Even where officials are personally committed to the partnership ideal, they can find themselves operating in an organisational vacuum, with little recognition or support for their efforts in their parent agency. Also, in many public service agencies, there is little tradition of working in partnerships. What is required here is a change in the administrative culture of public bodies that encourages and rewards its staff to engage with partnerships on issues of common concern. The current government initiative on reform of the public sector, referred to as the Strategic Management Initiative, is a potential vehicle for encouraging state agencies to develop links with other local actors. Finally, state agencies should adopt a pro-active approach to mainstreaming good practice from local partnerships.

Social Partners

For the social partners, local partnership demands a different approach to that practised under national agreements. In local partnerships, the emphasis is on a practical engagement and joint problem solving rather than an adversarial trade-off between vested interests. Thus, the effective trade union official or human resources executive in a private company may not be good as a representative on a local partnership. Clearly, a culture shift is needed for employers and trade unions to take on an active role in local partnerships. Furthermore, the centralist structures used by social partners are not conducive to the type of local focus required by local partnerships. While both employers and workers have sub-national structures, these are more talking shops on national issues rather than fora for addressing local concerns. (The exception here is the Chambers of Commerce structure.) Trade unions and employers need, therefore, to strengthen local mechanisms for engaging with local partnerships. A third issue is the limited extent to which the private sector has engaged with local partnerships in commercial ventures. This would bring a new dimension to local partnerships, as well as mobilising private resources.

Community and Voluntary Sector

There are huge challenges as well as opportunities for community and voluntary groups arising from local partnerships. A major challenge is the development of representative structures through which the views of disadvantaged communities can be communicated in local partnerships. While there is a general consensus that traditional methods of representation are inadequate, at the same time the current ad-hoc mechanisms for representing communities are deficient. To address this, community organisations in a number of local partnerships have established a community forum as a way of enhancing representation. Another issue is the fact that partnership-type relationships are relatively new to the community sector — self-help and campaigning are more traditional activities. Arising from this, community groups are challenged to adopt a more professional perspective than might have traditionally been the case. In particular, community groups must take on board new management practices such as needs assessment, strategic planning and quality assurance/assessment procedures. A third issue for community and voluntary groups is to balance their work with local partnerships with their more traditional activities. A strategic approach to local partnerships is therefore needed, so that existing work is not neglected.

Recommendations

- There should be a stronger engagement between local government and local partnerships on local physical development.

- State agencies should adopt a more pro-active approach to local partnerships, establishing a formal agreement outlining their commitment to local partnership and encouraging staff to develop new ways of working through these new structures. State agencies should also apply the lessons from local partnerships on service provision.

- The structural problems facing employers and trade unions in engaging in local partnerships should be addressed through administrative and cultural changes.

- The community and voluntary sector should adopt a strategic approach to the difficulties arising from local partnerships, so as not to be overwhelmed by the demands and requirements of being a partner in this new structure.

Conclusion

There is considerable evidence that local partnerships can make an important contribution to the fight against unemployment and social exclusion. At the same time, the application of local partnership as a policy instrument is still at an evolutionary stage of development, despite the popular usage of this model in mainstream government programmes. Local partnerships should still be treated as a problematic concept, whose potential is still to be refined and developed, rather than be treated as a definitive model for widespread replication in diverse policy contexts.

This chapter has outlined various ways in which local partnerships could be made more effective as an organisational form, focusing on the themes of structure, process and strategy. Local partnerships also pose a number of challenges for those involved in this experiment from a policy perspective. Local partnerships are not neutral entities that can be fitted into the existing policy framework without creating consequences for existing actors. This is especially the case for central government and the EU, whose creation local partnerships are in the first instance. They carry the major onus for supporting and mainstreaming the innovative work of these new structures. Equally, those involved as partner agencies are required to examine the implications of local partnerships for their traditional ways of working. Not to do so would be to put severe limitations on the inputs to be made to (and subsequent outcomes to be derived from) local partnerships by the various agencies involved.

Interviewees for National Policy Review

Central Government

Sylda Langford, principal officer, Department of Social Welfare

Dermot McCarthy, assistant secretary, Department of the Taoiseach

Frank O'Donnell, principal officer, Department of Agriculture

Julie O'Neill, assistant secretary, Department of the Tanaiste

Public Agencies

Tony Crooks, chief executive officer, Area Development Management

Tom Costelloe, programme manager, FÁS, the national training and employment agency

Hugh Frazer, director, Combat Poverty Agency

Rory O'Donnell, director, National Economic and Social Council

Employers and Trade Unions

Brian Geoghegan, director, Irish Business and Employers Confederation

Philip Mullally, director, Enterprise Trust

Peter Rigney, industrial officer, Irish Congress of Trade Unions

Community and Voluntary Organisations

Mike Allen, general secretary, Irish National Organisation of the Unemployed

Stasia Crickley, Community Workers' Co-operative representative on ADM

Seannie Lambe, Community Directors Forum and community director, Dublin Inner City Partnership

Anna Lee, manager, Tallaght Partnership and member, Planet

Researchers and Policy Analysts

Pauline Conroy, social policy analyst and central unit, Poverty 3 programme

Kieran McKeown, socio-economic consultant and evaluator, Global Grant for Local Development

Professor Jim Walsh, professor of geography, NUI Maynooth, and evaluator team, Leader 1 programme

Michael Mernagh, policy adviser, Irish research and development unit, Poverty 3

Appendix 2

Interviewees for PAUL Partnership Limerick Case Study

Directors Representing Community and Voluntary Groups

Tom Clancy, co-ordinating group, Moyross Partners

Joan Condon, director, Limerick Centre for the Unemployed

John Hannafin, chairperson, Southill Community Services Board

Rev Donough O'Malley, chairperson, Our Lady of Lourdes Community Services Board

Directors Representing State Agencies

David Deighan, regional manager, Shannon Development

Ger Dillon, housing officer, Limerick Corporation

Deirdre Frawley, adult educational officer, Limerick City VEC

Directors Representing Businesses and Trade Unions

Jim Leyden, employer, Irish Business and Employers Confederation

Tony Kenneally, trade union official, Irish Congress of Trade Unions

Others

Professor Joyce O'Connor, former chairperson, PAUL Partnership

Staff

Monica McIlvanney, social programmes officer and staff representative on the board

Denis O'Brien, economic programmes officer

Neil Walker, director

Funders/Support Agencies

Michael Mernagh, former research and development unit, Poverty 3 programme

Senan Turnbull, projects officer, ADM

TABLE A2.1: PARTNER PROFILE OF THE PAUL PARTNERSHIP, LIMERICK

Partner Name	Description
Moyross Partners	Umbrella body for community groups and voluntary service providers
Our Lady of Lourdes Community Services Group	Umbrella body for community groups and voluntary service providers
St Mary's Parish Awareness and Development Group	Community group concerned with development of area
Southill Development Co-operative	Locally managed economic development agency
Southill Community Services Board	Voluntary group providing social services
St Munchin's Action Centre Committee	Umbrella body for community groups and voluntary service providers
Irish Business and Employers Confederation	National representative body for employers and businesses
Irish Congress of Trade Unions	National representative body for trade unions
City of Limerick VEC	Local statutory provider of vocational and adult education services
Department of Social, Community and Family Affairs	Government department responsible for welfare services and policy
FÁS	National statutory provider of training and employment services
Limerick Corporation	Elected local authority for planning, development and social housing
Mid-Western Health Board	Regional statutory provider of health and social services
Shannon Development	Regional statutory economic development agency
Limerick Youth Services	Local voluntary provider of youth services
Limerick Centre for the Unemployed	Local voluntary provider of services for the unemployed

Appendix 3

Interviewees for Tallaght Partnership Case Study

Directors Representing Community and Voluntary Groups

Ben Murray, Disability Interests Forum

Maria Price-Bolger, Community Initiatives

Rosaleen Walsh, director, Tallaght Welfare Society

Philip Watt, project co-ordinator, West Tallaght Resource Centre

Directors Representing State Agencies

Jane Foreman, regional director, FÁS and chairperson, Tallaght Partnership

Aileen O'Donoghue, community worker, Dublin County Council

Dr Rosalea Waters, Eastern Health Board

Directors Representing Businesses and Trade Unions

Gerry Doyle, director, Tallaght Chamber of Commerce

Brendan Moorehouse, trade union official, Irish Congress of Trade Unions

Elaine Mulvaney, coordinator, Tallaght Centre for the Unemployed

Neil Ormond, employer, Irish Business and Employers Confederation

Staff

Anna Lee, manager

Aidan Lloyd, community co-ordinator

Funders/Support Agencies

Siobhan Lynam, projects officer, ADM

Liz Sullivan, projects officer, Combat Poverty Agency

TABLE A3.1: PARTNER PROFILE OF THE TALLAGHT PARTNERSHIP

Sector	Partner	Area of Work
Voluntary/ Community	Get Tallaght Working	Community-based enterprise
	West Tallaght Resource Centre	Community development
	Tallaght Welfare Society	Social services
	Disability Interests Forum	Issues relating to disability
	Women's Forum	Women's issues
	Youth Forum	Young people
	Barnardos	Services for children
	Community Initiatives, Tallaght	Network of community employment projects
Local Social Partners	Tallaght Centre for the Unemployed	Provision of services for unemployed people
	Tallaght Chamber of Commerce	Local business network
Social Partners	Irish Congress of Trade Unions	National trade union body
	Irish Business and Employers Confederation	National employer body
Statutory	County Dublin VEC	Education provision
	South Dublin County Council	Local Authority
	Eastern Health Board	Regional health authority
	Department of Social, Community and Family Affairs	Welfare provision
	FÁS	Training authority
	Forbairt	Industrial development

Appendix 4

Interviewees for South Kerry Development Partnership Case Study

Directors Representing Community and Voluntary Groups

Rev Michael Murphy, Kenmare area communities

Muiris O'Donoghue, Cahersiveen area communities

Sean O Suilleabhain, Mid-Kerry area communities

Paul Sweeney, Cahersiveen Centre for the Unemployed

Directors Representing State Agencies

Paddy d'Arcy, manager, Kerry County Council

Michael Donnelly, adult education officer, County Kerry VEC

Declan Murphy, manager, Cork-Kerry Tourism

Bill O'Brien, chief executive officer, Teagasc

Directors Representing Businesses and Trade Unions

Shiela Crowley, farmer, Irish Farmers Association

Tom McBride, employer, Irish Business and Employers Confederation and chairperson, South Kerry Development Partnership

Andrew McCarthy, trade union official, Irish Congress of Trade Unions

Others

Eamon Langford, ex-community director

Staff

Mary Lyne, education officer

Bill Thorne, general manager

Funders/Support Agencies

Senan Turnbull, projects officer, Area Development Management

TABLE A4.1: PARTNER PROFILE OF THE SOUTH KERRY
DEVELOPMENT PARTNERSHIP

Name	*Area of Work*
Cahersiveen community groups (3 places)	Mainly local and community development
Kenmare community groups (2 places)	Mainly local and community development
Killarney community groups (2 places)	Mainly local and community development
Mid-Kerry community groups (3 places)	Mainly local and community development
Irish Congress of Trade Unions (2)	National trade union body
Irish Business and Employers Confederation (2)	National employers representative body
Irish Farmers Association	National farmers representative body
Macra na Feirme	Representation of young farmers
Kerry Group plc	Food industry company
Kerry County Council	General purpose local authority
Kerry Co Vocational Education Cttee.	Education authority
Bord Fáilte	Tourism promotion
Forbairt	Industrial development (indigenous enterprise)
FÁS	Training and employment authority
Teagasc	Agricultural guidance and training
Bord Iascaigh Mhara	Fisheries development
Údarás na Gaeltachta	Gaeltacht development

Bibliography

A government of renewal, a policy agreement between Fine Gael, the Labour Party and Democratic Left, 1994

Area Development Management (1994), Report on the Area Based Response to Long-term Unemployment, 1991-1993, Dublin: ADM

Area Development Management (1994), *Community development within local development*, Proceedings of a seminar held in September 1994 in Navan, Dublin: ADM

Area Development Management (1995), *Integrated local development handbook*, Dublin: ADM

Area Development Management (1995), *Annual Report 1994*, Dublin: ADM

Area Development Management (1996), *Towards gender equality in integrated local development*, Dublin: ADM

Area Development Management (1996), *Annual Report 1995*, Dublin: ADM

Bailey, N. (1994), "Towards a research agenda for public-private partnerships in the 1990s", *Local Economy*, 8, 4, 292-306

Barrett, B. (1996), *LEDA local pilot actions, partnership study: Connemara, Galway, Ireland*, LEDA Programme, European Commission

Becher, U. et al (1994), *Partnership and the fight against exclusion, the lessons of the Poverty 3 programme*, Lille: EEIG

Breen, R., D. Hannan, D.B. Rottman and C.T. Whelan (1990) *Understanding Contemporary Ireland, State, Class and Development in the Republic of Ireland*, Dublin: Gill and Macmillan

Callan, T., B. Nolan, B. Whelan, Whelan and J. Williams (1996), *Poverty in the 1990s, Evidence from the 1994 Living in Ireland Survey*, Dublin: Oak Tree Press, Economic and Social Research Institute and the Combat Poverty Agency

Central Review Committee (no date), *Area Based Response to Long-term Unemployment, report on activities, 1992*

Chanan, G. (1992), *Out of the shadows, local community action and the European Community*, Dublin: European Foundation for the Improvement of Living and Working Conditions

Clohessy, L (ed) (1993), *Creating local enterprise through partnership*, report on a seminar workshop in June 1993 at the Environmental Institute, UCD

Coombes, D. (1991), "Political and administrative structures for effective local development", in J.A. Walsh (ed), op. cit.

Commins, P. (1991), "Rural change and development in the Republic of Ireland: global forces and local responses", Sociological Association of Ireland annual conference, Termonfeckin

Commins, P. (ed.) (1993), *Combating exclusion in Ireland 1990-94 — a midway report*, Dublin: Irish Inter-Project Committee of Poverty 3 Programme

Commins, P. and M. Keane (1994), "Developing the rural economy: problems, programmes and prospects", in NESC, *op. cit.*

Community work in Ireland, trends in the 80s, options for the 90s, Report of conference in September 1989 in Kilkenny, Dublin: Combat Poverty Agency *et al.*

Co-options, Journal of the Community Workers' Co-operative, special edition entitled "Consensus or censorship, community work in partnership with the state" (1992)

Craig, S. and K. McKeown (1994), *Progress through partnership, final evaluation report on the PESP pilot initiative on long-term unemployment*, Dublin: Combat Poverty Agency

Craig, S. (1995), *Community participation, a handbook for individuals in local development partnerships*, Dublin: Combat Poverty Agency

Craig, S. (1995), *Making partnership work, a handbook on involvement in local development partnerships*, Dublin: Combat Poverty Agency

Cullen, B. (1994), *A programme in the making,* Dublin: Combat Poverty Agency

Curtin, C. and T. Varley (1995), "Community action and the state", in P Clancy *et al* (eds), *Irish Society: Sociological Perspectives*, Dublin: Institute of Public Administration and the Sociological Association of Ireland

Curtin, C., T. Haase and H. Tovey (1996), *Poverty in Rural Ireland: A Political Economy Perspective*, Dublin: Oak Tree Press and the Combat Poverty Agency

Daly, M. and J. Walsh (1989), *Moneylending and low-income families,* Dublin: Combat Poverty Agency

Davoudi, S. and P. Healy (1995), "City Challenge: Sustainable Process or Temporary Gesture", *Environment and Planning C: Government and Policy*, 13, 79-95

Department of Enterprise and Employment (1996), *Report of City and County Enterprise Board Activities*, Dublin: Stationery Office

Donnison, D. et al (1991), *Urban poverty, the economy and public policy: options for Ireland in the 1990s*, Dublin: Combat Poverty Agency

Duggan, C. and T. Ronayne (1991), *Working partners, the state and the community sector*, Dublin: Work Research Centre

Eisenschitz, A. and J. Gough (1993), *The Politics of Local Economic Policy: The Problems and Possibilities of Local Initiative*, London: Macmillan

Economic and Social Research Institute, DKM Consultants, G. Boyle and B. Kearney (1993), *The Community Support Framework: evaluation and recommendations*, Dublin: Stationery Office

Fianna Fáil and Labour programme for a partnership government 1993-1997, 1993

Flanagan, N., T. Haase and J. Walsh (1995), *Planning for change, a handbook for individuals in local development partnerships*, Dublin: Combat Poverty Agency

Faughnan, P. et al (1996), *Gender equality in the partnerships: women's experience*, Dublin: Community Action Network

Geddes, M. (1997), *Partnership against poverty and exclusion? Local regeneration strategies and excluded communities in the UK*, Bristol: The Policy Press

Geddes, M. (1998), *Local partnerships: a successful strategy for social cohesion?* Luxembourg: Office for Official Publications for the European Communities and European Foundation for the Improvement of Living and Working Conditions

Harvey, B. (1994), *Combating exclusion: lessons from the Third EU Poverty Programme in Ireland 1989-1994*, Dublin: Irish Inter-project Committee of Poverty 3 Programme

Hasse, T., K. McKeown and S. Rourke (1996), *Local development strategies for disadvantaged areas, evaluation of the Global Grant, 1992-1995*, Dublin: Area Development Management

Humphreys, E. (1996), *LEDA local pilot actions, synthesis report*, LEDA Programme, European Commission

Ireland (1991), *Programme for economic and social progress*, Dublin: Stationery Office

Ireland (1992), Report of Interdepartmental Group on urban crime and disorder, Dublin: Stationery Office.

Ireland (1994), *Programme for competitiveness and work*, Dublin: Stationery Office

Ireland (1995), *Operational Programme: Local Urban and Rural Development, 1994-1999*, Dublin: Stationery Office

Ireland (1995), *Discussion paper by the Interdepartmental Policy Committee on the National Anti-Poverty Strategy*, Dublin: Stationery Office

Ireland (1996), *Devolution Commission interim report*, Dublin: Stationery Office

Ireland (1996), *Better local government: a programme of change*, Dublin: Stationery Office

Ireland (1997), *Sharing in progress, a national anti-poverty strategy*, Dublin: Stationery Office

Ireland (1997), *Supporting voluntary activity, a green paper on the community and voluntary sector and its relationship with the state*, Dublin: Stationery Office

Irish Business and Employers Confederation (no date), *Social policy in a competitive economy*, Dublin: IBEC

Joyce, L. and M. Daly (1987), *Towards local planning, an evaluation of the Pilot COMTEC Programme*, Dublin: Institute of Public Administration

Kearney, B., G. Boyle and J.A. Walsh (1994), *EU Leader I initiative in Ireland, evaluation and recommendations,* Dublin: Department of Agriculture, Food and Forestry

Kelleher, P. and M. Whelan (1992), *Dublin communities in action: a study of six projects*, Dublin: Community Action Network and Combat Poverty Agency

Kirby, P. and D. Jacobson (ed) (1998), *In the shadow of the tiger: new approaches to combating social exclusion* Dublin: Dublin City University

Local development: the Irish experience, the European context, Proceedings of conference held in Dublin in November 1996, Dublin: Department of the Taoiseach (no date)

Mackintosh, M. (1992), "Partnership: issues of policy and negotiation", *Local Economy* 6, 4, 210-224

McArthur, A. (1995), "The active involvement of local residents in strategic community partnerships", *Policy and Politics*, 23, 1, 61-71

McCafferty, D. (1996), "Urban deprivation in Southill east, Limerick city", Annual conference of the Geographical Society of Ireland, St Patrick"s College, Maynooth

McKeown, K. and G. Fitzgerald (1997), *Developing childcare services in disadvantaged areas*, Dublin: ADM

National Economic and Social Council (1990), *A strategy for the nineties: economic stability and structural change*, Dublin: NESC

National Economic and Social Council (1993), *A strategy for competitiveness, growth and employment*, Dublin: NESC

National Economic and Social Council (1994), *New approaches to rural development*, Dublin: NESC

National Economic and Social Council (1996), *Strategy into the 21st century, conclusions and recommendations*, Dublin: NESC

Nexus (1993), Evaluation of the pilot projects to combat moneylending and indebtedness, unpublished report for the Department of Social Welfare

Nexus (1995), Evaluation of Poverty 3 Programme, unpublished report for the Combat Poverty Agency

Nolan, B. and T. Callan (1994), *Poverty and Policy in Ireland*, Dublin: Gill and Macmillan

Nolan, B. et al (1994), *Poverty and time: perspectives on the dynamics of poverty*, Dublin: ESRI

Ó Cinnéide, M. and M. Keane (1987), *Community self-help economic initiatives and development agency responses in the midwest of*

Ireland, Galway: Social Sciences Research Centre, University College Galway

Ó Cinnéide, S. (1995), "Community response to unemployment", *Administration*, 33, 2, 231-257

Ó Cinnéide, S. and J. Walsh (1990), "Multiplication and divisions: trends in community development in Ireland since the 1960s", *Community Development Journal*, 25, 4, 326-336

O'Connell, P. and D. Rottman (1992), "The Irish welfare state in comparative perspective", in J. Goldthorpe and C. Whelan (eds), *The Development of Industrial Society in Ireland*, Oxford: Oxford University Press

OECD (1996), *Ireland: local partnerships and social innovation*, Paris: OECD

Office of the Comptroller and Auditor General (1994), *Report on value for money examination: the Leader programme*, Dublin: Stationery Office

O'Donnell, R. (1995), "Decision making in the 21st century: implications for national policy-making and political institutions", *Political Agenda*

O'Malley, E. (1992), *The Pilot Programme for Integrated Rural Development 1988-90*, Dublin: Economic and Social Research Institute

O'Neill, C (1992), *Telling it like it is*, Dublin: Combat Poverty Agency

Partnership in action: the role of community development and partnership in Ireland, Galway: Community Workers' Co-operative (1996)

Pringle, D. (1996), "Something old, something new . . . lessons to be learnt from previous strategies of positive territorial discrimination" annual conference of the Geographical Society of Ireland, St Patrick's College, Maynooth

Putting Poverty 3 into policy, Proceedings of conference held in Cavan in April 1995, Dublin: Department of Social Welfare (1995)

Rourke, S. (1994), *Local development in the Republic of Ireland, an overview and analysis*, Dublin: Combat Poverty Agency

Streeck, W. and P. Schmitter (1985), "Community, market, state - and associations? the prospective contribution of interest governance to social order", *European Sociological Review*, 1, 2, 119-138

Walsh, J. A. (ed) (1991), *Local economic development and administrative reform*, Dublin: Regional Studies Association

Walsh, J. (1993), "Pioneering a strategy for integrated urban development: The PAUL Partnership Limerick", in P. Commins (ed), *op. cit.*

Walsh, J. (1994), *Report on the implementation of the Third EU Poverty programme by the PAUL Partnership Limerick*, Limerick: PAUL Partnership Limerick

Walsh, J. A. (1995), "Local development theory and practice: recent experience in Ireland", International Society for the Study of Marginal Regions seminar on sustainable regional and local development, St Patrick's College, Maynooth

Walsh, J. (1996), "Tackling poverty through spatial interventions" annual conference of the Geographical Society of Ireland, St Patrick's College, Maynooth.

Walsh, J. (1998), "Local development and local government in the Republic of Ireland: from fragmentation to integration?", *Local Economy*, Vol. 12, No. 4.